Pressure

M000291286

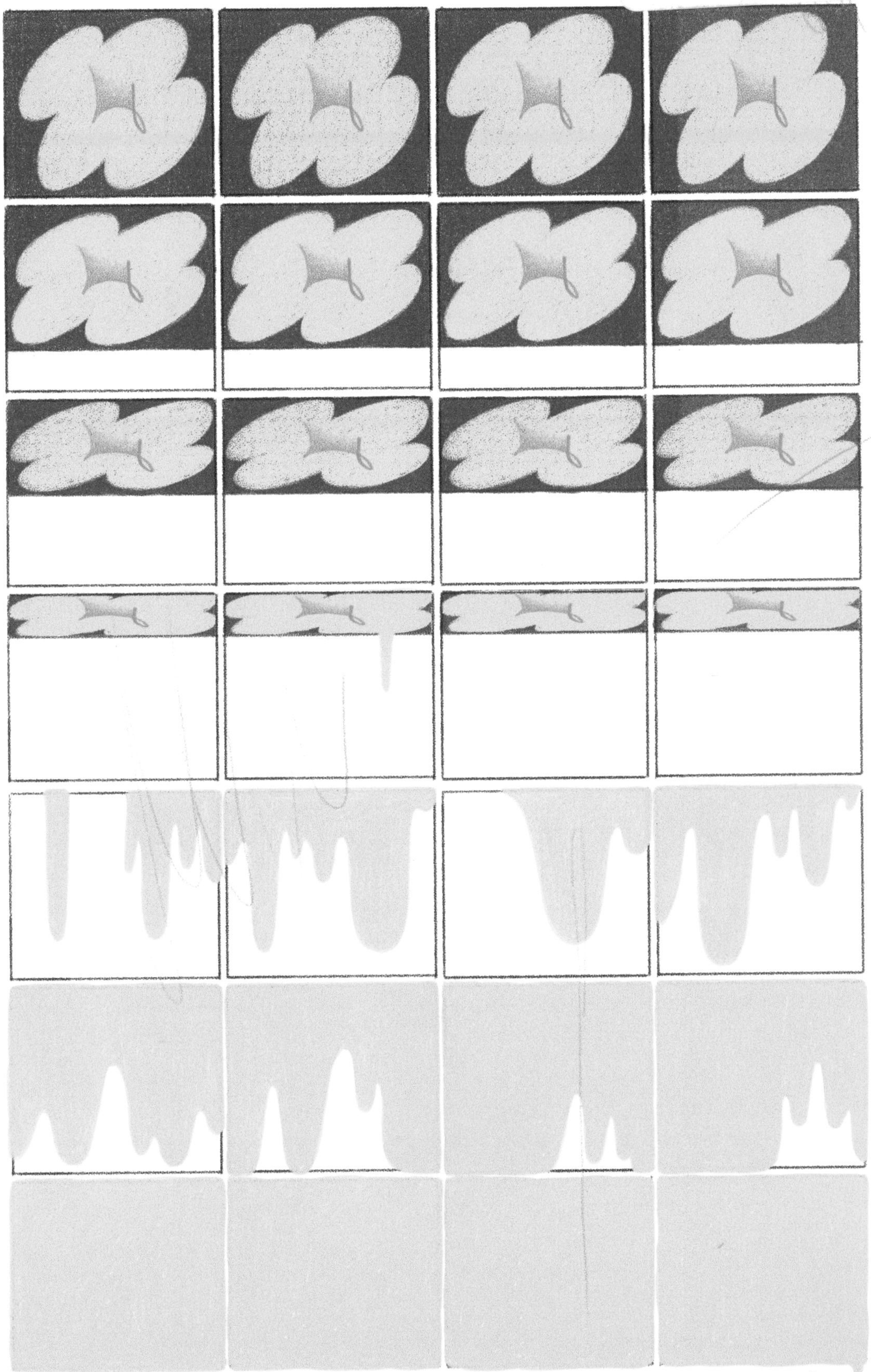

PUBLISHER'S LETTER

BY MICHAEL GERBER

MISSOURI SLEIGH RIDE

Black Lab 1, 9-year-old boy 0.

I can tell you precisely when I began to hate winter: January 1979. That's when I was deemed old enough to walk our dog.

My parents were the kind of parents who constantly scanned the horizon for opportunities to build my character, and by winter '79 they were concerned that the 9-year-old me might be getting a little soft. So one Sunday dinner, my father announced that, in addition to my other chores, I would now be responsible for walking Gus before I went to school.

From the other room, I distinctly heard Gus laugh. I didn't blame him — the entire proposition was absurd. First, I have a slight case of cerebral palsy that makes me rather unsteady on my feet. Second, Gus was half-Lab, half-tornado, as high as my waist and still growing; when he jumped up, which he did constantly, his big paws flopped onto my shoulders. Once, I held him there and began to waltz; Gus promptly took a snap at my nose. He felt he outranked me, and I couldn't really argue. Mom was tolerated because she fed him, but Gus truly recognized no authority save my father's.

Which is why Dad's encouragement didn't cheer me up. "You and I have walked Gus tons of times," he said. "It's just around the block. You'll be fine."

This was a lie. I don't remember whether all the sidewalks in Jefferson City, MO were humped and broken by tree roots, but the ones where we lived, next to the penitentiary (*yes, really*) tripped me constantly. Now I'd have to maneuver Gus, too? In the snow? He was like a broken shopping cart with four-wheel drive and descended testicles.

By the end of that bruising first week, Gus and I had settled into a routine. After a quick pee, he would go in search of breakfast. Rotting salmon out of a garbage can, roadkill marinated in motor oil, raccoon poop — each morning brought new delights. Because Gus outweighed me, and had four sturdy feet to my unsteady two, we went wherever he wanted to go, and stayed as long as he wanted to stay. All I could do was glance around guiltily, like the lookout at the world's grossest stickup, as Gus wolfed down some rancid giblets, or ate a chicken bone then noisily hacked it up. That dog could vomit like a Roman emperor.

After his hearty meal, Gus would then take a really awful poop — whatever went in had to come out, often spectacularly. Oh, I scooped, for a time. Then, one morning, I saw a screw in it, and something in me snapped; that was my own personal "Naked Lunch" moment. After that, all I wanted to do was get away. And forget.)

At first, the people on our route were friendly. But as Gus's landmines proliferated, they began hectoring us. "Oh, no you don't! Just keep on walking!"

The walk's final act commenced when, somewhere, a dog would bark. Gus would abruptly cease whatever he was doing — say, an eating/vomiting/eating cycle involving spoiled braunschweiger — and snap to attention. He would give a single loud "woof!," then listen for a response; I would begin preparing for the struggle to come, winding the leather leash several times around my palm and looking for something sturdy to hold onto — a tree, a lamppost. If Gus got an answering bark, he would immediately tear ass in the direction of his comrade. Then the question became: Could Gus reach escape velocity by the end of the leash? And if he did, did I let go, or have my shoulder pulled out at the root?

This was the low point of the walk. Humiliated and freezing my ass off, I'd tromp after the dog, me swearing at him, homeowners swearing at me, life sucking for everyone but Gus.

If I was lucky, Gus's quarry was far away; once I lost sight of him, I could reasonably head home. My mom wouldn't yell at me; she called Gus "that idiot" and openly questioned the wisdom of housing a wild animal in our home. But if I was unlucky, the other dog would be close, and I'd have to enter a canine maelstrom as Gus attempted to make friends in the most chaotic and destructive way.

Once when Gus was running figure-eights around a woman and her Dalmatian, she pulled something out of her pocket. Gus stopped dead, transfixed. I ran over and grabbed his leash. Using sleight-of-hand, she passed me the tennis ball. "You need this more than I do."

I walked the back half of my circuit that morning with the demeanor of someone who's finally figured life out. Until Gus knocked me down, and fished the ball out of my pocket — but by then we were close enough to the back door for me to drag him inside. Tennis balls were Gus's Kryptonite, and his expres-

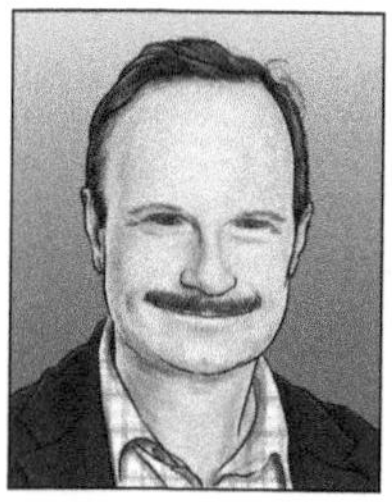

MICHAEL GERBER (@mgerber937) is Editor & Publisher of *The American Bystander*.

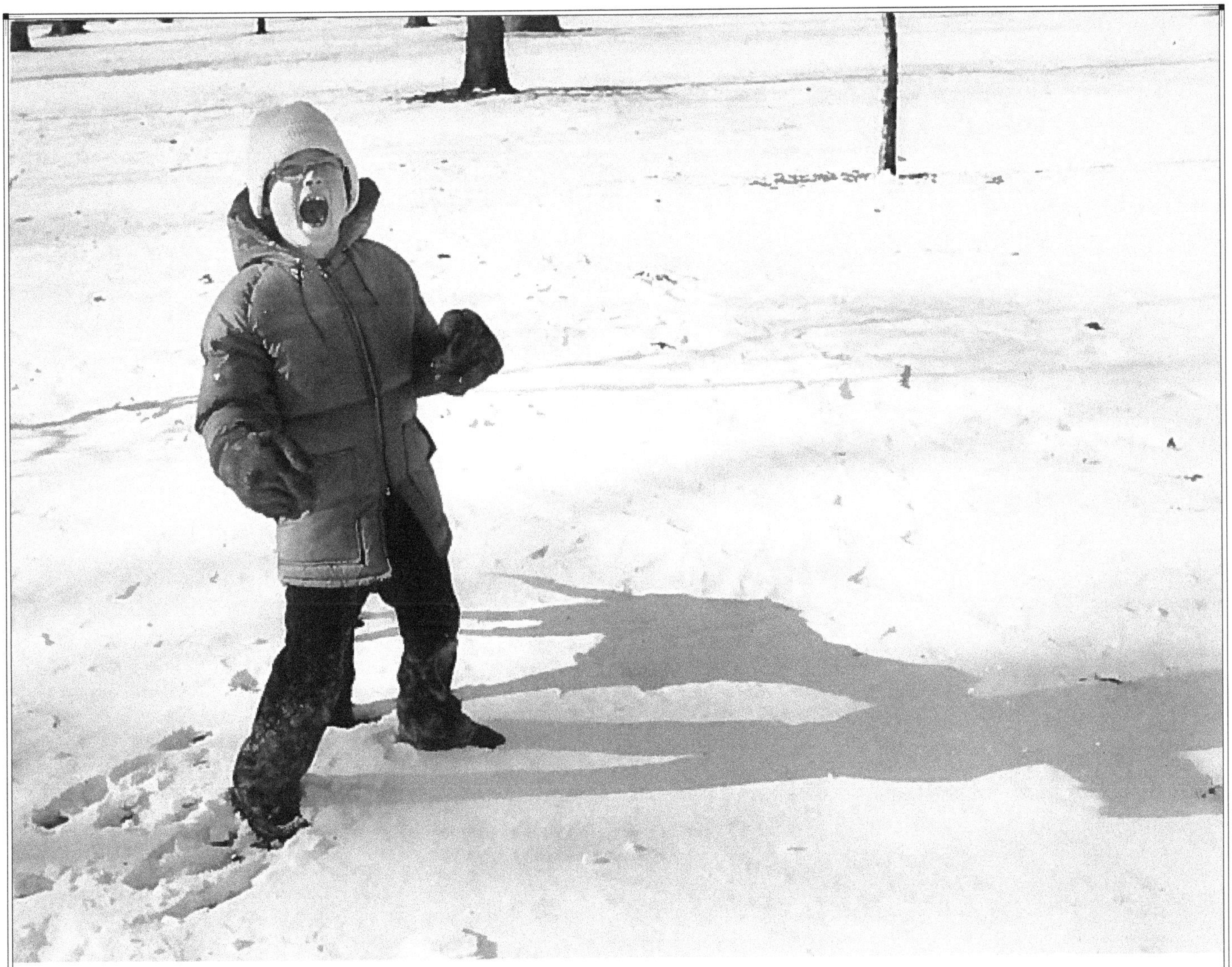

GREGORY GERBER

This picture of Gus and me, taken by my father right around the time our walks began, sums up our relationship perfectly.

sion was clear. "I know exactly what you're doing, but I'm powerless to resist. But know this: I will have my revenge."

Gus's revenge was what I called "a Missouri sleigh ride": He would knock me down, then pull me, via the leash, on my belly. As we tobogganed painfully over hill and dale, snow and ice would go down my shirt, into my boots, even down my pants. That's cold, my friends. That will make you hate winter.

One very snowy morning 39 years ago, Gus administered a sleigh ride so protracted, so violent, that my glove came off in the leash. The dog, predictably, took off. A crew-cutted dude — part of my regular audience, I'd often see him chuckling with a cup of coffee behind his picture window — saw the whole thing. "Go home and get your parents," he said as he helped me up. "It's dangerous for dogs to be out in a blizzard. They navigate by landmarks, and if something gets covered with snow, they can't find their way home."

Now, any sensible person would have thought, *Jesus Christ, if only.* But I was a very responsible, not to say neurotic, firstborn child so, wet and cold and near tears, I ran home as fast as I could, gave my news, and the family sprang into action: Mom called the school, giving me permission to be late. Then Dad and I went back outside, walking the neighborhood, calling Gus's name. Dad's booming voice reassured me, because it always made Gus come running. Except today.

We walked around for the better part of an hour; Dad said it wasn't my fault, but I could tell he was growing more and more worried. When we went back home to get the car, Mom met us at the back door. "Someone called," she said. "The idiot was out by the hospital."

"Jesus, that's five miles from here," Dad said. "Are you sure it was Gus?"

"The guy said, 'He let me get close enough to grab his collar, then slipped out of it and ran away.'"

"That's Gus," I said.

Dad grabbed the car keys. "Did he say where he went?"

"No." My mother and I shared a look. It's not that we wanted anything bad to happen to Gus, it's more that he'd made so many bad things happen to us, him freezing his ass off for a while felt like justice.

My dad isn't like that; Gus was part of his pack, and he had an obligation. "I'm going to go find him," Dad said. Just as he turned, we heard a familiar bark, and the sound of foreclaws hitting the thin aluminum of the storm door.

My mom was closest. She opened the door. "Come in, idiot."

Naturally we were all happy to see him. The worst thing was, Gus knew it. B

TABLE OF CONTENTS

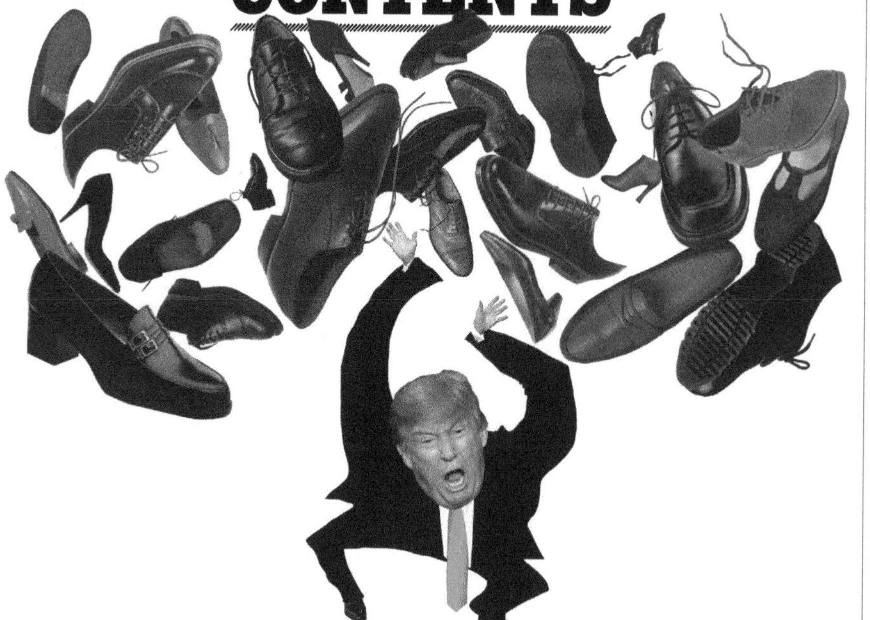

STEPHEN KRONINGER

DEPARTMENTS

GALLIMAUFRY

SHORT STUFF

FEATURES

The AMERICAN
BYSTANDER

#7 • Vol. 2, No. 3 • Winter 2017

EDITOR & PUBLISHER
Michael Gerber
HEAD WRITER Brian McConnachie
SENIOR EDITOR Alan Goldberg
DEPUTY EDITORS
Michael Thornton, Ben Orlin
CONTACTEE Scott Marshall
ORACLE Steve Young
STAFF LIAR P.S. Mueller
LIAISON James Folta (*New York*)

CONTRIBUTORS
Jaylee Alde, Ron Barrett, Charles Barsotti, R.O. Blechman, Rasika W. Boice, Harry Bliss, George Booth, Nate Bramble, M.K. Brown, Con Chapman, Roz Chast, Karen Chee, David Chelsea, Tom Chitty, Howard Cruse, Matthew Disler, Randall Enos, Xeth Feinberg, Alex Firer, Drew Friedman, Tom Gammill, Sally Gardner, Rick Geary, Gregory Gerber, Sam Gross, Tom Hachtman, Tim Harrod, John Jonik, Ted Jouflas, Lars Kenseth, Joe Keohane, Megan Koester, Stephen Kroninger, Peter Kuper, Sara Lautman, Stan Mack, Matt Matera, Zoe Matthiessen, Tom Motley, Ryan Nyburg, Joe Oesterle, Josh Perilo, Ethan Persoff, Mimi Pond, Mike Reiss, Blythe Roberson, Jay Ruttenberg, Mike Sacks, Nell Scovell, Maria Scrivan, Cris Shapan, Mike Shiell, Osman Siddique, Jim Siergey, Michael Sloan, Rich Sparks, Ed Subitzky, D. Watson, Evan Waite, Shannon Wheeler, P.C. Vey, Gizem Vural, Steve Young and Jack Ziegler.

COPYEDITING
Cheryl Levenbrown, God bless 'er
THANKS TO
Kate Powers, Rae Barsotti, Lanky Bareikis, Jon Schwarz, Alleen Schultz, Molly Bernstein, Joe Lopez, Eliot Ivanhoe, Neil Gumenick, Thomas Simon, Diana Gould, Greg and Patricia Gerber and many, many others.
NAMEPLATES BY
Mark Simonson
ISSUE CREATED BY
Michael Gerber

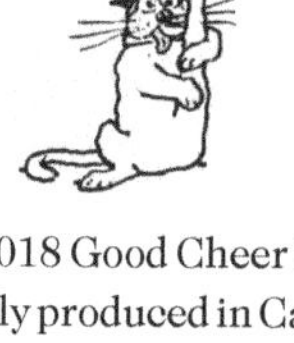

BOOTH

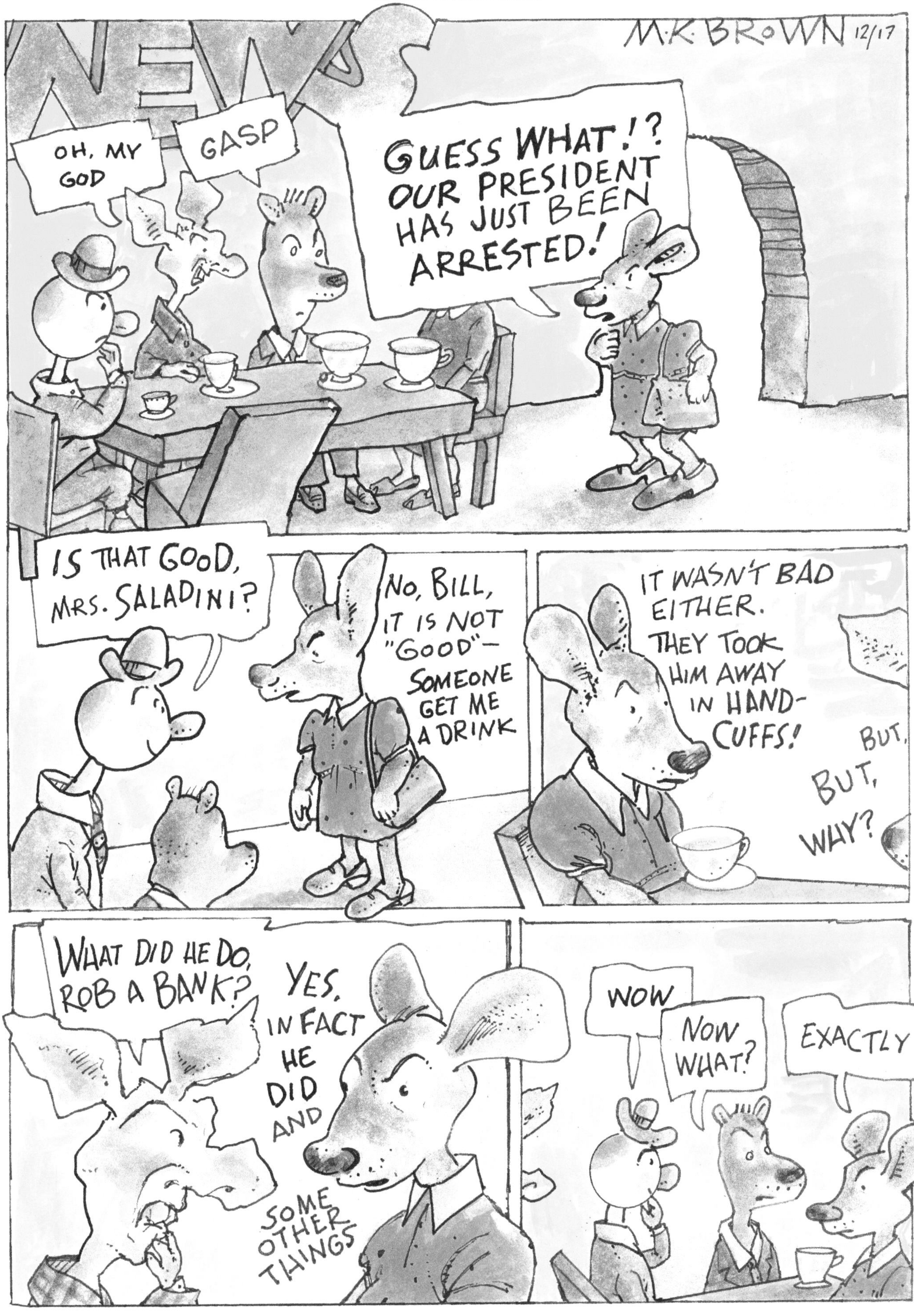
NEWS
M.K. BROWN 12/17
OH, MY GOD
GASP
GUESS WHAT!? OUR PRESIDENT HAS JUST BEEN ARRESTED!
IS THAT GOOD, MRS. SALADINI?
NO, BILL, IT IS NOT "GOOD"— SOMEONE GET ME A DRINK
IT WASN'T BAD EITHER. THEY TOOK HIM AWAY IN HAND-CUFFS!
BUT, BUT, WHY?
WHAT DID HE DO, ROB A BANK?
YES. IN FACT HE DID AND SOME OTHER THINGS
WOW
NOW WHAT?
EXACTLY

CARTOONS & ILLUSTRATIONS BY
R. Barrett, C. Barsotti, L. Bertman, H. Bliss, G. Booth, R. O. Blechman, N. Bramble, M.K. Brown, R. Chast, D. Chelsea, T. Chitty, H. Cruse, R. Enos, X. Feinberg, D. Friedman, T. Gammill, S. Gardner, R. Geary, G. Gerber, S. Gross, T. Hachtman, J. Jonik, T. Jouflas, L. Kenseth, S. Kroninger, P. Kuper, S. Lautman, S. Mack, S. Marshall, Z. Matthiessen, B. McConnachie, T. Motley, P.S. Mueller, J. Oesterle, E. Persoff, M. Pond, M. Scrivan, M. Shiell, C. Shapan, M. Simonson, M. Sloan, R. Sparks, E. Subitsky, P.C. Vey, G. Vural, D. Watson, S. Wheeler and J. Ziegler.

*"Of course we love you. That's why we give you
so much shit."*

COVER

This issue's cover comes courtesy of Mr. Bob Blechman, who classes up every joint he hangs around in (especially this one). I was determined to get him on our cover within the first 10, so there's a certain extra glow of satisfaction. Bob's one of those illustrators — and we have many of them here at *Bystander* — who pose a bit of a problem: *I love everything he sends me.* So you can also see him in *Marvy*, our comics section (which is begging for its own spin-off magazine, don't you think?). Thanks also to Zoe Matthiessen, Mark Simonson and Scott Marshall, for their Photoshop and InDesign wizardry.

ACKNO
WLEDG
MENTS

THE AMERICAN BYSTANDER, Vol. 2, No. 3, (978-0-692-06585-3). Publishes ~4x/year. ©2018 by Good Cheer LLC. No part of this magazine can be reproduced, in whole or in part, by any means, without the written permission of the Publisher. For this and other queries, email *Publisher@americanbystander.org*, or write: Michael Gerber, Publisher, *The American Bystander*, 1122 Sixth St., #403, Santa Monica, CA 90403. Subscribe at www.patreon.com/bystander. Other info, really *too much* info, can be found at www.americanbystander.org.

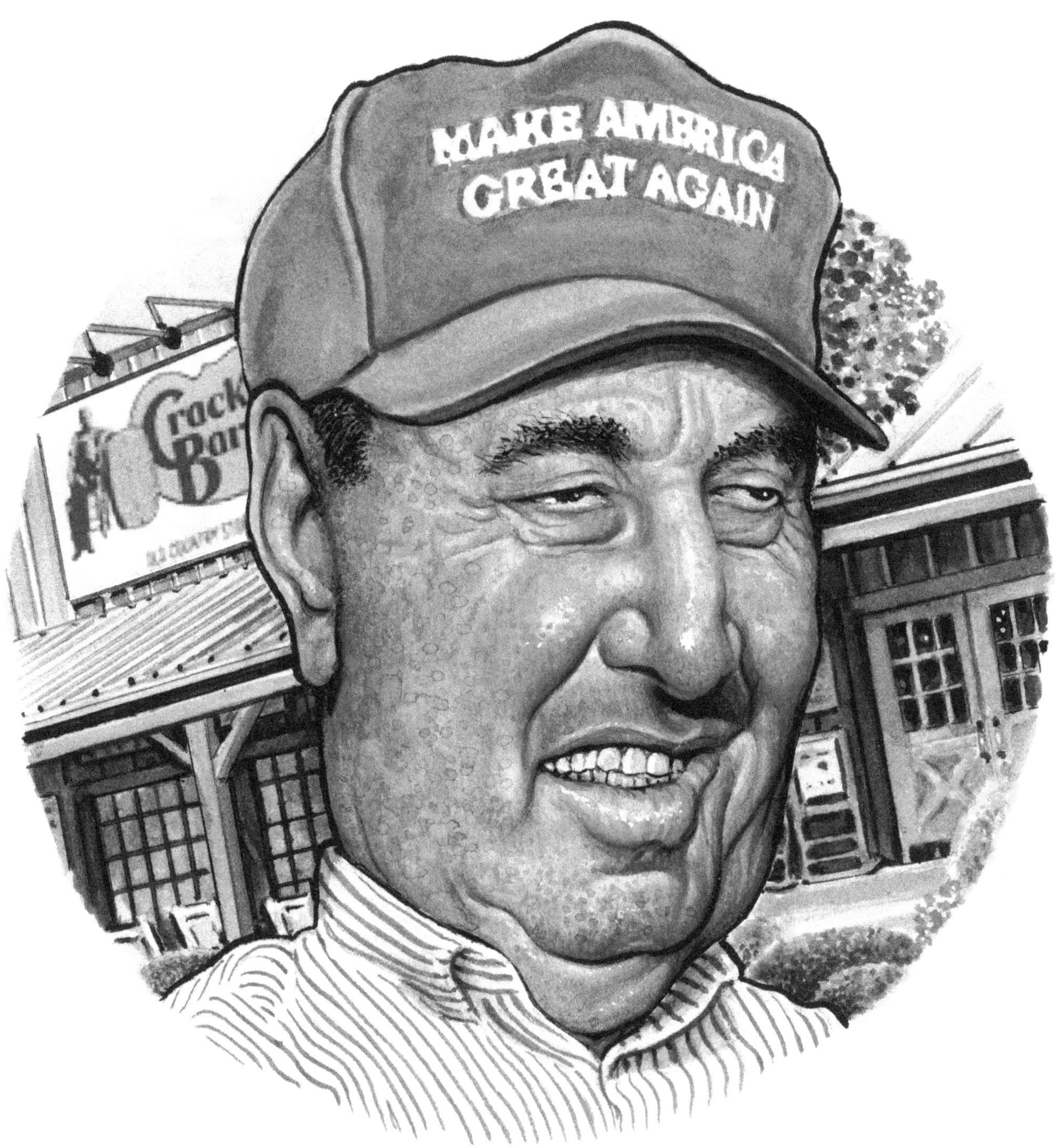
MAKE AMERICA
GREAT AGAIN

American Bystanders #4

A. Schmuck

THE HOT LIST

Snoods? **HOT!** *Lederhosen?* **NOT.** *Mitosis?* **HOT!** *The Krebs Citric Acid Cycle?* **NOT.** *Pogs?* **HOT!** *Pugs?* **NOT.** *Oral surgery?* **HOT!** *Outcroppings of schist?* **NOT.** *Bora Bora?* **HOT!** *Baden-Baden?* **NOT.** *Joseph Cotten?* **HOT!** *Broderick Crawford?* **NOT.** *Butterscotch blondies?* **HOT!** *Ouzo blondies?* **NOT.** *Clement Attlee?* **HOT!** *Bonar Law?* **NOT.** *Large, flightless birds?* **HOT!** *Algae?* **NOT.** *Coriander?* **HOT!** *Cilantro?* **NOT.** *Pantone 300 C?* **HOT!** *Pantone 17-1544 TCX Burnt Sienna?* **NOT.** **ON OUR RADAR:** *Bangs…Icecubes from a tray…Egg noodles…Nightlights…The 25th Amendment… Potpourri that smells like feet.*

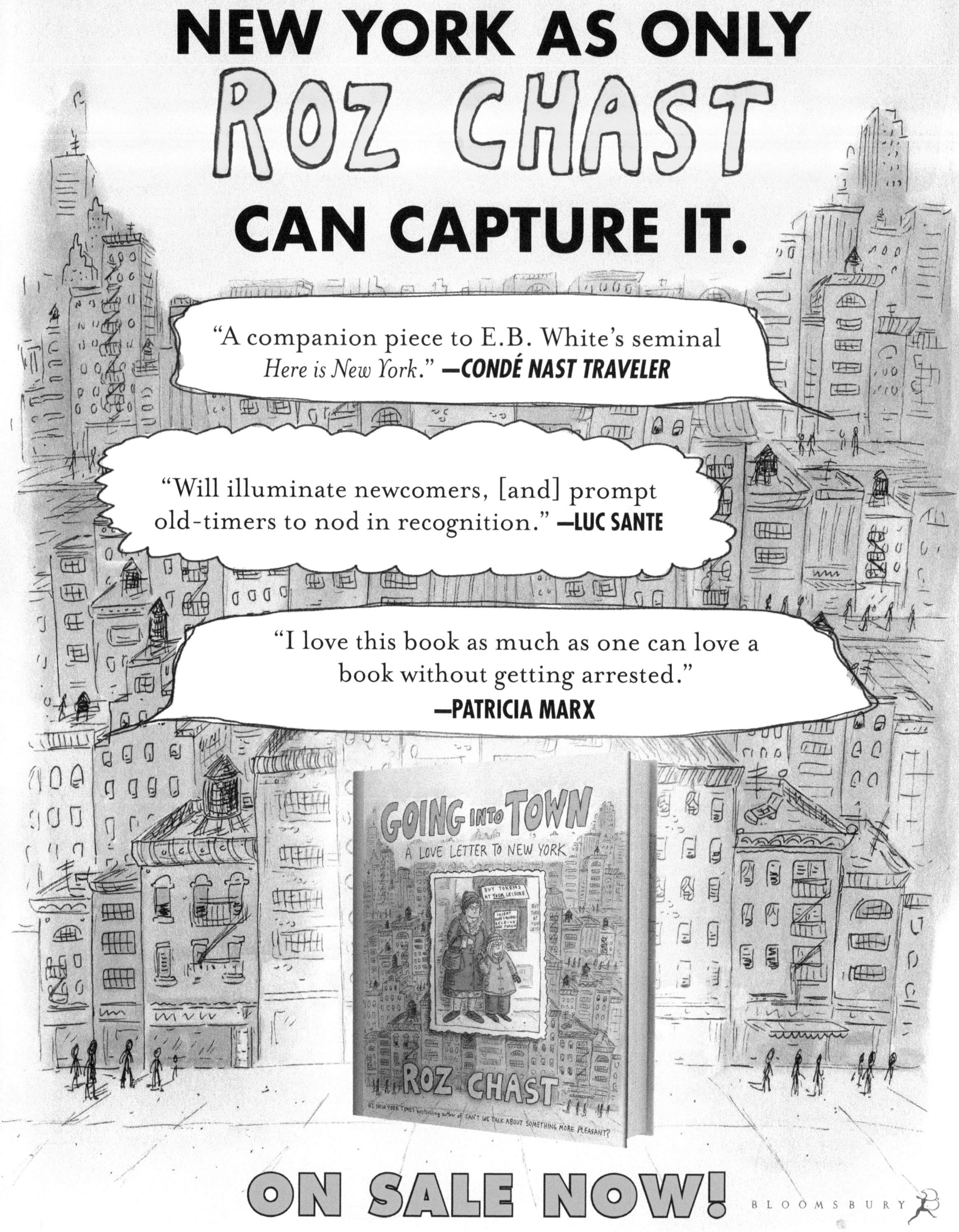
NEW YORK AS ONLY
ROZ CHAST
CAN CAPTURE IT.
"A companion piece to E.B. White's seminal *Here is New York*." —CONDÉ NAST TRAVELER
"Will illuminate newcomers, [and] prompt old-timers to nod in recognition." —LUC SANTE
"I love this book as much as one can love a book without getting arrested." —PATRICIA MARX
GOING INTO TOWN
A LOVE LETTER TO NEW YORK
ROZ CHAST
#1 NEW YORK TIMES bestselling author of CAN'T WE TALK ABOUT SOMETHING MORE PLEASANT?
ON SALE NOW!
BLOOMSBURY

NEWS & NOTES

What's going to happen in 2018? Our contributors have a few ideas...

RANDALL ENOS

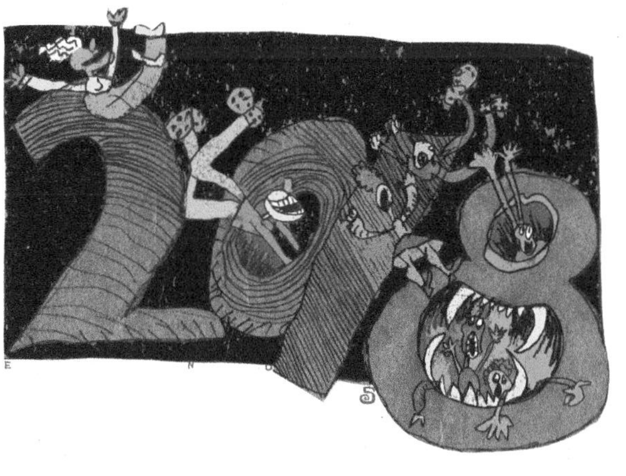

Instead of the usual folderol, I asked our contributors, "Do you have any predictions for 2018?" Boy, did they. A question like that is like *Bystander*'s Karaoke Night. With half-priced Long Islands.

The following is just a smattering of the vast flood of prophecies offered up by our crew. Strangely, none are as outlandish as our current reality... I don't know whether that's reassuring or not. Let's say that it is.

To **STEVE YOUNG**, 2018 will be a time of troubles. "In the wake of scandal, topaz will be removed from Moh's Hardness Scale... The U.S./Mexican border wall will be built, but on the night of Nov. 9th, tens of thousands of East Germans will breach the wall and flood into the U.S.... Hackers will steal data from thousands of Wi-Fi-enabled refrigerators, and sell information on the dark web about who's low on half and half." He also predicted trouble coming from a rather unexpected source. "Arbor Day is renamed Tree Day after a majority of Americans complain that the word 'Arbor' is confusing and smacks of elitism. The phrase 'smacks of elitism' is then replaced by the phrase 'sounds stuck-up.'"

P.S. MUELLER offered up the following: "Scientists will create the world's first test-tube ribeye steak and everyone on earth will love the perfect guilt-free balance of texture and flavor. This new meat will also have a mortal soul that most people will push around their plates or take home for the dog. (I'll have the shrieking salmon, please.)"

Not surprisingly, many predictions were political. **ED SOREL** sees dismal times ahead: "I predict that Mike Pence will become president and lower the voting age to embryos." **HOWARD CRUSE**, on the other hand, provided a future we all can believe in: "I predict that the famous comet Kahoutek will make a surprise reappearance and turn Mar-a-Lago into a crater. All political dinosaurs will immediately become extinct."

More wish fulfilment came from **PAUL LANDER**: "Jared Kushner turns his focus to prison reform... from the inside." But **DYLAN BRODY** hedged his bets: "I would like to predict impeachment, but I guarantee continued impairment." Sunny though it was, **ERIC BRANSCUM**'s prediction was probably wrong before he finished typing: "In 2018, I predict there won't be a single bad tweet." Then again, depends on what you consider "bad" — the goalposts keep getting moved on us, don't they?

JOE KEOHANE's predictions stuck mostly to the homefront: "That thing on your neck will turn out to be benign. But that rumble in your tummy will turn out to be a 17-foot-long foot tapeworm... Your dog's love will prove somewhat conditional after all... You will be justifiably underestimated by a work rival... You will become, ever so slightly, shorter....It will be bedbugs... You will shoot for grandiose and wind up with fiasco." But, Joe concludes, "It will have all been worth it, nevertheless."

NOAH JONES ranged widely; in addition to "robot clothes," he forecast "The Five Stages of Allegation Denial. Driverless golf clubs. In June, it will be revealed that Six Degrees of Kevin Bacon is actually made up of 2 Associate's degrees, 2 diplomas for HVAC classes, a Vulcan Language Certificate of Proficiency, and an honorary degree from a now-defunct Philadelphia beauty college for being 'sexy cum laude.' August will bring the discovery of glinp. September, glinp intolerance. In the fall, a typo in *The New York Times* Sunday crossword leads puzzle fanatics on a yearlong quest to find the mythical "5-word letter" for browning bread. My degree of certainty on these," Noah assures us, "is pretty high."

DAVID INFANTE got personal — very personal. "In 2018, you're going to get a promotion. A big one. From associate something to senior associate something. Look at you go.

"To celebrate, you're going to go out to dinner with your significant other. During this meal, unfortunately, you will choke to death on the seafood risotto. You will try to swallow a mussel, it will lodge in your windpipe, and you will die. At first you rise from your seat only slightly, clasping at your throat with a sense of rising but not overwhelming urgency, because you don't yet know that 'this is it.'

"You'll feel embarrassed to be making such a scene. This is a nice restaurant, after all, and you're a senior associate something. Your significant other has dressed up, and he/she was planning on giving you a handjob tonight. How humiliating. (The scene, not the handjob. Unless you're into that sort of thing.)

"In a few moments you'll realize that the squishy little mollusk in your throat is stuck there. This will scare you, and suddenly you won't feel so bad about causing a disruption. But you will feel a flicker of outrage: the thing that's killing you binds itself to rocks in tidal pools; it doesn't have a job;

it has never been the senior associate something of anything. Who does it think it is?, you will wonder to yourself indignantly.

"At this point, your significant other and nearby diners will also have realized that you are choking to death on some slacker bivalve. They will set about trying to evict it from your airway, using their fists to thwack you on the back and their phones to call 9-1-1. None of this will matter, of course.

"As the last oxygen molecules in your lungs are absorbed into your bloodstream, you are going to throw your head back in a silent scream. One last pantomime of existence, grimly prophesying the eternal silence of the grave. You were a senior associate something, master of all you surveyed (sort of). Damn this wretched world, and the cruel mussels that attach to the worthless rocks in its brackish tidal pools. Damn the risotto, and the handjobs. *Damn it all to hell.*"

I think I'll have the shrieking salmon.

"Thanks for asking," **KIT LANDER** replied to my email. "You are clearly aware of my keen insight into the paranormal. (Everyone is, Kit. We sneak into your house when you're asleep, and whisper "Give us lottery numbers" in your ear.) "In 2018, rather than arranging play-dates via their parents, elementary school children will begin using the new app Kinder." Kit, if you drop everything and make that app, I predict in 2019, you will buy *Bystander*.

ANDREW BARLOW clearly has his finger on the pulse of… something. "In the coming year," he writes, "women will be called 'dwarves.' Hence, schoolboys will be heard to yell, 'I love dwarves!'"

Unsurprisingly, our contributors aren't bullish on Bitcoin. "The Bitcoin economy finally tanks," wrote **JACQUELINE DETWILER**. "It's replaced by a new speculative market in Botcoin, which is just covering pennies in aluminum foil and making beep-boop noises." **OSMAN SIDDIQUE** went even further. "The US government will crack down on cryptocurrencies by making it illegal to be a dork." But, says **RICARDO ANGULO**, dorks will have their revenge: "Congressional Field Day ends with Mitch McConnell puking on the Capitol steps during a rousing game of 'dizzy bats.'" I'd pay to see that, Ricardo.

President Trump was all over our predictions. **LARS KENSETH** said, "The Presidential Fitness Challenge will add 'straining on the toilet' to its list of approved physical activities."

The Trump administration is wearing out **JAMES FINN GARNER**. "An alien race will arrive on Earth in September," he predicts. "When they announce they are enslaving every man, woman and child, we will eagerly agree, because of the sweet final certainty of it."

I particularly liked **LUKE ATKINSON**'s prediction: "Climate change's stronger winds cause sail cargo to overtake air, road, rail and shipping as the leading form of freight transport." Here's to a quieter 2018.

"A team in such and such sport will win such and such championship, helping heal such and such city after such and such tragedy," opines **JONATHAN ZELLER**, aiming for the fat part of the target. "American children's grammar skills will deteriorate so badly they start falling into goods. Sorry, that prediction may not be so well."

JAMES FOLTA is similarly downcast about the coming year. "In 2018, you'll realize that all those pretty words you were told about 'reliability,' 'family,' and 'trust' were just a ploy to sell you a cellphone plan." And the news will give you no comfort, either: "For another year in a row, a lot of people are going to go to jail. But yet again, it's not going to be the guys you want."

GEOFFREY GOLDEN and **AMANDA MEADOWS** go even further: "To increase profitability and shareholder value, major tech companies will begin blackmailing users with their own data. Alexa will threaten to release recordings of couples drunkenly talking shit about their other friends. Google will release webcam videos of users searching terms like 'crying when I get an erection' and 'recipe for guy fieri guy-talian fondue dippers.' And somehow, Apple knows everyone who voted for Trump in Berkeley, CA." Faced with this hellscape, Geoffrey and Amanda also believe that "in 2018, Americans will eat at least 10% more of their feelings" — and **CHERYL LEVENBROWN** tells us what they will be eating: "Starbucks will start selling Tide Pods Frappuccinos." But there's a silver lining: "They're gluten-free."

According to **DAVID HARNDEN-WARWICK**, 2018 will be a year of surprises. "In November, an NRA investigation will conclude Oswald acted in self-defense." Stand your ground, Lee Harvey. David also thinks that "the Supreme Court will decide volcano cults must accept anal virgins." But ultimately, David thinks the year's going to be a downer, after "Alabama launches America's largest Civil War re-enactment since 1865."

Even so, says **J.A. WEINSTEIN**, "The New York Jets will still suck." B

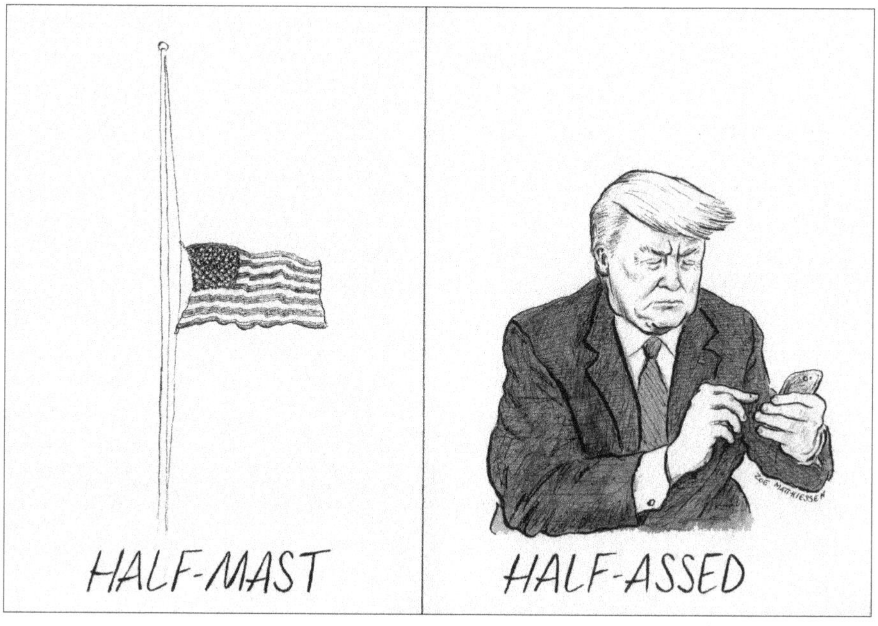
HALF-MAST
HALF-ASSED
ZOE MATTHIESSEN

KUDOS KORNER: *This illustration by* **ZOE MATTHIESSEN**, *first published on our blog, was selected by the Society of Illustrators for its annual book and exhibition.*

BY SHANNON WHEELER

HOW TO CHOKE A CHICKEN

Paging Jack Kevorkian, D.V.M.

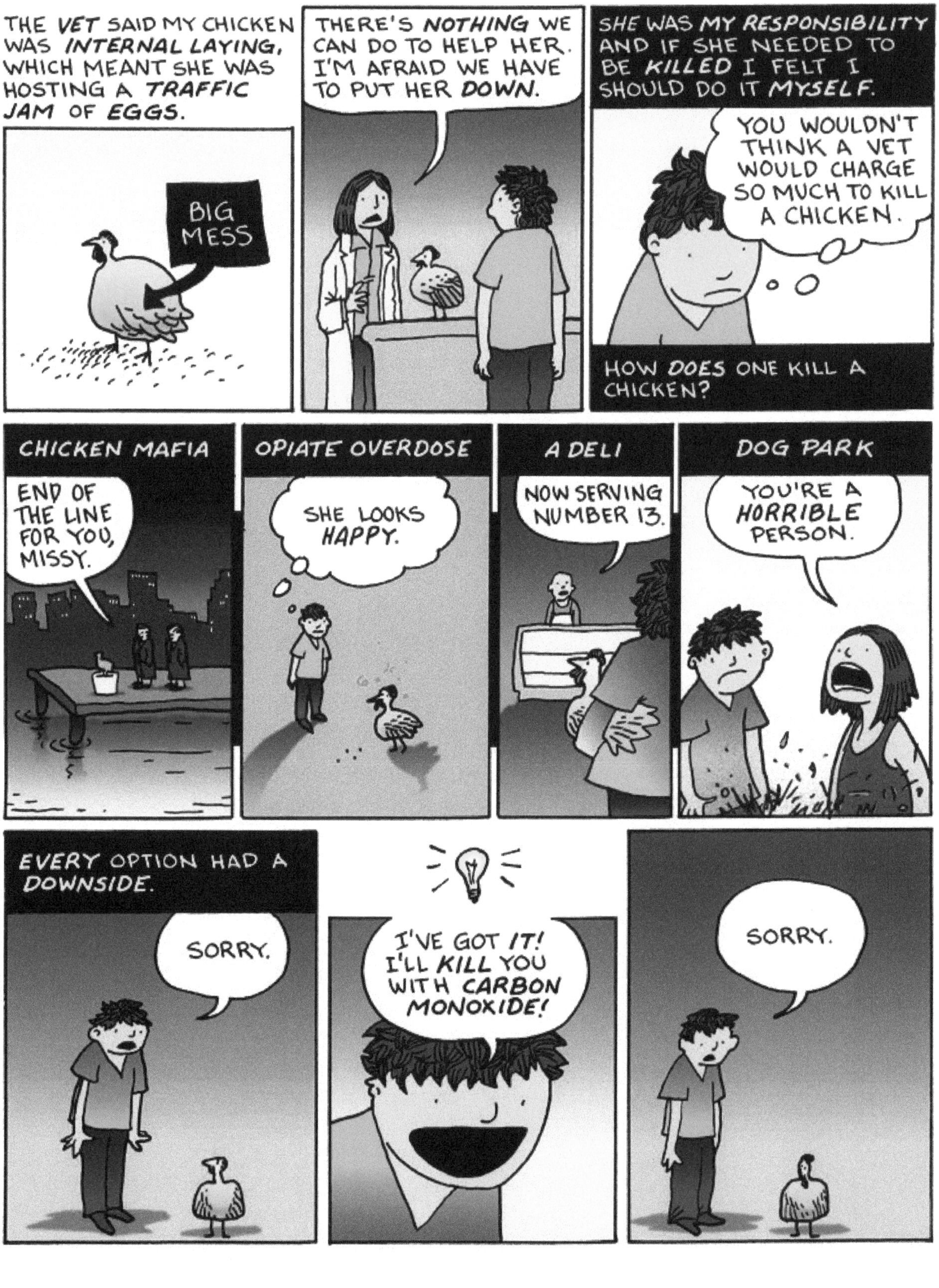
THE VET SAID MY CHICKEN WAS INTERNAL LAYING, WHICH MEANT SHE WAS HOSTING A TRAFFIC JAM OF EGGS.
BIG MESS
THERE'S NOTHING WE CAN DO TO HELP HER. I'M AFRAID WE HAVE TO PUT HER DOWN.
SHE WAS MY RESPONSIBILITY AND IF SHE NEEDED TO BE KILLED I FELT I SHOULD DO IT MYSELF.
YOU WOULDN'T THINK A VET WOULD CHARGE SO MUCH TO KILL A CHICKEN.
HOW DOES ONE KILL A CHICKEN?
CHICKEN MAFIA
END OF THE LINE FOR YOU, MISSY.
OPIATE OVERDOSE
SHE LOOKS HAPPY.
A DELI
NOW SERVING NUMBER 13.
DOG PARK
YOU'RE A HORRIBLE PERSON.
EVERY OPTION HAD A DOWNSIDE.
SORRY.
I'VE GOT IT! I'LL KILL YOU WITH CARBON MONOXIDE!
SORRY.

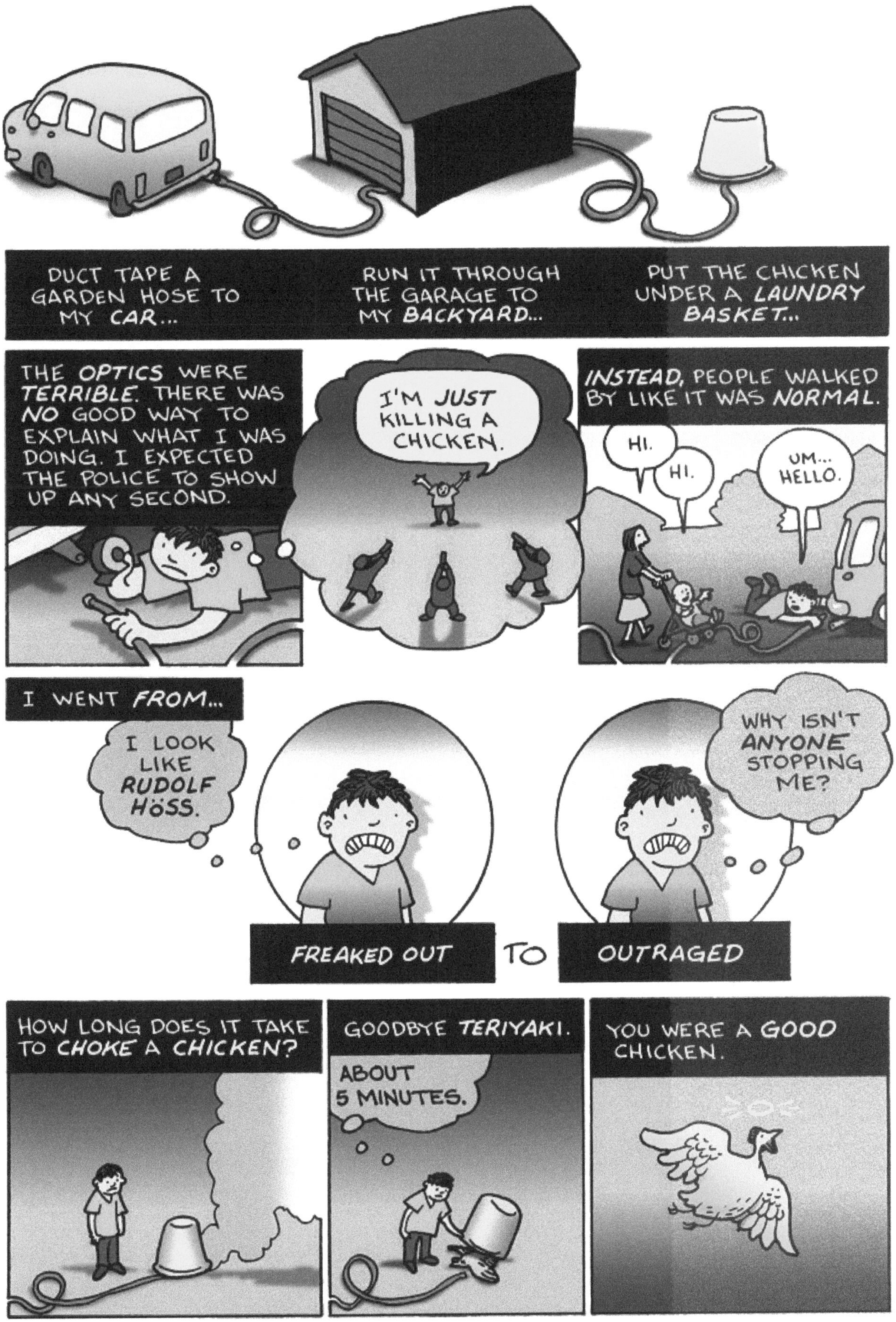
DUCT TAPE A GARDEN HOSE TO MY CAR...
RUN IT THROUGH THE GARAGE TO MY BACKYARD...
PUT THE CHICKEN UNDER A LAUNDRY BASKET...
THE OPTICS WERE TERRIBLE. THERE WAS NO GOOD WAY TO EXPLAIN WHAT I WAS DOING. I EXPECTED THE POLICE TO SHOW UP ANY SECOND.
I'M JUST KILLING A CHICKEN.
INSTEAD, PEOPLE WALKED BY LIKE IT WAS NORMAL.
HI.
HI.
UM... HELLO.
I WENT FROM...
I LOOK LIKE RUDOLF HÖSS.
WHY ISN'T ANYONE STOPPING ME?
FREAKED OUT
TO
OUTRAGED
HOW LONG DOES IT TAKE TO CHOKE A CHICKEN?
GOODBYE TERIYAKI.
ABOUT 5 MINUTES.
YOU WERE A GOOD CHICKEN.

SHANNON WHEELER *lives in Portland with his twin sons (and the ghost of Teriyaki). A contributor to many publications, he created the iconic* **Too Much Coffee Man**.

Gallimaufry

"You cannot buy the revolution. You cannot make the revolution. You can only be the revolution. It is in your spirit, or it is nowhere."

Ursula K. Le Guin (1929-2018)

SOMEONE BUILT A McDONALD'S INSIDE A WALMART INSIDE AN AMERICA.

I can't stop watching *Zootopia* and the entire county is flooded, but the good news is someone built a McDonald's inside a Walmart inside an America.

My dad never comes up from the basement, even if he's bleeding. But he will if I tell him we're going to a place with hamburgers, hamburger buns, and the Civil War. It's like when I found a cigarette dipped in caramel inside a Ferris wheel.

Think about it: for under $10 you can eat chicken nuggets, buy a plastic cup and have a congressman that used to coach high school football.

Whoever thought this up sure had my family in mind. My deceased sister Amelia ate McDonald's every single day. She lived on a motorcycle, and her children are currently in a legal battle over possession of her bike-house. I have an uncle that worked his entire life at Walmart.

He died peacefully in his sleep at the age of 19. My uncle and sister both would've gotten a kick outta the place.

I was at the McDonald's-inside-a-Walmart-inside-an-America last week, and the milkshake machine was down, the self checkout wasn't working and there was a factory explosion in South Bend, IN. But you know what? I went back the next day, and everything was back to normal.

Lately, I've found myself caught up in that opioid epidemic. It's not what they make it out on the news, trust me. The fish filet gets a bad rap, too. And really, you're gonna tell me you don't want a DVD with four different Kevin Hart movies?

Food isn't bad just because it doesn't cost an arm and a leg. A store isn't bad just because every last aisle is blocked by pallets stacked sky high with Pop-Tarts. And a country isn't bad just because 12 to 150 times a year something goes horribly wrong.

I have to go because I can hear Dad coughing. I hope he lives to see the day billions served turns to trillions served. I hope he lives to see the day Walmart finally makes a car. And I hope he lives to see the day America finally makes its own sun that it doesn't have to share with anyone else.

—*Osman Siddique*

EVERY NEW YORKER'S SECRET REACTION TO EVERY TERROR ATTACK.

1. Where was it?
2. How bad was it?
3. Is everyone I know okay?
4. If it was close by, can I help?
5. If not: Do I have to get down to that area to do something tonight or tomorrow morning?
6. If so: Is this going to be a big pain in my ass?
7. If not: Am I often in that area?
8. If so: Why wasn't I there during the attack? Was it because the line at the coffee shop was long? If so: If I had caught that F train where the conductor slammed the doors in my face like an asshole, even though the train just sat there for another 30 seconds, would I have beat the line at the coffee shop, and then been right at the scene of the attack at that exact moment? Huh. Makes you think. Well, maybe there's an upside to the MTA falling apart. Maybe I should consider this the next time I spend my whole commute flaming the governor on Twitter.

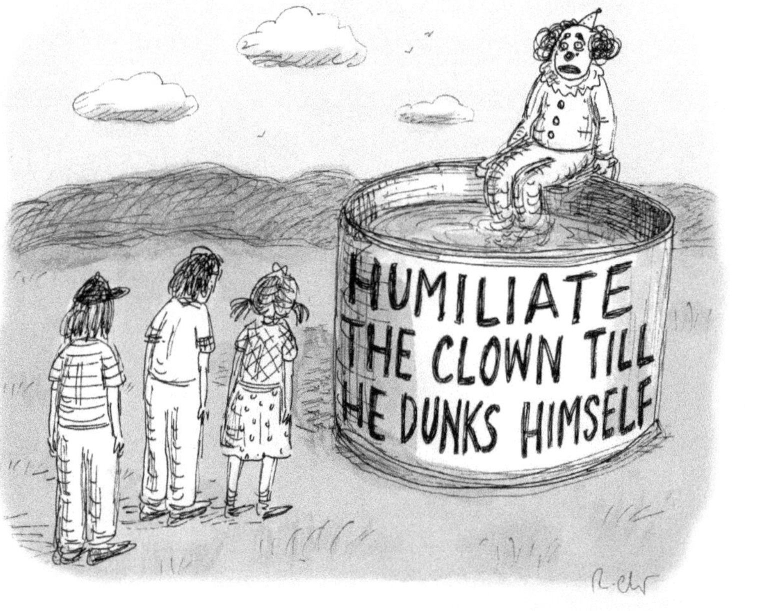
HUMILIATE THE CLOWN TILL HE DUNKS HIMSELF

9. If not: Fuck Cuomo. I'll vote Eric Trump's gums for president before I pull the lever for that bum.

10. Who was the attacker?

11. If white: Prepare social media post about media and political double standards in reacting to lone wolf terror attacks perpetrated by white men.

12. If Muslim: Prepare social media posts about how the supposed national mental health crisis never seems to apply to Muslim lone wolf terrorists, only white ones.

13. Then be extra cool to your Pakistani bodega guy this morning. Let Fahad know that we know that he's one of us, not one of them.

14. Even though, you know, frankly, this bagel could use a couple more minutes in the toaster. Would you mind? You're the man, Fahad.

15. Where was the attacker from?

16. If he was here legally: Prepare social media posts about how a giant wall and/or extreme vetting wouldn't have mattered in this particular instance.

17. If he was here illegally: Change the subject. Point out that the GOP shrugged off 58 dead in Vegas but is freaking out about this. The hypocrisy is sickening. Dead is dead.

18. You know, not for nothing, but if I had to live in Paterson, NJ, and Tampa, FL, like this guy did, I'd probably wind up a terrorist, too. Throw in Phoenix, and I'd be Hitler.

19. And I'll tell you something: If I were a terrorist, I'd be a hell of a lot better than this guy. You're going to do a truck attack in Manhattan, and you don't go after Herald Square, or Union Square, or any hellishly crowded unguarded Midtown area at rush hour? You pick... a bike path? At 3 pm? And then you run out with... a BB gun? Bush league.

20. Take stock. How do you feel? Are you sad? Are you reminded for a brief moment of the inherent vulnerability of living in a place like this? A place thick with people, with a big target on its ass? Of course you are. Are you afraid? Never. Fear is for people in the flyover who live in places ISIS has never heard of. And you've got too much shit to do to worry.

21. This is just another reason to avoid the West Side. Like we needed one.

—*Joe Keohane*

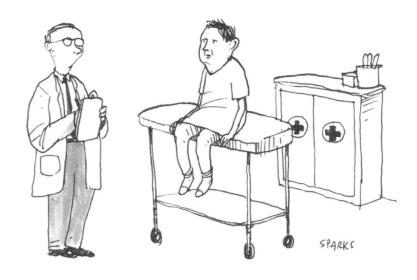

"It hurts when I pay."

CYNTHIA FROM H.R. IS BEING SUPER H.R.-Y RIGHT NOW.

Here it goes. All because you couldn't be cool, Cynthia. As you requested, I logged my bar shift from last night. You wanted me to break down the events that led to my second verbal warning of this month so I broke it all the way down.

ENJOY ALL THIS TRUTH, CYNTHIA.

Hour 1: I turned both TVs to ESPN3 because that's where they keep the weird shit like logrolling or high school basketball. The simple syrup was low so I made a fresh batch. I set up the bottles, cut limes and refilled the straws. I sat in the cooler for 20 minutes and screamed.

I DO THIS SOMETIMES, CYNTHIA. IT CENTERS ME.

Hour 2: Happy Hour. It was Taco Tuesday so the place was lit.

Hour 3: I looked over toward my co-worker. He was aggressively scrolling through Pinterest. I didn't dare interrupt him. He was obviously hurting.

I BET YOU WOULD INTERRUPT, CYNTHIA. I BET YOU WOULD HAVE HIM FILL OUT A FORM INSTEAD OF LETTING HIM HEAL IN HIS OWN WAY.

Hour 4: I ate a gross amount of french fries. I ate them very fast, and standing up, and with my legs crossed because I had to pee so bad. I also had to make a lady a cappuccino, which is just the worst.

Hour 5: A guest of the hotel asked me to explain Mezcal. He did the same thing two days ago. So again, I poured him a sip. And again, I winked when I did it. But this time I added: "Bud, have you ever dreamt of befriending a wolf, or becoming a breakdance champion, or maybe mastering an ancient wind instrument? Have you ever dreamt outside the narrative your life fell into but didn't necessarily want? Bud, you are not an accountant, or medical supplies salesman, or whatever the fuck boring job you obviously do. You are your boyhood dreams. You are the dude the wolves want to hang with. In short, would you describe the tint of these dreams as 'smoky'? Because Mezcal is smoky...like your dreams."

He drank his sip. We then tightly hugged. And then we went to the valet parking lot and we smoked about two grams of medicinal marijuana.

HAVE YOU EVER CONNECTED WITH A STRANGER IN SUCH A DEEP WAY, CYNTHIA? OR ARE YOU CONSTANTLY TRYING TO SIGN PEOPLE UP FOR SIX-HOUR TRAININGS THAT SHOULD ONLY LAST FIVE FUCKING MINUTES?

Hour 6: I had come to the realization, during the making of a gin and tonic, that there is very little sincerity in the act of whistling.

THINK ABOUT IT, CYNTHIA.

Hour 7: It was right around this time that I had begun to crave a leftover piece of garlic bread in my fridge. I just couldn't shake it from my mind. I

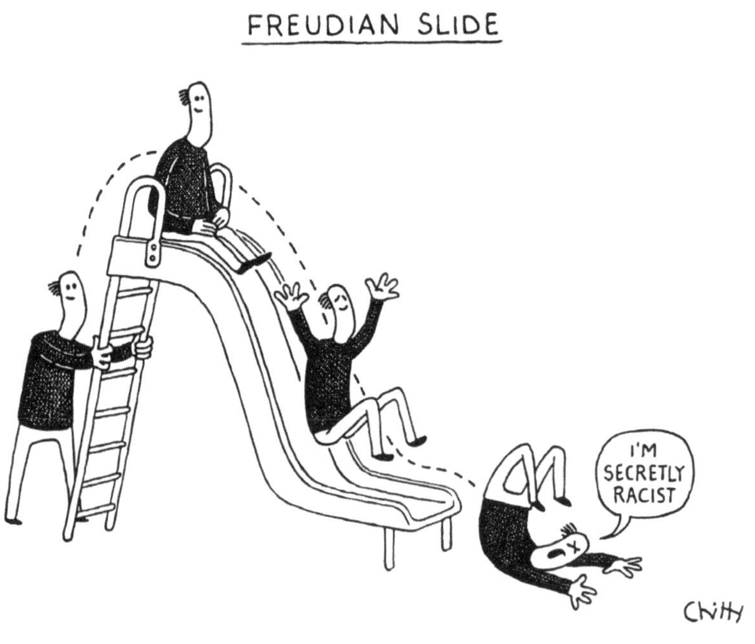
FREUDIAN SLIDE
I'M SECRETLY RACIST

wanted to really fuck it up, you know? And I was certain it still had a good amount of Alfredo sauce smeared on the bottom of it, too.

Hour 8: Mill Valley High Crusaders won against the Falcons of St. Lutheran School for Boys with the final score being 42-34. Up next was Regional Dart Throwing. I then clocked out and ran home as hard as I could.

ALL THIS BECAUSE I FORGOT TO TURN THE TVS OFF AGAIN. THE BALL IS NOW IN YOUR COURT, CYNTHIA.

—Jaylee Alde

THE IMPLIED CONTRACT FOR WHEN A STRANGER ASKS YOU TO WATCH THEIR THINGS WHILE THEY USE THE BATHROOM.

THIS is the implied and very legitimate contract agreed to on TODAY'S DATE, between YOU (henceforth known as "Bathroom User") and ME (henceforth known as "Kindly Appearing Stranger"), who just met in this random cafe (henceforth known as "Starbucks.")

IN CONSIDERATION of bladder-related needs and other good and valuable benefits, the sufficiency and receipt of which are hereby acknowledged, the two (2) parties agree as follows:

I. The interaction "Would you mind watching my stuff?" and "Sure," counts as official, binding signatures by both parties.

II. Upon completing the interaction in which Bathroom User's request is acknowledged, Kindly Appearing Stranger assumes full responsibility of Bathroom User's belongings, up to and including a laptop, purse, cute dog or small child.

III. Upon the commencement of this contract, the small child is legally renamed "Horatio." The cute dog is to be set free, as all dogs are inherently wild beasts.

IV. Kindly Appearing Stranger is now solely responsible for "watching [their] stuff." If the items are obtained by a third party during the time that Bathroom User is absent, the Kindly Appearing Stranger must watch these goods grow smaller and smaller, until they finally leave their frame of vision. This, and only this, is the meaning of "watch" as put forth in this contract.

V. THEREFORE, it is in Kindly Appearing Stranger's best interest to obtain the watched items, then bolt.

VI. Having done so, Kindly Appearing Stranger has the full legal right, but not the obligation, to assume the identity of Bathroom User.

VII. Bathroom User may attempt to regain their previous life, but there is no legal ground to do so. Bathroom User's former partner, parents, Horatio, etc. are no longer their own biological relations. Even Bathroom User's partially used Chapstick now belongs to Kindly Appearing Stranger, though that is a little gross.

VIII. In any case, Bathroom User must wash their hands. Otherwise that is also gross.

IX. Should Bathroom User track down Kindly Appearing Stranger and accost them, Kindly Appearing Stranger has the right to mumble "for keepsies."

X. Horatio is vegan, loves polo and must be nourished with bread that is not risen.

XI. Horatio is a good boy. He is not gross. Kindly Appearing Stranger is lucky to have him.

(Note: Kindly Appearing Stranger, by virtue of their kindly appearance, may already be in custody of multiple Horatios. They are encouraged to adopt more until they have a full polo team of Horatios.)

IN WITNESS WHEREOF the parties have hereunto set their hands wherever they like as long as Bathroom User washes theirs afterward. (Seriously, they must do this. Otherwise, it is gross.)

—Karen Chee

JOKES LOST IN TRANSLATION.

JAPAN — A man receives a very close haircut. His wife, who has worked hard all day, sees him and complains, "I married a husband, not an old bald one!"

KENYA — CHILD: Mother, when will I be as big and strong as Father?
MOTHER: Child, when the wind returns from the mountain.
CHILD: Today or tomorrow?

SAUDI ARABIA — Q: How do you get a camel into a helicopter?
A: First, you must calm it with some tea.

FRANCE — The prime minister enters a busy cafe and orders a plate of bread and Brie de Meaux. The waiter, finding no Brie de Meaux, serves Brie de Melun, reasoning, "His Honor will not know the difference." The prime minister takes a bite and says, "The Provençal will be invading shortly, yes?"

GERMANY — It's no use to try to escape a bear trap, but you can always scream until help arrives.*

CHINA — POLICEMAN: Did you see the man who burgled your shop?

WOMAN: No, his face was covered by a turnip bag.

POLICEMAN (*writing*): "He has the features of a *Zhejiang*."

BELARUS — Last winter was so cold, the state produced half as much oil.

TURKMENISTAN — Gurbanguly Berdimuhamedow, Akja Nurberdiýewa and Yaylym Berdiev are walking down Saparmurat Turkmenbashi Avenue when a beautiful nude woman approaches them. Berdimuhamedow says, "I am pleased to see that Turkmen agriculture is reaping high yields this year." Nurberdiýewa says, "I am pleased to see that the Turkmen military is in fine form this year." Berdiev fires his pistol into the air and shouts, *"All horses to the starting line!"*

—Tim Harrod

A GENTLE REMINDER.

A few months ago, I bought some Greek yogurt that I wanted to take to work. But I kept forgetting to grab it in the morning.

Well, one evening, while frustratedly staring at that grocery bag full of uneaten yogurt in my fridge, the answer to my problem finally came to me. The solution was so simple, it was embarrassing.

What I did was, I took my car keys, and I put them in my butt. That way, in the morning I would remember to take the yogurt. I'm happy to report I've been doing this for weeks and haven't forgotten to take the yogurt once.

—Osman Siddique

EXCERPTS FROM THE DVD COMMENTARY.

(The following is taken from the commentary for **Born to Lose, Dying to Win** *(1978), recorded by the director Homer Hornbecker for the 2010 Criterion Edition.)*

00:02:00 This opening scene came almost verbatim from a dream I had after my third wife left me for the chimp handler on that show *B.J. and the Bear*, and I'd gone out and gotten whacked on Everclear and set fire to a cactus in Joshua Tree National Park. Woke up the next morning and found I'd vomited a perfect pentagram around myself and was handcuffed to a coyote that was wearing a wedding veil and some Indian fella told me I was the mayor of a local shantytown. I looked him right in the eye and then and there said, "Son, I got an idea for a movie." Sometimes you're just a... channel, y'know?

00:10:03 [sound of vomiting]

00:11:47 Gas station attendant here was our producer's coke dealer. I only gave him the part because he put a hex on me.

00:21:19 Lot of people miss it, but I put a motif of big fuckin' titties in this film. If you look for it you start to see 'em everywhere, just jigglin' around. Feminists get on my ass, but really I'm just showing my appreciation for the female form. Like Picasso. Also, sweater meat gives me a mega-boner.

00:23:22 [sound of vomiting, followed by fervent prayer]

00:30:51 I don't remember this scene. That's not too surprising, though. I don't remember my fourth wife, five of my kids' names or most of the mid-to-late 1980s.

00:37:09 You see right there where Johnnie stabs that guy? That really happened. I mean, he's really getting stabbed right there. Knives got mixed up, so basically Johnnie killed a guy. Since we were shooting without a permit, an accident like that would have shut us down, so I made the crew sign a blood oath, then had craft service chop the body up and we ate it. Few beers, a little salsa, didn't go down too bad. Problem was there was like 50 of us, so there wasn't enough to go around. That's why we filmed this second killing here, I think it was some local. Everyone got a human bone as a crew gift.

We should probably cut this part out.

00:46:39 [here begin 10 minutes of spoken-word Carpenters lyrics]

00:58:17 You see that quick little jump cut there? We had to stop filming when we got into a gang war with the local townsfolk — because of all the people who went missing after we showed up. It was pretty brutal. I'm *pretty sure* that's when I lost my left pinky. Or was that the right one? Either way, some old lady bit it off. Our gaffer ended up beating the chief of police into a coma with a length of dolly track, and I'm pretty sure someone set a church

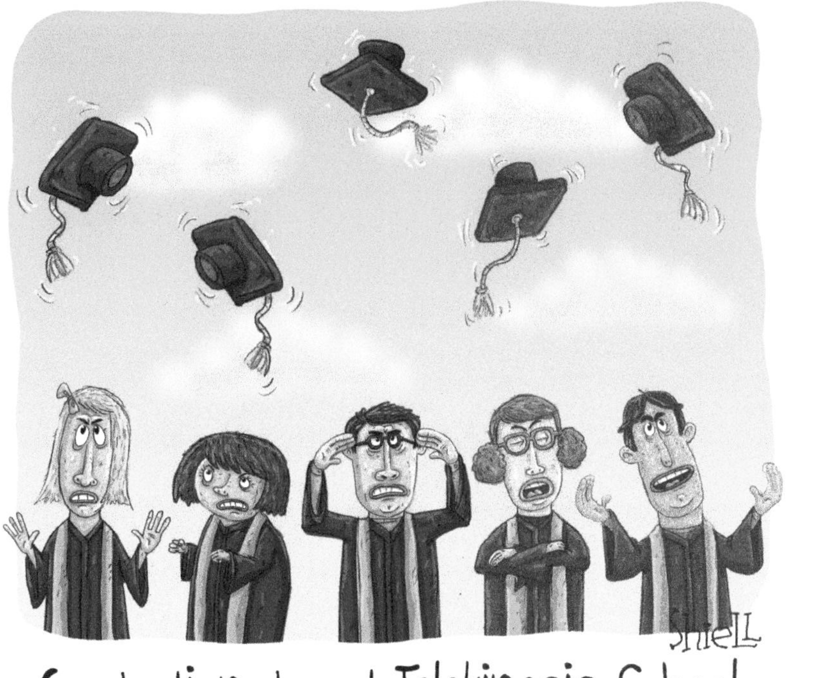
SHELL

Graduation day at Telekinesis School.

* *CORRECTION: This has been translated flawlessly.*

EMBROIDERED PANT PROFILING

Anchors Guy: You're attracted to novelty, like the limited-edition Oreos in the Peeps and Firework flavors. You prefer the beach in the fall. You strive for that perma-windburn look of extreme pro athletes (or someone who lives by the sea). And you're getting close! Kids would draw you with the pink crayon. In second grade, you secretly fed the class guinea pig ham, just to see what would happen.

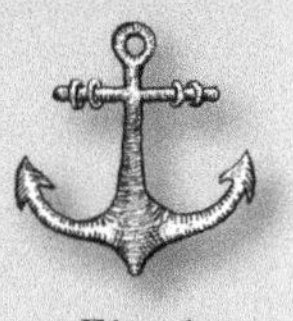

Fig. 1

Black Lab Guy: You don't look cops in the eyes. Ever. You like cold beverages (G. Love #rideordie). You pair pastels with pastels, bolds with bolds, primaries with primaries. Nothing too matchy, though. Generally you avoid black, the exception, of course, being the dogs on your pants. Your go-to brunch cocktail is red sangria — so solid. At college, you did a bad thing in the dining hall.

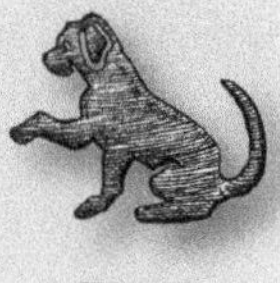

Fig. 2

Martinis Guy: You limit your facial hair to just around your mouth and covering your chin. You trim it over the sink once a week, carefully moving the toothbrushes and hand soap inside the medicine cabinet so no little hairs get on them. For dinner on Tuesdays, you make salmon in a tinfoil packet with rosemary and lemon. Sometimes you fake showering before work à la sticking your head under the sink plus CK Be.

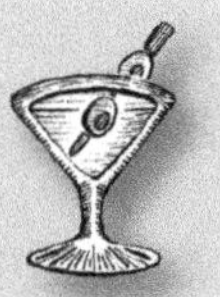

Fig. 3

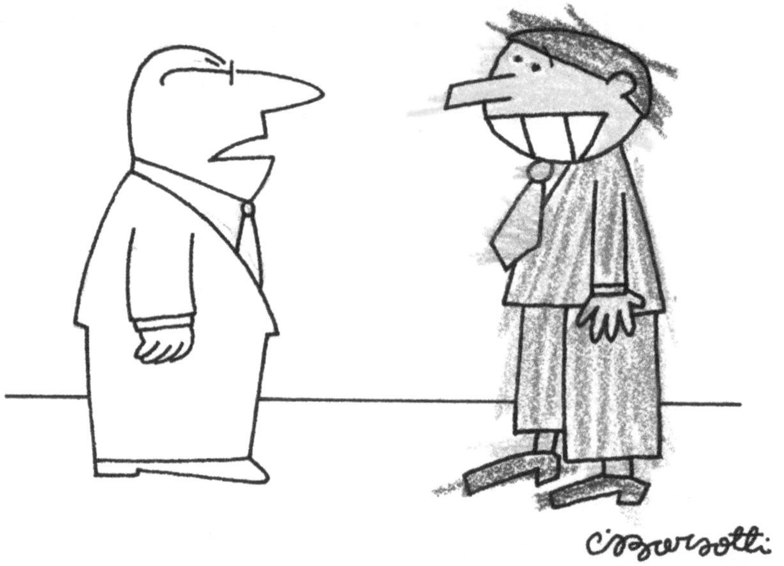

"Until you're top management, Warrick, I strongly suggest you stay within the lines."

on fire. Anyway, you were asking why Johnnie goes suddenly from wearing a leather jacket to wearing a severed dog's head as a hat.

01:11:59 [sound of cigarette being lit and a few minutes of grunting]

01:13:36 This dream sequence is an actual dream I had. How the fuck did we film my dreams, is what I want to know.

01:20:03 [sound of cigarette being lit, inaudible mumbling, occasional prayer; a few final dry heaves]

01:33:43 The ending here has caused some debate apparently, but it's pretty straightforward. We ran out of money, so we just set everything on fire for the insurance, then planned to flee the country. I had just chugged an entire coffee thermos of DMT and was trying to start a knife fight with my own skeleton, so I was up for any idea the goat I had dressed in a tux and called "executive producer" said was worth trying.

After we wrapped, I spent a lot of time in Nicaragua, mostly on purpose. I completed the editing by sending death threats via telegram to my ex-wives and a few key political figures. Eighteen months later, I woke up in an ancient lava bed with a note stapled to my chest telling me I'd won the Palme d'Or. Go figure.

—Ryan Nyburg

ABBOTT & STELLA.

I don't know about yours, but in my house, a comedy routine can break out at any moment. Just last week, I ordered some Indian takeout for dinner. As usual, I got a little carried away, and soon our kitchen table was filled with appetizers, entreés, mango lassis, papadum and naan. As my wife, Stella, and I dug in she said, "Be sure to save me some of that Indian bread." Mouth full, I nodded in agreement.

Several lip-smacking minutes later, Stella spoke up."I'm ready for some naan now. Is there any left?"

"There's naan left."

"You jerk! I asked you to save me some."

"We have naan."

"Aw, I was really looking forward to it!"

"But there is naan."

"I know! Quit rubbing it in."

"No, no, naan exists!"

"I get it, Buster. You can shut up about it now!"

I pawed through a rubble of containers and napkins. "Look, there's naan on the table…somewhere…"

"You're gonna be on the *floor* if you don't stop teasing me!"

"I'm trying to tell you! We! Have! Naan!"

"God, you can be such an asshole!"

"But — oh, never mind."

After a chilly silence, Stella asked: "Is there any more of that lamb dish? What's it called?"

"Goan."

"THAT, TOO!?"

Third base.

—Jim Siergey

OUR 'ALL-TIME BEST' CHARITY AUCTION!

The Beatrice and John McKenzie Center for Vascular Surgery at the Boston University Hospital is proud to present our "all-time best" silent charity auction! (You'll understand why we're calling it that in a second.) Every year is special, given the lifesaving work we do here at the Center, but this year you're in for a real treat: We've been given access to a time machine! Just like in the movies!

Of course, in the movies, bad things always happen when you monkey with the awesome force of Time itself, but this is reality. Also, it's for a good cause. So bid with confidence.

1.Ultimate Yankee Takedown! *(Minimum bid: $100,000)* It's the dream of every Red Sox fan: sweet revenge, served very cold. Mere seconds after stepping into our time machine, you'll be facing hated Yankee greats Babe Ruth, Lou Gehrig, Joe DiMaggio and Reggie Jackson. Because they can hear you, but not see you (you'll appear as a shimmering pinkish mist) the winning bidder is encouraged to goad the players with racial epithets and question their sexual preferences — be as nasty and childish as you want! For an extra $10,000 donation, Mr. Ruth has agreed to wear lipstick, rouge and a novelty Red Sox bikini, so you can snap a selfie with him in this degrading getup. How would *that* look in your BoSox mancave? (Not to mention in every subsequent Ruth biography.)

2. Always the Twain Shall Meet! *(Min. bid: $100,000)*: Do you hate co-op board meetings as much as we do? So boring; so serious.

Why not have Samuel Clemens himself run your next one? Instead of spluttering with barely contained rage at that pompous ass of a treasurer, let the silver-tongued Father of American Wit handle your retort instead! America's master wordsmith will perfectly skewer your building's antiquated recycling policies, leaving everyone in the room shaking with laughter. (NOTE: Mr. Clemens re-

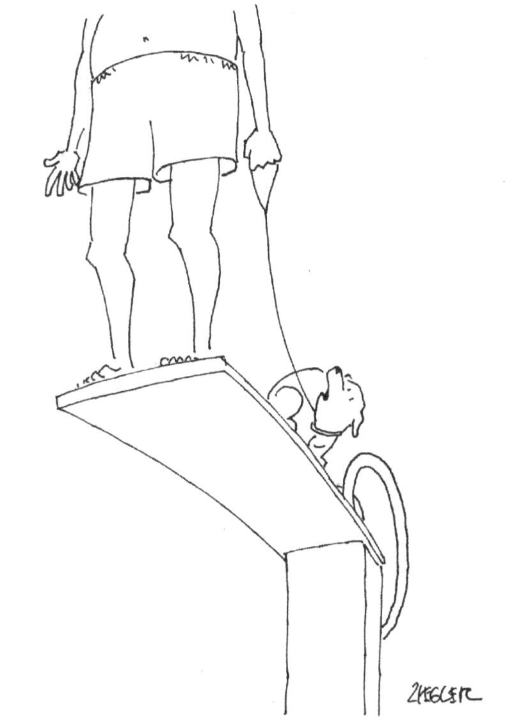

"Excuse me, Ed, but I stopped enjoying this walk about 5 minutes ago."

Mallards in Flight Guy: If you met Bryce Harper, you'd be friends. You have a nice camera, and your favorite bird to photograph, despite what these pants may suggest, is the robin. You're built like a football player and use that muscle to craft exquisite gardens around office buildings. When your little sister, now not so little and in her 20s, sings Pink's "What About Us", you a) have never heard it before, b) are into it, and c), decide to listen to more new music that isn't by Lin-Manuel Miranda (but he really is so talented). Your middle school years were largely colored by shoplifting.

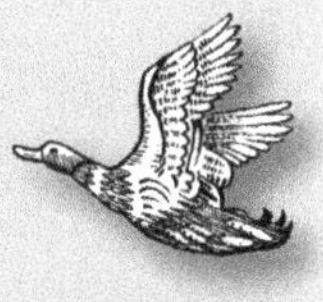

Fig. 4

Hula Girls Guy: You start planning your next vacation as soon as you get home, sometimes even on the way home. Your TV is mounted, has been for years now, and you have a sectional couch with a chaise longue at one end. You prefer curly to straight hair, and "business casual" makes you weary. That scene in *Forrest Gump* where he wipes his muddy face on a yellow T-shirt and says, "Have a nice day," thus sparking, you know, that entire thing — gets you every time. Once or twice, you've woken up unable to remember where you've left your belt.

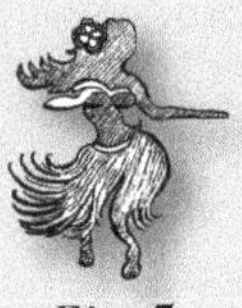

Fig. 5

Fish Bones Guy: You like your IPAs with juicy hops, preferably drunk from a can while in a canoe. You know that a good campfire requires a perimeter of large rocks. On the weekend, you almost exclusively wear waffle-knit tees. At the office, because of your regular attendance and general dependability, they've assigned you fire warden. Your best friend is your orange tabby cat, Sam. And, if you're being entirely

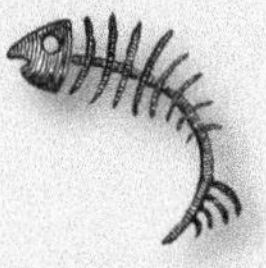

Fig. 6

honest, you could never ever date someone heavy.

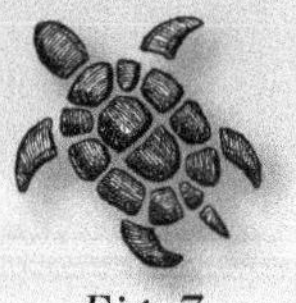
Fig. 7

Sea Turtles Guy: At the playground, you sit on the bench while your 5-year-old son woos the other kids with his remote control car. The search history on your phone includes "How to re-caulk your tub" and "Homeland season premiere?" Your college friends still call you by your last name, even though no one keeps in touch with the other Pauls anymore. You'd like to do one of those bike tours in Scotland of all the whisky (no "e") distilleries. You often wonder about your parents' wills.

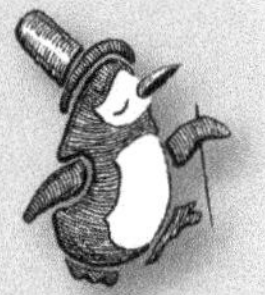
Fig. 8

Dapper Penguin Guy: You carry your messenger bag by its top handle. You're diligent about changing your pillowcase once a week. You wear spectacles, not glasses. You do not have a mounted TV, but you do have a bike mount. Breakfast is scrambled eggs cooked very slowly over medium-low heat. The last time you wore sweatpants was in elementary school. You wish homeless people would just go away. And you don't care how.

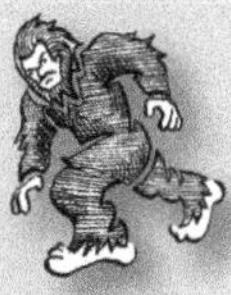
Fig. 9

Yeti Guy: You believe clouds are made from cotton balls, UB40 is led by Kevin Bacon, Sunny Delight holds the cure for cancer, and we need more guns. 2017 was your all-time favorite year.

What's that? Doesn't sound like you at all?

Huh. This is awkward. I wish there were something I could do. But the thing is, I believe it very deeply, so my mind's made up: It must be true.

—Rasika W. Boice
illustrations by Zoe Matthiessen

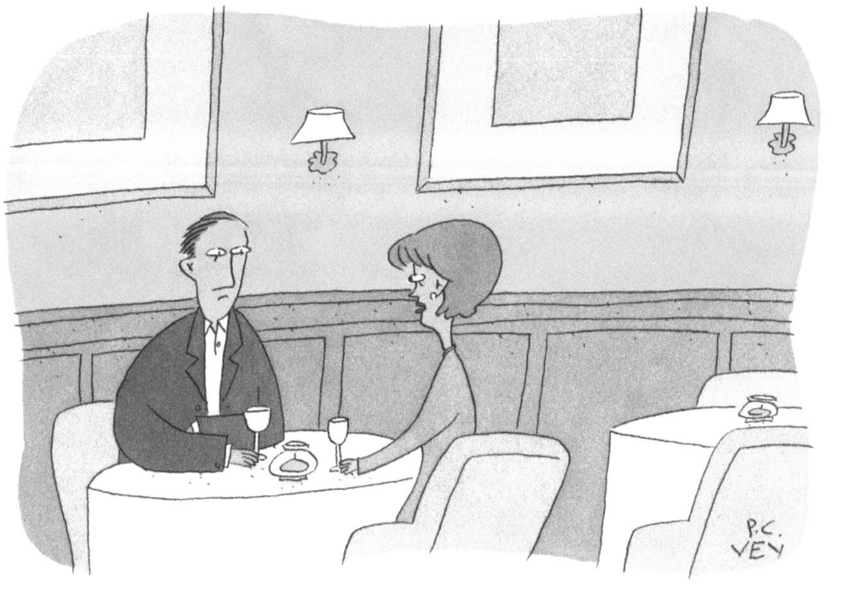
P.C. VEY
"Would you like to come back to my place and face some uncomfortable truths?"

quires expenses covered for cleaning and drying of his suit, a two-horse carriage to and from the meeting, and a three-course dinner at Delmonico's.)

3. The Butterfly Affect *(Min. bid: $350,000):* What's better than last year's catered lunch with Ashton Kutcher, star of the early 2000s *The Butterfly Effect*? Actually making one! Trek back to your choice of three prehistoric periods, all within the Paleozoic Era (Cambrian, Ordovician or Silurian). Once there, you can sneeze, stomp and touch to your heart's content. What will happen next? Perhaps a single step of your tassled Cole Haan loafer onto an ancient water bug will cause Connecticut's public school system to rank higher than New Jersey's. Or cause Reggie Jackson and Babe Ruth to be lovers. Who knows, that's where the fun comes in! This exciting prize also includes a catered, post-trip lunch with Ashton Kutcher. (Lunch is contingent upon Ashton Kutcher still existing in the timeline you return to.)

4. Smoke 'Em if You've Got 'Em *(Min. bid: $600,000):* Even the docs in the Vascular Ward will admit it: There's nothing better than a good cigar. But we aren't here to sell you a box of 1954 Romeo y Julietas, like last year. Thanks to this time machine, we're offering you the only lighter worthy of your Churchills: The Big Bang! You and one "smoking buddy" will be transported to where our universe began, to light your stogies on one 7.2-trillion-degree flame! We will also throw in matching monogrammed heat suits, and two four-ounce pours of Remy Martin Louis XIII Grande Champagne Tres Vieille Age Inconnu.

5. ??????????? *(Min. Bid: $1.5 million)*: As we were preparing for this very special evening of giving and celebration, one of the Center's interns bumped into the time machine's confusing control panel (we're assuming it was a control panel, but hey... we're not rocket scientists!). After an impressive display of flashing lights, sirens and spoken warnings to power down the machine, a humanoid figure with a rat-like head and mucous-covered tentacles protruding from its "mouth" tumbled to our feet. He (or she) thrust a beautiful, powder-blue piece of stationery toward us with one of its five hands, just before emitting a sound that can only be described as a dump truck barreling through a no-kill pound. He/she released a copious amount of a pinkish-yellow opaque liquid, then expired. The following was written on the stationery:

wWHrningg peepled of 0t43rRRR RRth+yOArr eQperrim3NT hAth PHAILD++
dUE n000t pRRRoseed+++

After some tinkering with the machine, we were able to find the coordinates that our rodent squid-faced friend originated from... and it turns out that he/she is actually from our exact time, only one or two alternate realities over!

So, it is with great excitement that we present this final (and, frankly, unexpected) auction item: the opportunity to travel to rodent-squid's alternate reality of origin for a chance to return his/her rapidly decomposing body and visit with the men and women of his/her bizarre world. While you're there, pick up a copy of *The Goldfinch* and read the alternate reality ending. Travel to parallel universe Montauk for the weekend to see where your summer home was relocated. Find out if alternate Earth Babe Ruth took a male lover or publicly dressed in women's clothing. Even take in an alternate-parallel Broadway show. Who knows, maybe Andrew Lloyd Webber is that dimension's Stephen Sondheim!

—*Josh Perilo*

THE CONVERSION.

Taking advantage of the beautiful weather, Waldo took a stroll through the park. Flowers were blooming, birds were chirping, and squirrels were scampering — but sitting forlornly on a bench was his old friend Emerson.

Waldo took a seat next to his disconsolate amigo and inquired about his downcast demeanor.

"It's my neighbor." wailed Emerson, "He's driving me crazy."

"The Hungarian?"

"Yes, Gergó. He has decided to become a Buddhist."

"What's wrong with that?" asked Waldo, as he produced a banana from his coat pocket and began to peel it.

"Nothing, nothing at all. It's just that he keeps trying to convert me. All week long, it's been *karma*-this and *dharma*-that. If I hear about Zen just one more time, I'll…"

Waldo swallowed his mouthful of elongated fruit. "Well, he is from Budapest."

Emerson's groan sounded almost like *ommmm*.

—*Jim Siergey*

WHY I DON'T GO TO THE CAR FIGHTS.

We don't have a lot of entertainment out here in Crane County. Our one movie house went out of business six months back when the glass factory closed. The AA baseball team left. Our Dairy Queen is a "Dairy King" and it can't legally sell soft-serve. Finn O'Connor can give you rides in his 1992 Corolla, but that's no big whoop.

You'd think we'd be bored, but nah. Because we have the car fights.

The car fights is simple. Out in the junkyard, there are these two cranes with magnets on the end of them. And those magnets can pick up cars and make them fight.

My dad waited until I was 5 to take me to my first, so's I wouldn't be too scared when those cranes fired up and just smashed the cars into one another. Sparks fly when they smack, and the whole town gets a-cheering. It's the purest joy we know.

There ain't too much joy when there ain't no work. In Crane County, you gotta find joy where you can. Joy like touching the magnet. Rubbing our hands on it. Talking to the two local celebrities — the two crane operators, Grippy-X and Cale's dad, Robbie.

There are also the death row inmates who volunteer to sit in the car in lieu of a proper execution — they're celebs, too. You can commit the awfulest crimes, but you sit in one car fight car, you'll be a hero until the minute you die. The local pastor even told them they'll probably go to heaven even though they murdered all those little girls. He did!

Yeah, accidents happen. Oncet the car flew off and crushed Mrs. McNeil's arm, and now she can't weave the Official Car Fight Blankets. And yes, it's true, that NASCAR man was considering licensing the car fights, when his pacemaker went all crazy because of the big magnet. That NASCAR money woulda really helped us out, but that's car fights! Anything can happen.

You don't believe me? Last year at this time, the last time I went, the car fights were going per usual. Our small dirty faces peeking out of the crowd, trying to see if Grippy-X was really going to wale on Cale's dad, and if the man who we knew at this point was innocent, but the justice system was too corrupt to save, was going to cry before the cranes hit him. Then we heard someone from outside the stadium shout. "Eyy, anyone ordered a brand new city!?"

We turned and gawked — and normally we gawk in pain, but this time, in joy!

There it was. A new city on the back of those trucks. Sixteen gleaming flatbeds each carrying a little piece of salvation. There were chain restaurants like Subway, there was a bus system

complete with organized, well-timed and helpful routes — there were movie houses — heck, a brand new glass factory to send all of our men to work — and on every truck — skyscrapers. Skyscrapers to reseed our small little town. Skyscrapers reaching back into the distance. Our poor little town was about to be saved. We didn't care it was government help. We were about to be saved.

But the car fights had other plans.

"Big city!?" cried Cale's dad angrily. He whipped his crane around quickly, and the car from it flew, knocking down the first skyscraper. The building fell over simply, quickly, knocking down the next skyscraper. Which knocked down the skyscraper behind it — exactly like a domino. Which knocked over the next one and the next one and the next one. I wish they bolted them to the ground better, but they kept falling and toppling. This continued on for hours, and all we could do was watch in terror. And not all of the buildings were empty. The Subway restaurant, for example, was fully operational. In total, we lost 52 lives that day, 641 skyscrapers and any hope Crane County ever had.

We beat up Cale pretty good at school the next day, and I decided to go sign up for a war so I could see a sexy pinup when the boys would pass it around.

But when I get back — if I get back — I ain't going to any more car fights. Too painful. Too many memories.

—*Alex Firer*

TO OUR LOYAL CUSTOMERS.

For years, we have marketed Wild Eagle to a special kind of whiskey drinker: the cool, discerning, independent man. A man always ready for action. A man who knows exactly what he wants.

But we were wrong.

After a year of extensive market research, we've realized that's just not who's drinking Wild Eagle. Now, when we think of our ideal customer, we picture an old railroad tycoon in a waistcoat, pouring himself a stiff drink while gazing out the window and wondering what he has become.

That's a Wild Eagle Moment.

Some in corporate couldn't handle the truth. "Seems risky," they said. "Let's just run the same old commercials showing generic images of American wilderness, to convey an aura of adventure."

But the data is the data. So our new commercial is this: a portly, mustachioed man holding a tumbler while pacing back and forth in front of a rain-streaked window before finally saying, "It's best that you sit down, my boy."

Wild Eagle drinkers don't want wilderness. They don't want adventure. They want a whiskey that an aged titan of industry can sip before saying: "I knew one day I would be on top of the world. And here I am, son. I've done unspeakable things, but here I am." Wild Eagle is the perfect complement to lapsing into a reverie of memories and guilt, the condensation on the side of the glass dripping onto the floor, the only sound coming from the ticking of a pocket watch.

So we'll let other brands go after debonair, adventurous bachelors. They can have tough, savvy ladies who play a mean game of Texas Hold'em and can steal your heart with a glance. That's their crowd. Our crowd is elderly tycoons who open a safe hidden behind a painting and pull out a thick envelope, explaining, "This holds the secrets to everything I've done, and more importantly, my boy, it includes a letter formally handing over control of this corporation."

That's a Wild Eagle Moment.

The sales figures don't lie: For the

last three quarters, while the overall market for brown spirits has been soft, Wild Eagle's orders have quintupled in regions where our customers' spendthrift children reach out to grab the outstretched envelope before their fathers yank it back and chuckle: "Oh, this isn't for you, Harry. I am going to give this letter to your brother when he comes back from the war. Now refill my glass."

We'll leave it to other whiskeys to try to attract customers with TV spots showing pine forests or hunting dogs or time-tested distilling processes. We'll focus on the next generation of Wild Eagle drinkers: aged industrialists' frustrated sons who pour another dram and hand it over as their father gruffly states, "I've made my decision, and Cornelius is to be my successor."

We are lucky that we can expand to this untapped market even while Wild Eagle remains a favorite among old men with prodigious mustaches and sad eyes who finish their second tumbler then ask their profligate sons: "Was there anything else in that drink? It tasted a little different," to which their progeny respond in the negative while surreptitiously hiding a small vial in their sleeve. That's right — our market research has made us confident that in such situations, our loyal customers will still say, "This is some damn fine whiskey," then clutch their throats and point a shaking, accusatory finger at their second sons before collapsing to the floor, the empty tumbler rolling across the Oriental carpet to rest on the hearth of the massive fireplace.

So no fancy ad campaigns for the new Wild Eagle. No celebrity spokespeople. No expensive sports sponsorships. Our whiskey will stay what it's always been: something passed down from generation to generation, mostly because it is the only drink that sons see when they rifle through their recently deceased father's cabinets and carefully place a forged letter giving them control over the family corporation, tossing the original into the crackling fireplace and watching the paper disappear into the flames.

In that moment, Wild Eagle tastes perfect. *That's* a Wild Eagle moment.

—*Matthew Disler*

STAN MACK'S CHRONICLES

UP HIS ALLEY

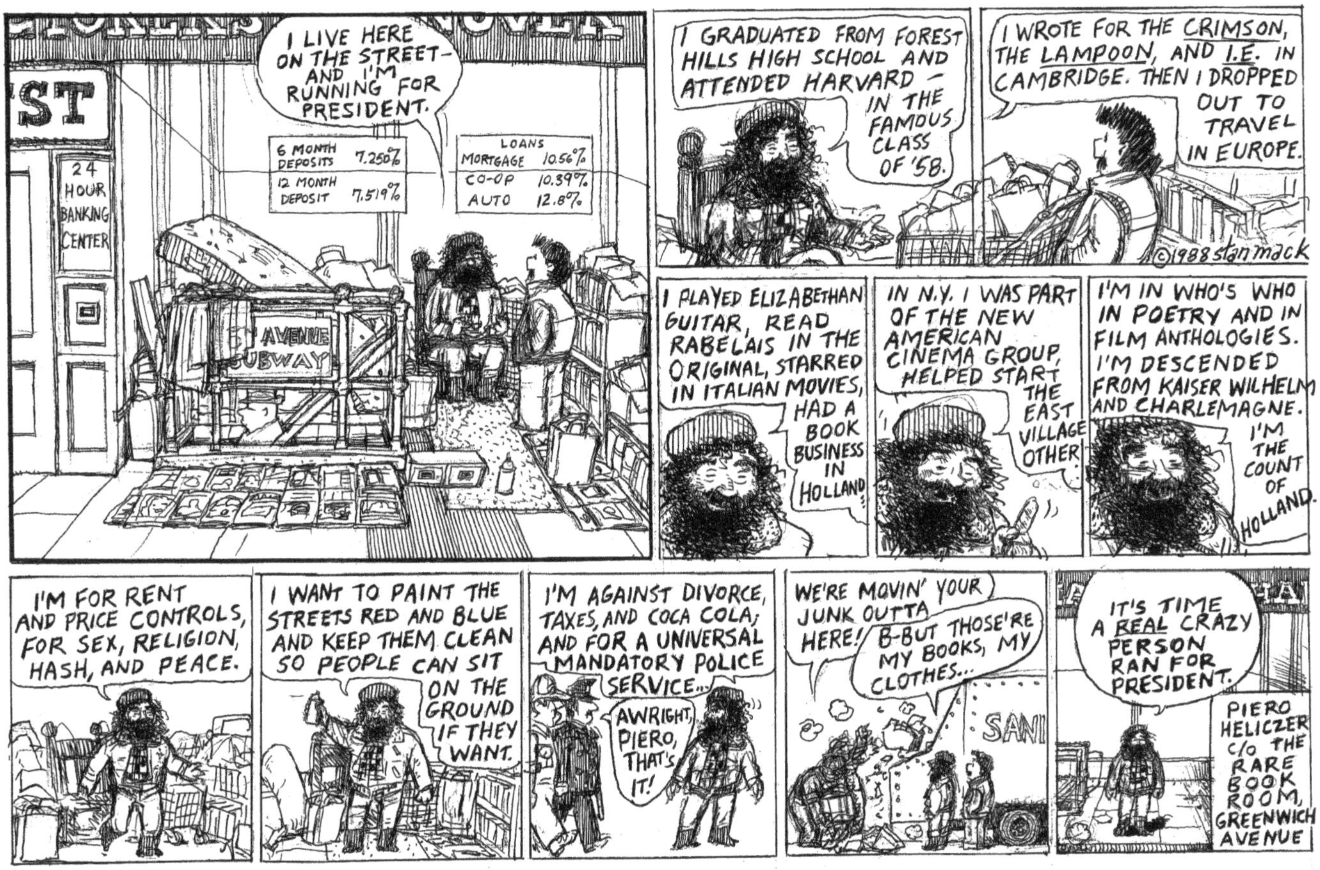
ST
24 HOUR BANKING CENTER
I LIVE HERE ON THE STREET- AND I'M RUNNING FOR PRESIDENT.
6 MONTH DEPOSITS 7.250%
12 MONTH DEPOSIT 7.519%
LOANS
MORTGAGE 10.56%
CO-OP 10.39%
AUTO 12.8%
AVENUE SUBWAY
I GRADUATED FROM FOREST HILLS HIGH SCHOOL AND ATTENDED HARVARD - IN THE FAMOUS CLASS OF '58.
I WROTE FOR THE CRIMSON, THE LAMPOON, AND I.E. IN CAMBRIDGE. THEN I DROPPED OUT TO TRAVEL IN EUROPE.
©1988 stan mack
I PLAYED ELIZABETHAN GUITAR, READ RABELAIS IN THE ORIGINAL, STARRED IN ITALIAN MOVIES, HAD A BOOK BUSINESS IN HOLLAND
IN N.Y. I WAS PART OF THE NEW AMERICAN CINEMA GROUP, HELPED START THE EAST VILLAGE OTHER
I'M IN WHO'S WHO IN POETRY AND IN FILM ANTHOLOGIES. I'M DESCENDED FROM KAISER WILHELM AND CHARLEMAGNE.
I'M THE COUNT OF HOLLAND.
I'M FOR RENT AND PRICE CONTROLS, FOR SEX, RELIGION, HASH, AND PEACE.
I WANT TO PAINT THE STREETS RED AND BLUE AND KEEP THEM CLEAN SO PEOPLE CAN SIT ON THE GROUND IF THEY WANT.
I'M AGAINST DIVORCE, TAXES, AND COCA COLA; AND FOR A UNIVERSAL MANDATORY POLICE SERVICE...
AWRIGHT, PIERO, THAT'S IT!
WE'RE MOVIN' YOUR JUNK OUTTA HERE!
B-BUT THOSE'RE MY BOOKS, MY CLOTHES...
SANI
IT'S TIME A REAL CRAZY PERSON RAN FOR PRESIDENT.
PIERO HELICZER c/o THE RARE BOOK ROOM, GREENWICH AVENUE

QUESTIONABLE ADVICE FROM AMERICA'S BEST.

Jeff Bezos: Don't be afraid to fail. Be afraid to succeed. Success is a bad thing. Always screw up.

Kevin Durant: You miss 100% of the shots you don't take. So take every shot, no matter what your coach says.

Simone Biles: The journey of a thousand miles begins with a single step, unless you're moonwalking. Then you're getting farther away from your destination, but it's worth it because of how cool you'll look.

Elon Musk: You can be anything you want to be, except the CEO of Space X. That's *my* job.

Sheryl Sandberg: Lean in. Lean out. Shake your hips all about. Do the Sandberg Shuffle!

—Evan Waite

TO ALL PLAYERS AND COACHES.

New League rules allowing touchdown celebrations have been a great success! Every Sunday, players are expressing their creativity (and their senses of humor), and fans are loving it. After years of being called the "No-Fun League," fun has returned to the NFL!

However, there have been a few times recently when things have gotten out of hand. So as we head into the Super Bowl, we want to remind everyone of a few common-sense guidelines.

1. End zone celebrations involving velvet-roped VIP areas are strictly verboten. Any player caught retaining the services of a gender ambiguous, clipboard-wielding bouncer to issue catty judgments regarding which teammates may pass the goal line into the party will be fined $15,000. Also note that, following an incident during the Saints/Jets game in December, all end zone festivities involving bottle service will be flagged. No exceptions!

2. Upon scoring, any receiver wishing to dance the hora is free to do so. However, only the last two players to touch the ball, as well as their immediate family members, will be permitted to be raised in chairs. Those players hiring klezmer bands to perform "Hava Nagila" are asked to remind the musicians that this is not a Grateful Dead concert — please make sure they rein in any extended solos and instrumental showboating. Any toasts given by distant uncles and the like should be kept under 20 minutes.

3. Evites are acceptable but, let's be honest, annoying. Note that while the League has instituted a ban on the offering of gifts in the end zone, there is also a ban on invitations that explicitly request that guests "shouldn't feel obligated to bring gifts." We all know what this means. (No passive-aggressive charity requests either — looking at you, Jacksonville Jaguars.)

4. Culinarily-inclined players who wish to celebrate a touchdown by preparing a meal in the end zone are free to do so. However, the League asks that banquets not spin out of control. Making a big show of the fact that you baked your own bread, for example, is overkill and, it must be said, not really that impressive. I

TAXONOMY.

—Zoe Matthiessen

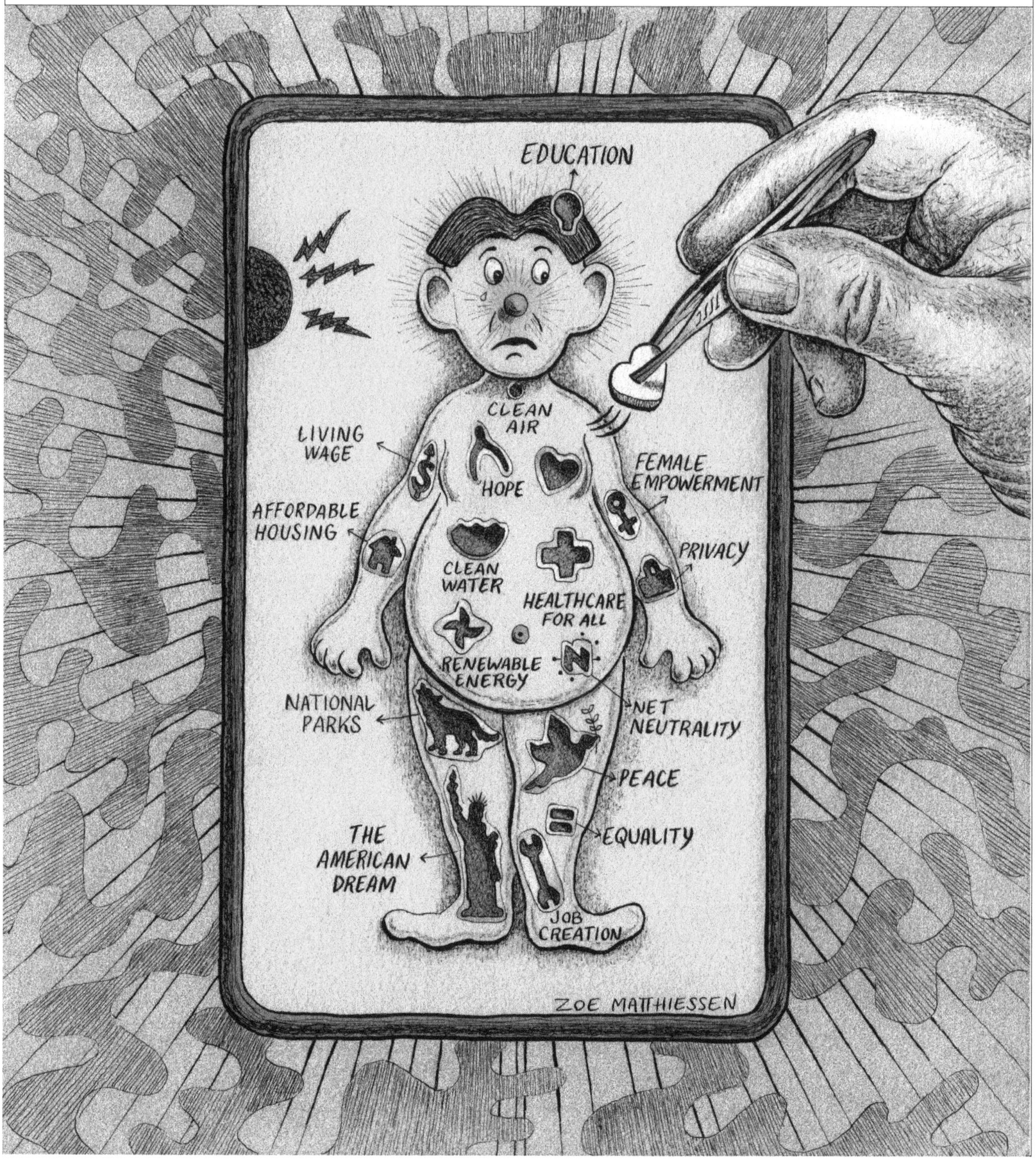
EDUCATION
CLEAN AIR
LIVING WAGE
HOPE
FEMALE EMPOWERMENT
AFFORDABLE HOUSING
CLEAN WATER
PRIVACY
HEALTHCARE FOR ALL
RENEWABLE ENERGY
NATIONAL PARKS
NET NEUTRALITY
PEACE
EQUALITY
THE AMERICAN DREAM
JOB CREATION
ZOE MATTHIESSEN

mean, my God, Aaron Rodgers, just buy a loaf at the store! Also, remember that as NFL players, you are role models — mind your table manners, and take care to match silverware to its corresponding course. Finally, be sure to tidy the end zone after the aperitifs, so that play may resume in a timely manner.

5. In accordance with the League's ban on taunting, hiring an exotic dancer to impersonate an opposing quarterback's mother in the wake of an interception will be flagged. Employing a rapper to perform a "diss track" from the sidelines is allowed, so long as the rapper's fame does not eclipse the moment. (Think Soulja Boy, not Jay-Z.) On-field fat-shaming and Trumpian mean tweets will not be tolerated.

6. Finally, while spiking the football following a touchdown is permissible, welcoming Bill Nye the Science Guy into the end zone to inject the game ball with a concoction of confetti, marshmallows and military dynamite is not. Even if you *are* Tom Brady.

—Jay Ruttenberg

"Nate Dern may not be quite a genius. Still, he has written a book that is very smart, funny, thoughtful, and that might be just what the world needs."

—THE NEW YORK TIMES BOOK REVIEW

From the senior writer at *Funny or Die* and former artistic director at the Upright Citizens Brigade Theater, a collection of absurdist, hilarious stories and essays on relationships, technology, and society.

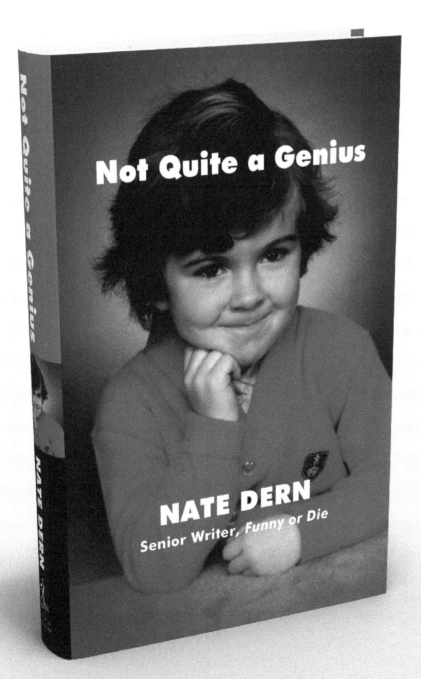

Not Quite a Genius

NATE DERN
Senior Writer, Funny or Die

"Nate Dern's brain is a VitaMix that chops up Kafka, the internet, Republicans, and thousands of other cultural ingredients and blends them into hilarious little treats... Highly recommended reading for those hungry for surprise."

—A.J. JACOBS, *NEW YORK TIMES* BESTSELLING AUTHOR OF *THE KNOW-IT-ALL* AND *DROP DEAD HEALTHY*

"A breath of fresh air that you can eat up bit by bit or all at once like a huge hoagie. His book is, in a lot of ways, like a really wonderful sandwich."

—ABBI JACOBSON, CO CREATOR AND STAR OF COMEDY CENTRAL'S *BROAD CITY*

AVAILABLE WHEREVER BOOKS ARE SOLD.

SIMONANDSCHUSTER.COM SIMON & SCHUSTER
A CBS COMPANY

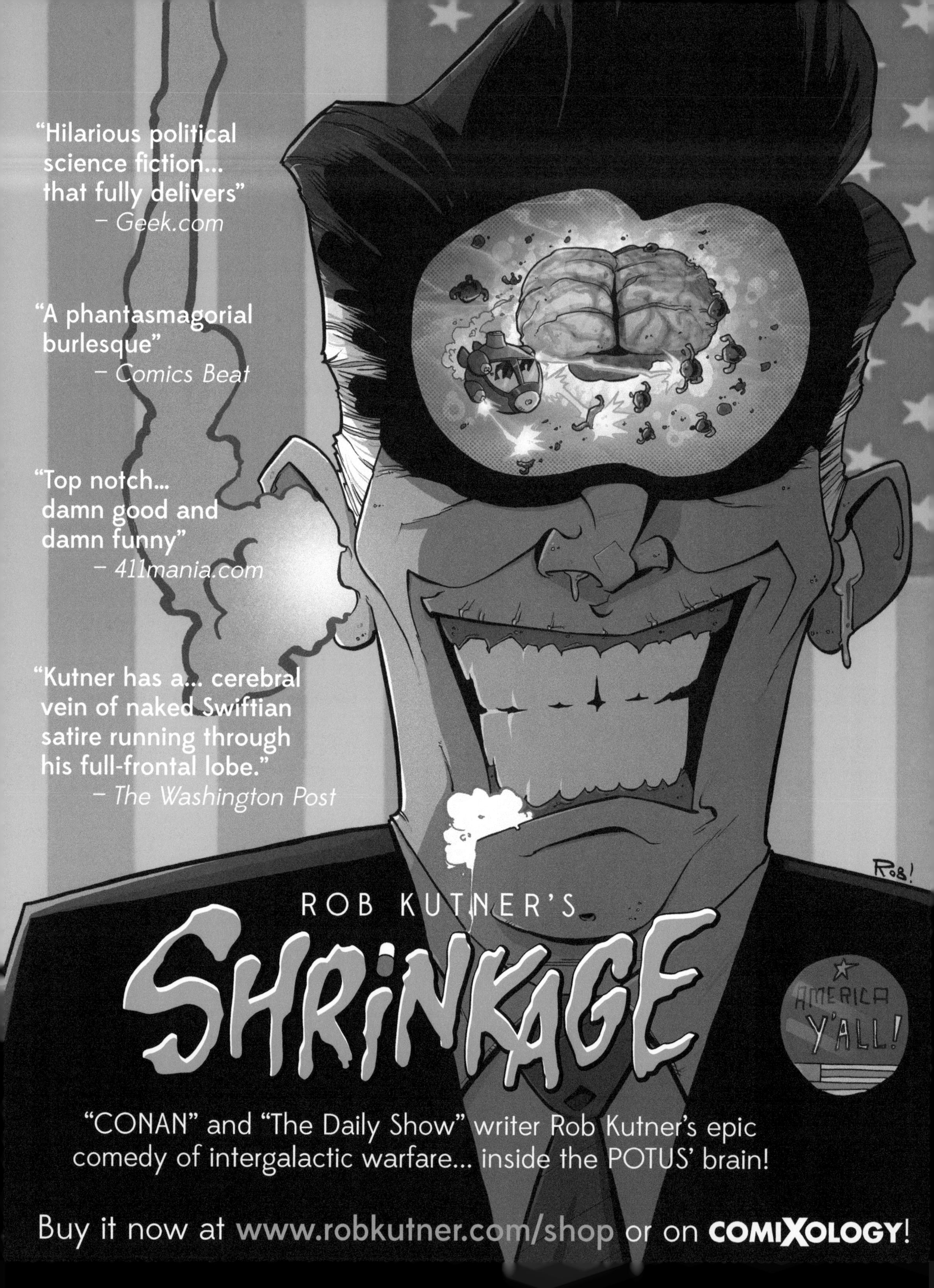

"Hilarious political science fiction... that fully delivers"
– Geek.com
"A phantasmagorial burlesque"
– Comics Beat
"Top notch... damn good and damn funny"
– 411mania.com
"Kutner has a... cerebral vein of naked Swiftian satire running through his full-frontal lobe."
– The Washington Post
ROB!
ROB KUTNER'S
SHRINKAGE
AMERICA Y'ALL!
"CONAN" and "The Daily Show" writer Rob Kutner's epic comedy of intergalactic warfare... inside the POTUS' brain!
Buy it now at www.robkutner.com/shop or on COMIXOLOGY!

BY STEVE YOUNG

DONALD TRUMP'S LIES TO ANIMALS

In fact, lobster attacks on raccoons are exceedingly rare

LOUISA BERTMAN

We're all familiar with the long, dispiriting list of lies Donald Trump has told — to humans. Unfortunately, his lies directed at animals, many of which are extremely gullible, have received less attention. Here are some of the more egregious lies told to animals by Mr. Trump. Feel free to show this list to animals.

"You goats love me. I'm honored. I got over 80% of the goat vote." (Nationwide, goat support for Mr. Trump was under 30%.)

"Fish used to drown in the water. It was a disaster. Then I said, What if fish had gills? That's what turned it around. If you're a fish and you enjoy living in the water, you should thank me." (Fish have had gills for hundreds of millions of years. It is unknown whose idea it was.)

"Can I get a roar? In just a few short months since taking office, I've created over half a million good-paying middle-class jobs for the bear community." (Bear employment has actually declined slightly during the Trump administration.)

"Listen, I'm gonna protect you guys from the lobsters. 78% of attacks on raccoons are committed by mean, pinchy lobsters." (Lobster attacks on raccoons are exceedingly rare.)

"Chuck Schumer wants us to believe that snakes don't have legs. Of course you have legs. How could you walk otherwise? Stand up, snakes, and be proud of your legs!" (Snakes do not have legs. Mr. Trump later claimed that he was referring to lizards.)

"You're a good boy, aren't you? Who's a good boy? You are, yes, you are!" (The dog in question is vicious and ill-tempered.)

"This is why I want to open up the libel laws, pigeons: as you may know, when the parrots talk, they say terrible things about you." (There is no evidence of parrots or parakeets badmouthing other bird species. Libel laws would not apply anyway, since they pertain to written or published, not spoken, defamation by birds.)

"Just because you're a mule doesn't mean you have to be sterile. We're creating terrific affordable new health insurance that will cover mule fertility treatments." (Mules, the sterile offspring of male horses and female donkeys, are not mentioned in any version of Republican-sponsored health insurance legislation.)

"My duck friends tell me that you and your fellow ducks have been devastated by cheap Peking duck dumped on the market by China." (This represents a complete misunderstanding of the duck economy. Also, Mr. Trump has no duck friends.)

"Don't let the lying media call you a 'platypus.' It's pronounced 'plapy-tus.'" (It's pronounced "platypus.")

"I say to Siamese cats: You have been ripping off the government, and it stops now. Look, it's sad that you're stuck together, but we will no longer spend taxpayer dollars to cut you apart." (Siamese cats are not typically conjoined. The few cases in which conjoined Siamese cats have been surgically separated have been paid for with private funds.)

"You can take pride in your heritage. Did you know that our 19th president was one of you, a big, beautiful, smart horse named Mr. Jingles? Unbelievable horse, led us through the tough times of World War I." (The 19th president was Rutherford B. Hayes, whose term occurred nearly 40 years prior to World War I. President Hayes was a human.)

"The liberal Ninth Circuit Court of Appeals ruled that bunnies are not adorable. Crazy, right? Anyone can see you're extremely adorable!" (The case concerned one particular bunny, not bunnies in general. The Supreme Court upheld the ruling, agreeing that the individual bunny was not adorable.)

"A lot of elk at our rally here today. Great to have your support, elk!" (They were moose, and they were protesting.)

"Turtles have been hurt the most by our failing economy. In the past 20 years, it's gone from most of you owning your shells to most of you renting." (Turtle shell ownership has hovered around 65% since 1990, with only a brief dip under 60% during the 2008-2009 recession.)

"I love what you cows do. I'm a big supporter. Every morning I eat your delicious eggs, your delicious cow eggs." (Cows give milk. They do not lay eggs.)

"The so-called 'experts' say you're fossilized, but you're just very thin, and that's Obama's fault. We're going to help you and you're going to get better and it's going to be fantastic!" (The dinosaurs had been extinct for 65 million years prior to Mr. Obama taking office.)

ℝ

STEVE YOUNG (@pantssteve) *is a veteran* **Letterman** *writer who's also written for* **The Simpsons.** *He recently worked on NBC's* **Maya & Marty** *variety show and is teaching a course at NYU's Tisch School.*

BY BRYCE DURDEN, ASSOCIATE

MY BOSS AT PINKBERRY IS PUTTING RAT FECES IN THE YOGURT AND I WILL NOT STAND FOR IT ONE SECOND LONGER

My honored colleagues, I rise today with no small measure of regret. Regret because of the state of our disunion. Regret because of the coarseness of our leadership. And regret that a certain individual keeps putting rat feces in the frozen yogurt.

In recent months, a phrase has entered the language to describe the accommodation of a new and undesirable order, that phrase being "the new normal." But we must never allow ourselves to fall into thinking that that is just the way things are now at our Placid Hills Pinkberry—that every man, woman and child is doomed to unknowingly ingest what is really quite a significant amount of rat feces, every time he or she enjoys one of our premium frozen treats.

Colleagues, we have fooled ourselves for long enough believing that things would change. They have not. We have fooled ourselves for long enough hoping that a certain nameless individual would mend their ways. They have not. If anything, there is even more rat feces in the yogurt than ever before. So much so that we've been forced to sell the vanilla as chocolate chip on more than 12 separate occasions. Including a child's birthday party.

Well, I rise before you today to say, enough.

Now, I'm aware that some people, Associates more savvy than I, will caution against such talk. "Think of the big picture," they'll say. "Keep your head down. Don't take your freebies from the left-most spigot." But the notion that we should say or do nothing in the face of such behavior is ahistoric and, I believe, profoundly misguided. After all, what if someone hadn't spoken up when Stoner Jerry was caught touching all the plastic spoons with his penis? What if someone hadn't raised an alarm when Shelia ran a hundred gallons of dog milk through the yogurt machine and then sold it to people?

I'll tell you what: Neither of them would have been put on secret probation for three days.

Acting on conscience and principle is the manner in which we express our moral selves and as such, loyalty to conscience and principle should supersede loyalty to any man. We can all be forgiven for failing in that measure from time to time. I certainly put myself at the top of the list of those who fall short in this regard. I am holier than none. I have put some pretty fucked up shit in the yogurt over the years myself.

But too often we rush to excuse our failures, so that we might accommodate them and go right on failing until the accommodation itself becomes our principle. In that way and over time, we can justify almost any behavior. I am afraid that this is where we now find ourselves at the Placid Hills Pinkberry.

I, for one, will not be complicit or silent. That's why I've decided that I would be better able to serve the valued customers of Pinkberry by resigning my position as Associate. It is clear at this moment that an Associate who objects to animal feces being put in the yogurt will face unfair and perhaps insurmountable barriers to career advancement at this Pinkberry. It is also clear that the Pinkberry in Watertown pays a little more, and my cousin says he can hook me up with a job if I so desire.

My fellow colleagues, I will not call the Health Department, nor notify Pinkberry corporate, nor do anything that could result in certain individuals being disciplined or removed for knowingly and repeatedly contaminating the yogurt with animal feces. I care too much about the Pinkberry brand to take such heedless action. But I will do this: I will say, Something must be done. Your children and grandchildren will judge you on the course of action you determine to take in the days and weeks ahead. Mine won't, of course, because I'll be over in Watertown. But yours definitely will. Act wisely. History is watching.

Thank you. I yield the floor.   B

JOE KEOHANE *is a NYC-based journalist whose work has appeared in many publications of varying repute over the years — from* **Esquire** *and* **The New Yorker**, *to several others that he will never cop to.*

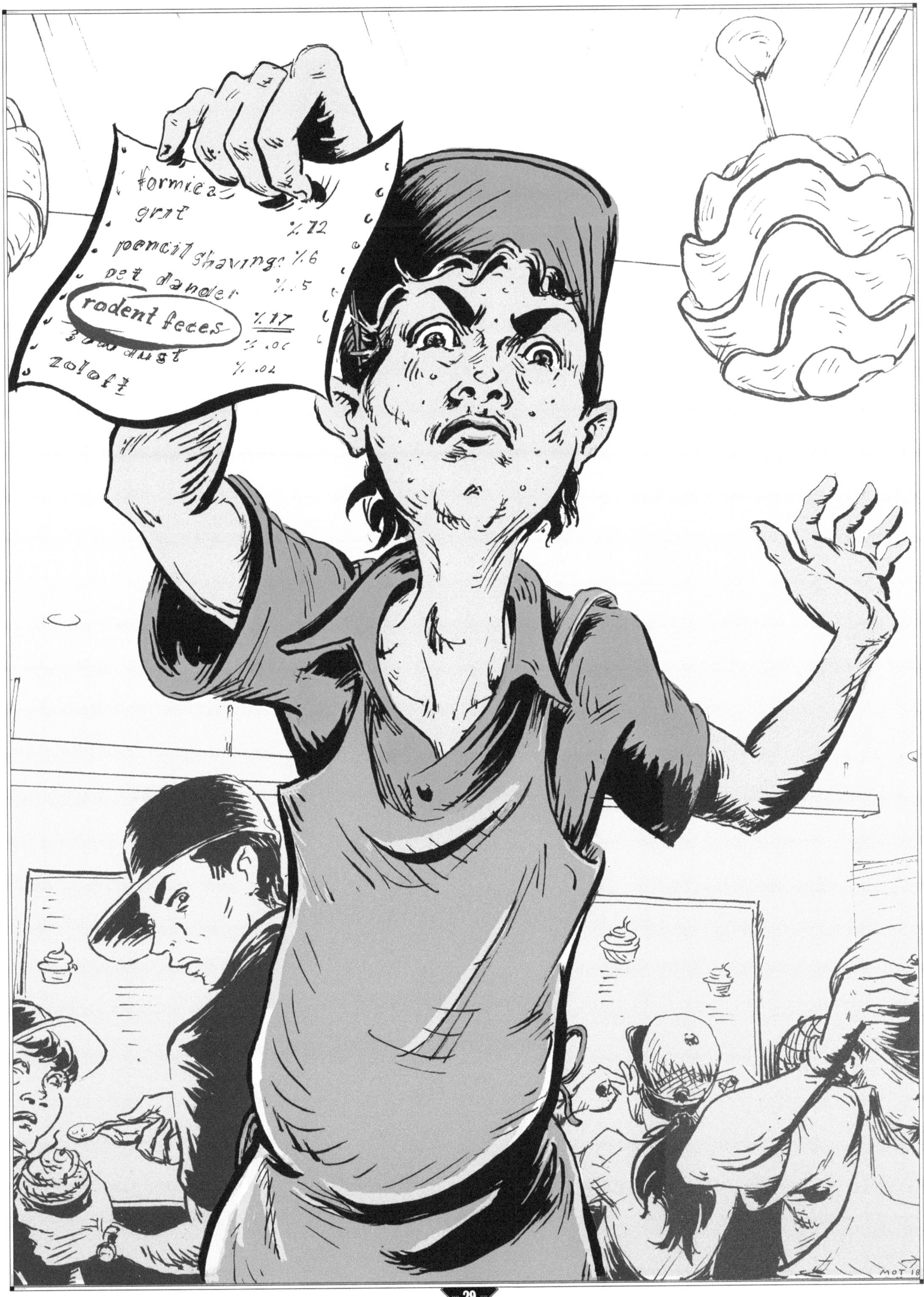
formica
grit %72
pencil shavings %6
pet dander %.5
rodent feces %17
dust %.06
zoloft %.02
MOT '18

TOM MOTLEY

BY MEGAN KOESTER

THEIR WONDERFUL LIVES

An algorithm-led tour of the dark night of your soul

Instagram is like the film *It's a Wonderful Life* in reverse. Instead of a kindly guardian angel showing you how unpleasant the world would be devoid of your presence, a coldly inhuman app allows you to see how joyful folks are, and would continue to be, were you out of the picture. Let's let the algorithm take us on a tour of the dark night of your soul, shall we?

Look! It's your ex-boyfriend, Greg, lounging by the pool with his new girlfriend, Kelly. Look how trim, happy and well adjusted he is. He's miles away from the man who once threw a highball glass at your head because you said you were "too menstrual for sex." You're just a distant memory — a discarded remnant of a former life, the human equivalent of a comically large size pair of jeans disposed of by someone who has gotten lap band surgery. The time you spent with Greg could best be described as "existential." Three years of dating required a decade's worth of therapy to rectify, yet you still feel a nagging twinge of jealousy toward his latest victim. What does she have that you don't, other than a dermatologist and personal trainer? Is she just menstrual enough for sex?

And here's your friend Meredith, the one you always cancel brunch plans with the hour before you're supposed to meet. The last time you canceled, you said you had food poisoning. But how does one acquire food poisoning if they've yet to consume their first meal of the day? Regardless, it was clear you had no desire to keep the plans she had guilted you into making. Sure, you had already blown her off four times, but she constantly uses the phrase "you go, girl" and refers to her dog as if it is her child. Meredith is brunching with someone else — she's brunching with Diana, that woman you loathe because she insists on her name being pronounced "Die-ANNAH." They're at that insufferably trendy place on Sunset where hungover hipsters stand in line for bread. You'd never stand in line for bread. You're not a Soviet-era Russian. And yet, still, you feel like a pariah, an outsider looking in, as you dip your saltines into cottage cheese with one hand

and vacantly scroll with the other. It is 8 PM on a Sunday. Your Monday has been ruined before it has even begun.

Ooh, here's Christina. The girl who's always taking "tasteful" photos of her tits. You make your living with your mind, not your body, thank you very much — you don't need to desperately attract the male gaze in order to feel valid as a woman. The idea of your inbox filling with messages from blue-balled mouth breathers has absolutely no appeal, no siree. Frankly, you feel sorry for Christina. Clearly she has father issues. But God. Her tits do look great, don't they? You look down at your own, artlessly drooping in a ragged T-shirt that somehow has a menstrual blood stain on the collar. You haven't felt the touch of a man in months. You've stopped even attempting to masturbate, as you "fail to see the point." Whenever you close your eyes and try to conjure up a sexual fantasy, you only see the void, a vacuous, all-accompanying darkness.

Ah, James! It looks like his career's going pretty well...he got staffed on another show! He says you should watch it premiere at 11 tonight on a channel you've never heard of. Wait, it's not a channel. It's an app you've never heard of, accessible only by people who own Samsung Galaxy S8s. But you don't own a Samsung Galaxy S8. You're still paying off the Apple iPhone 5s you were forced into buying because the planned obsolescence kicked in on your 4s. Most children you pass on the street have better phones than you. You're a grown woman who envies the phones of children and has never been staffed. Even though you're much funnier than James. Is it because you didn't go to Harvard? Oh, you're sorry you didn't go to fucking Harvard. James is bloated and looks borderline indigent, but it doesn't matter. He's a man; his ghoulish ass will be employable forever. Must be nice.

You close Instagram, open your phone's front-facing camera and examine the ample bags under your eyes. The phone crashes, but you can still see your haunted visage in the blank screen. Were you to die in this instant, you wonder how long it would take the landlord to find your body. **B**

MEGAN KOESTER *(@bornferal) doesn't mean to brag, but multiple television writers twice her age have hit on her. As of press time, none of them have done anything for her career.*

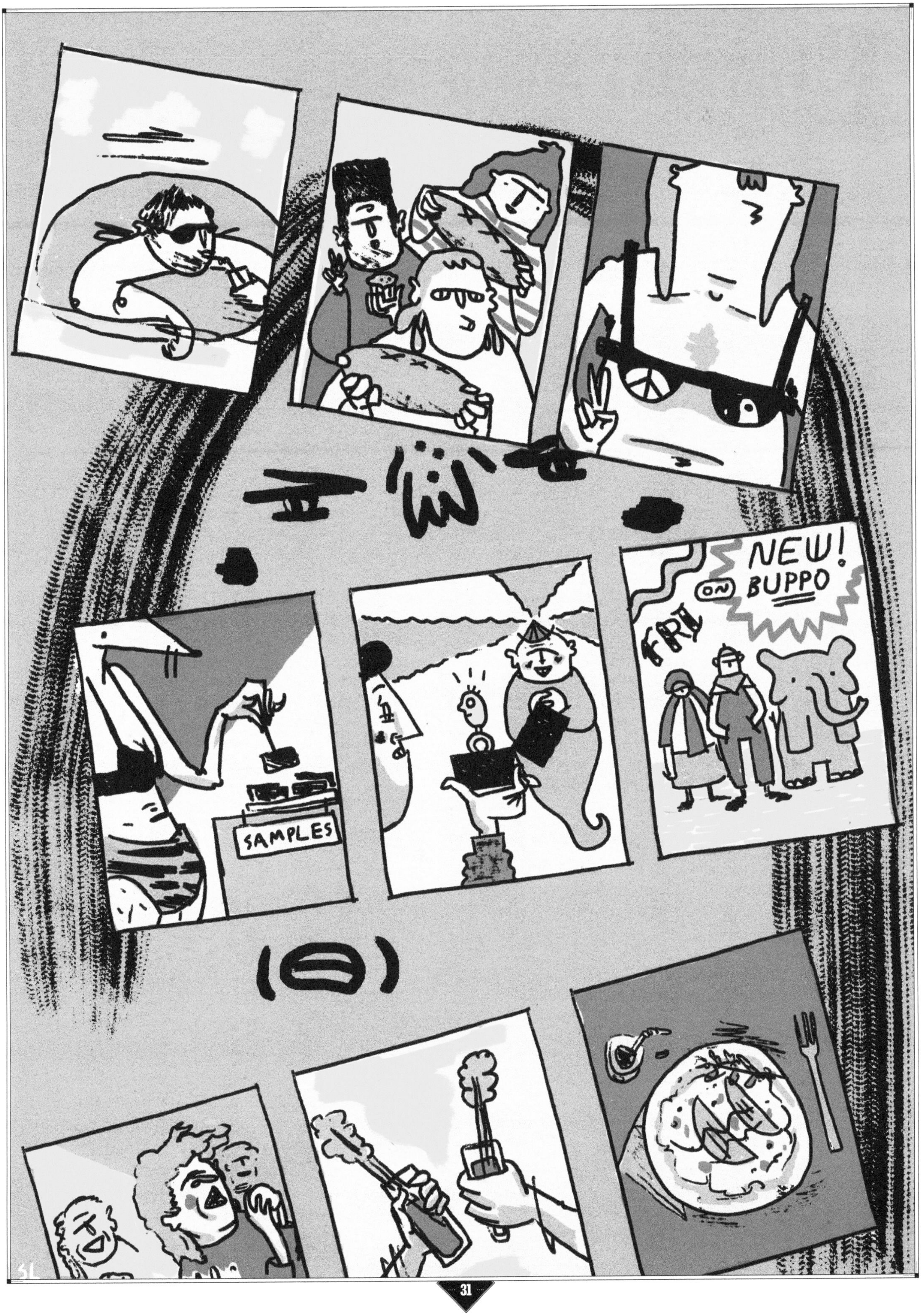
SAMPLES
NEW!
ON
BUPPO
FRI
SL

BY LARS KENSETH

EVERYDAY MINDFULNESS

In the end, just three things matter: How well we've lived, how well we've loved, and do we have any penicillin?

By now, we all know mindfulness meditation is great for stress reduction, longevity and helps treat a myriad of ailments… so why aren't you doing it? Sure, we're all busy. But you don't need to spend an hour perched on a buckwheat pillow surrounded by candles and Tibetan singing bowls in order to meditate. You can be mindful anywhere, at any time.

In fact, you can be mindful all the time. Whether you're washing the dishes, writing a letter, or lighting a tallow candle for the fallen, you can be mindful.

Here's an example. A week ago, I was in the tower research library trying to find a way to make penicillin. Unfortunately, we have precious few texts on curative molds. Mostly it's Clive Cussler novels. Long story short, I flew into a tearful rage — throwing paperbacks around the room and screaming out the embrasure: "Death!! The smell of death is everywhere!!" But then I realized, it doesn't have to be this way… I can be mindful. I focused on my body — tense and shaky under my armor made from old metal trashcan lids. My breathing — staccato and raspy like the infected waifs in the pinfold of the damned. Then I shifted my attention to the sounds in the room. The cackle of the witch doctor's crow, the drip from the sewage conveyor belt in the hall, the distant erotic chants of the Hill Raiders raping one another behind their walls of mud. And that's when I got curious about the sounds I was making. When I hurled Clive Cussler's *White Death* into our research lab — a children's chemistry set — what did it sound like? Sort of a plinky glass breaky sound with a flop at the end, it turns out. Before I knew it, I was completely calm.

Don't think of mindfulness as a chore. It's a tool. And it's there for you when you need it. Like this morning, when I got stopped at the Zone 2 crossing by Zone 1 sentries who took all my ration credits. As they laughed at me through their respirators and got back into their riding lawnmowers painted to look like angry dinosaurs, I had an unpleasant thought: "Maybe I'll sneak into their barracks at night and spray them down with infected waif urine." I was horrified! Why would I even think that? And why did it make me cackle like when the witch doctor's crow fellates himself with his beak? Rather than get sucked in by the thought, I just noticed it, gave it some space, and pretty soon I was walking to the credit reclamation office with a clear head and a tranquil mind.

Anybody have trouble falling asleep? I sure do. Whether it's a lumpy mattress, too much coffee or being visited by the faces of all the small children you've had to kill to stay alive, mindfulness can help! Just take a few deep, cleansing breaths, close your eyes and just *be*. If the blood-soaked faces of the slain appear, their haunting gaze seemingly fixed on your very soul, imagine them saying something like, "I wish you loving kindness," or, "Let go and let glow."

Welcome to dreamland.

You can even be mindful in the shower! Feel the water on your body, your feet in the plastic basin. If you don't have feet, feel the water run down the healed portions of your extremities. If your extremities aren't fully healed from previous trauma, make sure the water has a beta particle content that does not exceed two parts per million. If it does exceed that threshhold, go for a spot clean instead. If you're already in the shower, exit the shower as quickly as possible — but do it mindfully. Feel the burning sensation as the water singes your skin — don't judge it. Feel it. If you can't feel the water burning due to pre-existing numbness or scar tissue, just exit the shower.

It's important to remember that there's no such thing as flawless mindful awareness. You're going to face challenges. Say you're having a great meditation session and all of a sudden you feel the corners of your mouth upturn and your hunger pains dissipate. Don't be alarmed. This is what the before tribes called "happiness." You are happy and, believe it or not, it's a good thing. Label it in your mind, "happiness." Or if that's too foreign to you, try "reverse dread." Sometimes just putting a word or phrase to a difficult feeling can help you accept it.

Bottom line: Mindfulness isn't a cure-all; that's penicillin. Mindfulness takes practice. But once you master it, you'll have it for life. Or at least until winter, when the Hill Raiders will surely come. And remember, if you have any ideas on how to produce penicillin, please contact me immediately. **B**

LARS KENSETH *(@larskenseth) is a cartoonist for* **The New Yorker**, *a Sundance Fellow and is currently baking a big loaf of weird for* **Adult Swim**. *Feel free to troll him on Instagram.*

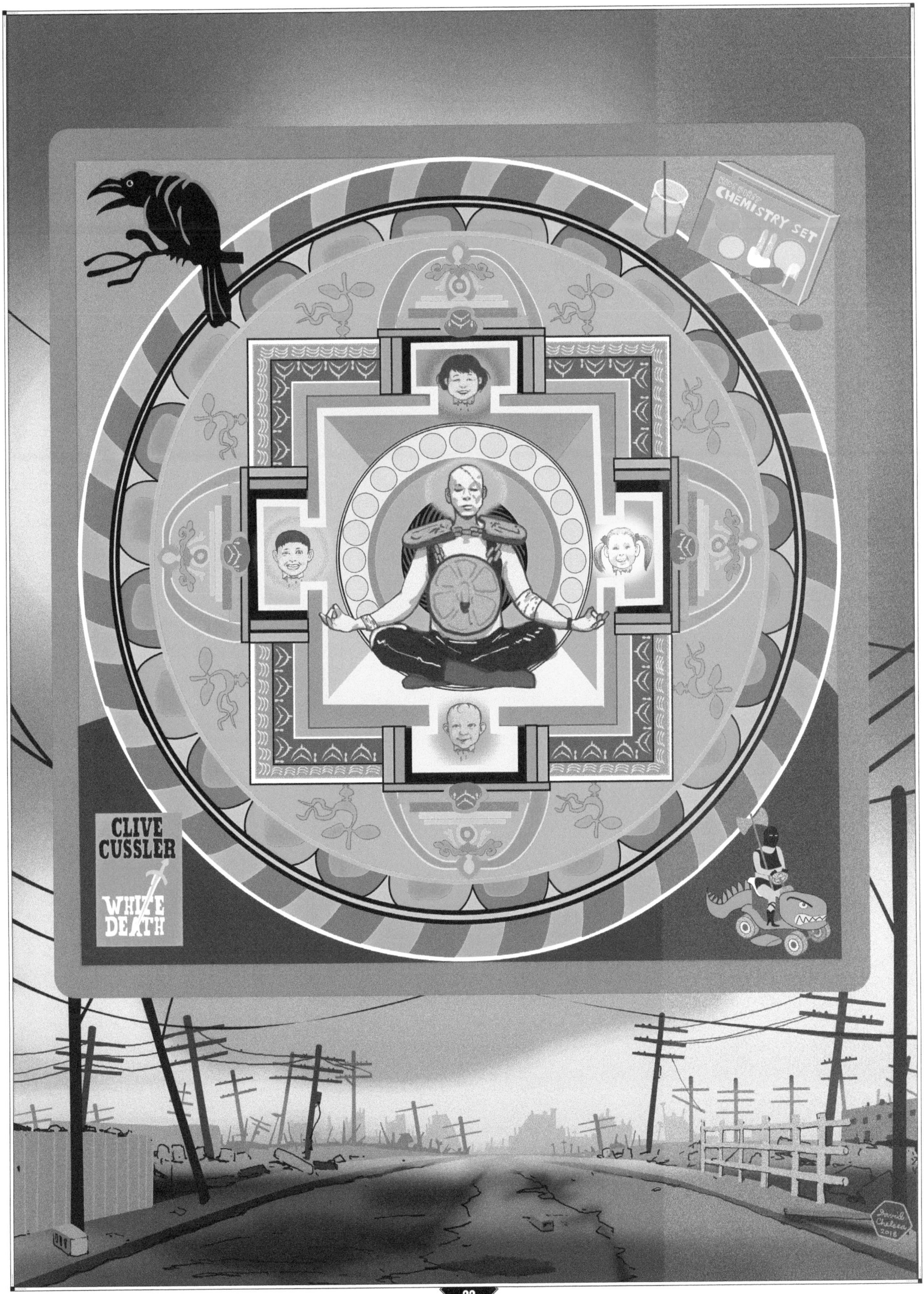
CHEMISTRY SET
CLIVE CUSSLER
WHITE DEATH
Chelsea
2018

BY BLYTHE ROBERSON

CORPORATE FEMINIST TIPS FOR SURVIVING THIS PLANE CRASH

"In a 1970 Civil Aeromedical Institute study of three crashes involving emergency evacuations, the most prominent factor influencing survival was gender (followed closely by proximity to exit). Adult males were by far the most likely to get out alive. Why? Presumably because they pushed everyone else out of the way." — Mary Roach, **Stiff**

Listen, ladies. Men have been disproportionately surviving plane crashes for too long. *You* deserve to make it off this plane. And *you* are the only one to blame if you don't.

Remember: Feminism is all about making sure that good things happen to *you*, specifically. You have heard that it's about helping other women, or any person of any gender identity who faces oppression. Not true! It's about figuring out how you personally can acquire the most money and perks. Taylor Swift's a great example of a woman who has used feminism to greatly benefit her and absolutely no one else. And: She's never died in a plane crash!

The following are some important things to think about as you punch, kick and shove your way free.

SETTING GOALS

Maybe your problem is that you never *aspired* to survive a plane crash. Maybe you think: "Life is constant pain." "I am harassed every day on the basis of my gender." "Two senile heads of state are trying to blow up our planet anyway, just let me die." Well, ladies, men aren't going to *save* you from this plane crash. You need to *chase your goals*.

PUT YOURSELF WHERE THE ACTION IS

If you're not a man who is willing to punch his way off a plane, your next best bet is sitting in the exit row. But maybe you don't feel *qualified* to sit in an exit row? Maybe you have imposter syndrome? Maybe you've asked yourself: "Do I *really* know how to open a door??" Men are hired on the basis of their potential, whereas women are hired on past performance. Like, "Oh, sure, that guy looks like he knows how to open a door," whereas if you're a woman, the flight attendants are like, "Tell me about the three most difficult doors you've opened in the past." The key to this is to *fake it 'til you make it*. Even if it turns out that you don't know

how to open a door and everyone on the plane dies because of it, you shouldn't have to miss out on the chance.

LIKABILITY

If a woman punches a ton of people while trying to survive a plane crash, she's a "bitch." If a man does it, he is "authoritative" or "hot."

FIND A MENTOR

Find someone who will use their structural power to give you a leg up because you look like them. Male allies are better, because men are better than women. So ladies: Follow directly behind a man who is already punching his way off of this plane. Feminism is all about taking these violent power structures that men have already created and using them to our advantage.

(Oh, just a quick break to say, I love capitalism!!)

MANAGING YOUR ROLE AS A MOM

Maybe, for likability reasons, you decided to have kids. Women are often saddled with the bulk of the child-rearing responsibility. You might say, "I am solely responsible for making sure my kids get off this plane!!" But we need to insist on equal partnership: Neither I nor my husband deal with our kids, because we pay another woman to do it. You might ask, "Shouldn't there be some sort of universal, tax-funded child-care system?" The answer is no, because taxes stress me out.

WORK WITH OTHER WOMEN

This means… don't criticize me, just because I refuse to help other women!

So, if you follow all of these tips, you can be the one woman out of 15 people who survive this plane crash. And remember: The only thing holding you back is yourself. It's not like the whole plane is sexist and racist and that's why it's crashing in the first place.

If *you* survive this plane crash, it is good for *all women* on the plane. And who knows: Maybe, one day, there will be a whole generation of girls willing to punch people on planes, just like you. B

BLYTHE ROBERSON (@blythelikehappy) *is a contributor to* **The New Yorker** *and* **The Onion**. *She is currently writing* **How To Date Men When You Hate Men** *for Flatiron Books.*

"Who better to tell the story of the legendary *New Yorker* cartoonist Peter Arno than another legendary *New Yorker* cartoonist Michael Maslin? And what a delight to discover that Maslin's gift for writing equals his talent for drawing. From start to finish, this is book is masterful and unforgettable."

—ANDY BOROWITZ, *New York Times* bestselling author and *New Yorker* columnist

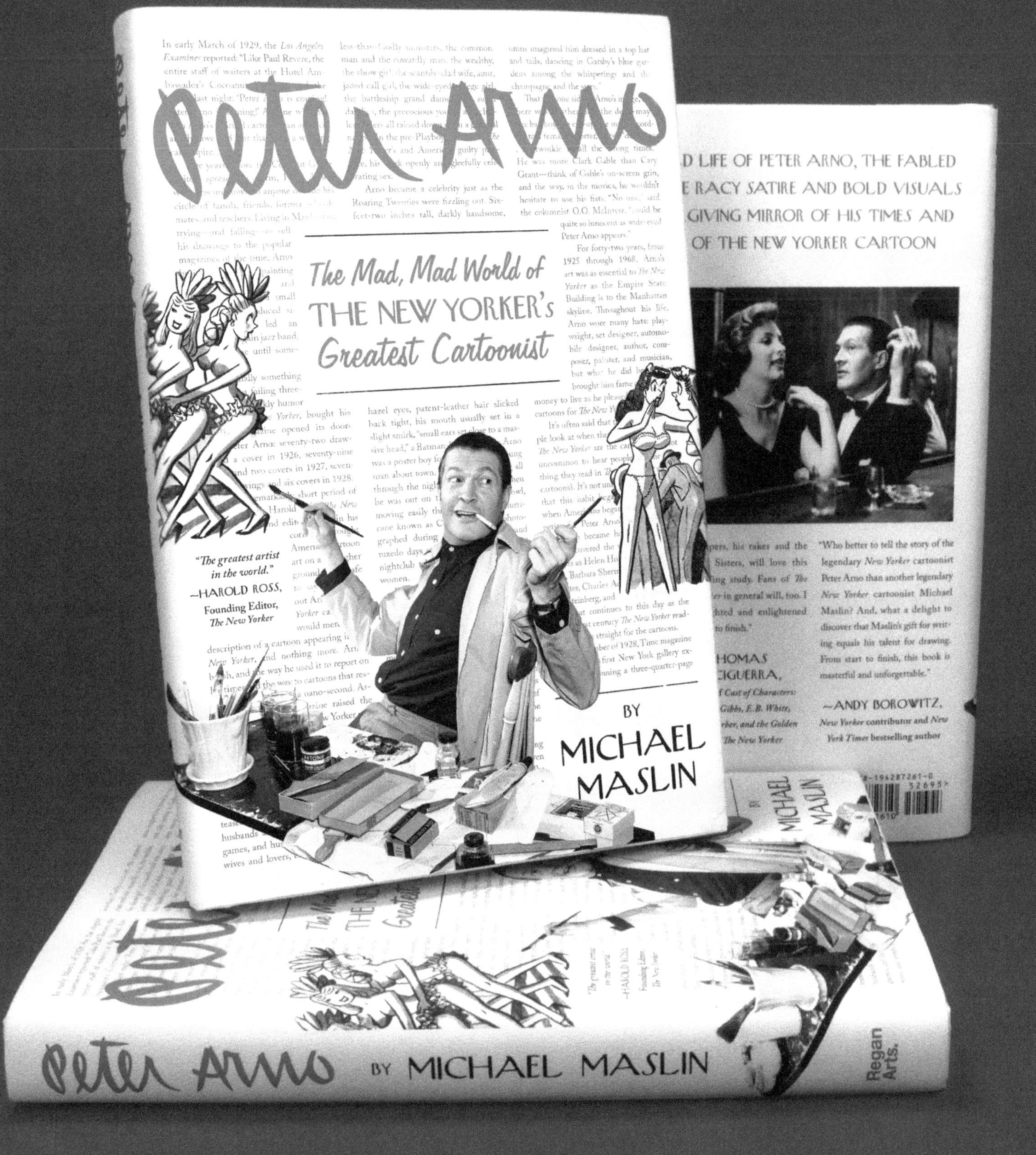
Peter Arno
The Mad, Mad World of THE NEW YORKER's Greatest Cartoonist
"The greatest artist in the world." —HAROLD ROSS, Founding Editor, The New Yorker
BY MICHAEL MASLIN
Peter Arno BY MICHAEL MASLIN
Regan Arts.

AVAILABLE NOW AT

WWW.REGANARTS.COM/BOOKS/2016/PETER-ARNO/

"IF BARRY BLITT IS ANYTHING IT'S BRILLIANTLY PROVOCATIVE."

—JAMES RAINEY, *LOS ANGELES TIMES*

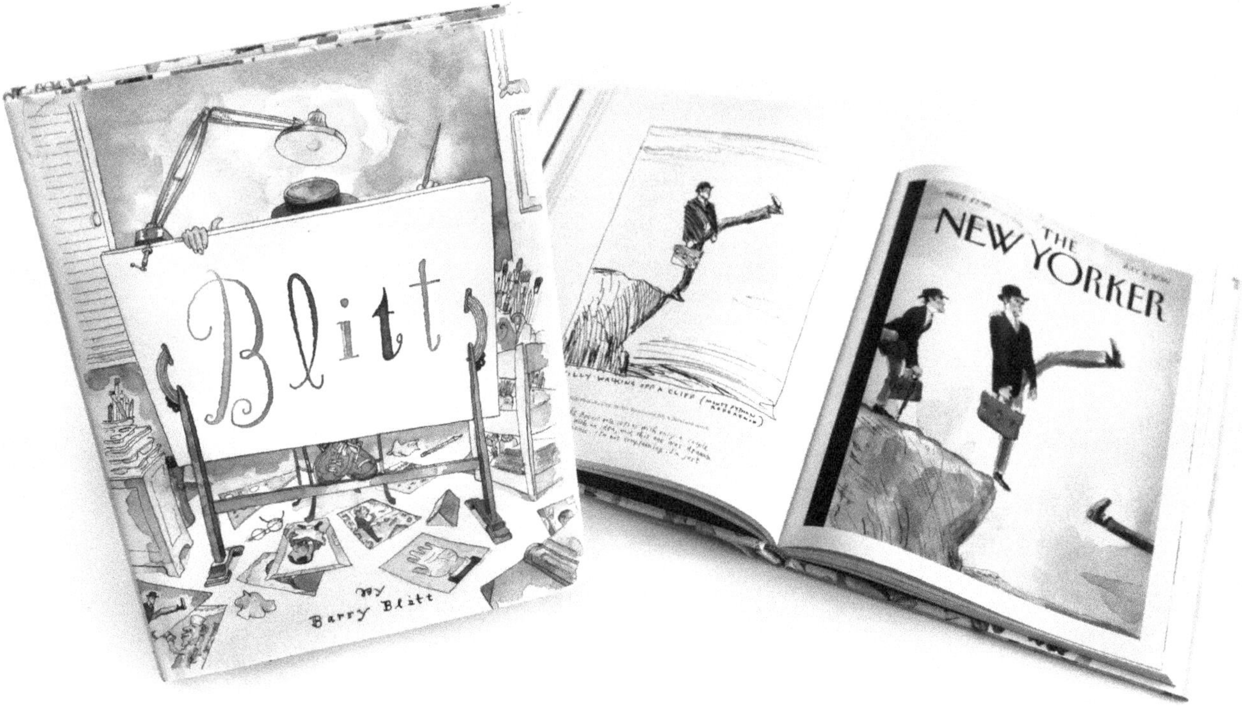
Blitt
by Barry Blitt
THE NEW YORKER

"By turns fascinating and entertaining . . . The beauty of [Blitt's] art is that it rarely needs explaining. You just *get* it."

—*MOTHER JONES*

A gorgeous, hilarious, and provocative compendium of the award-winning artist's illustrations for *The New Yorker*, *The New York Times*, *Vanity Fair*, and more.

- Featuring more than 100 never-before-seen sketches and unpublished illustrations with insightful and satirical annotations by the artist
- Including original essays by Frank Rich, Françoise Mouly, Steve Brodner, David Remnick, and Steven Heller
- Gorgeously designed, an essential coffee-table book for discerning political spectators and fans of comic art alike

ON SALE NOW

A story about a little boy who lives in the White House

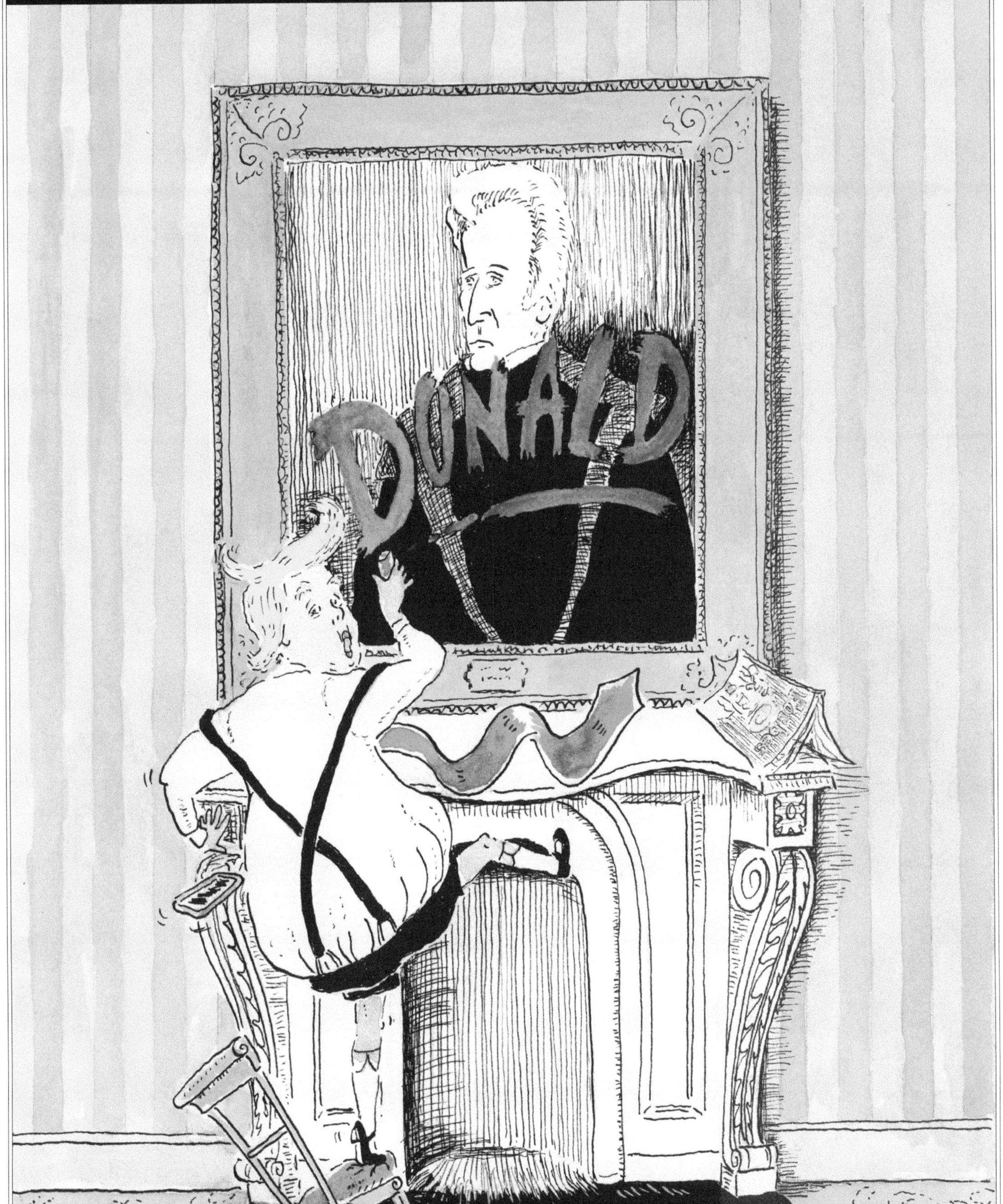
DONALD
A PARODY BY
MIMI POND & NELL SCOVELL

I am Donald Trump
I'm raw-ther important
I live at 1600 Pennsylvania Avenue
I am the most famous person to
ever live there

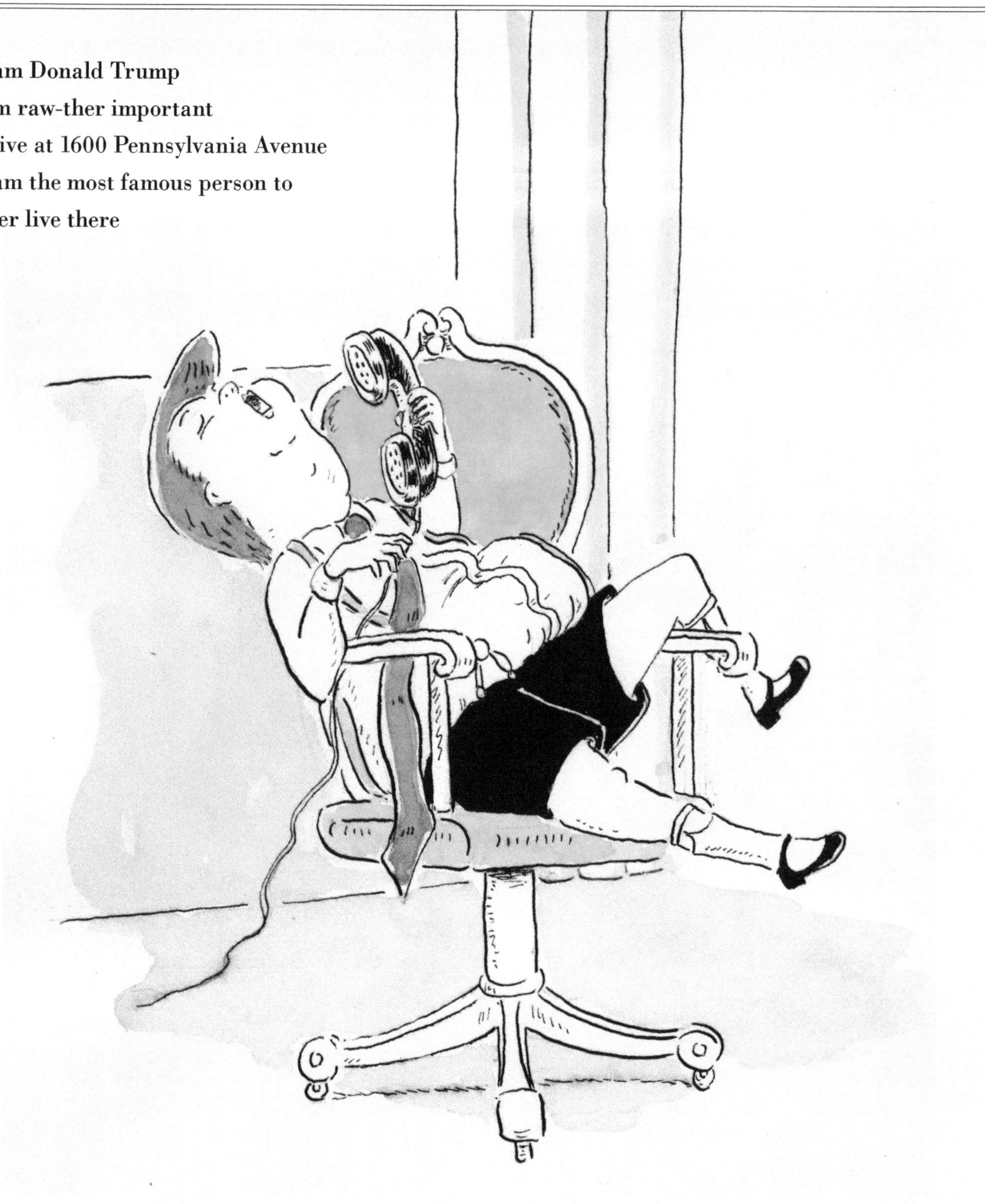

I spend an awful lot of time watching TV.
When I'm bored I call my friend V. Putin.
"Hello, Putie," I say.
"Who is zees?" he asks.
I say, "It's me — Donnie!"

I have an office that is oval
Many people don't know but that is a shape
I have a desk that has the name: Resolute
I also named my chair: Swivel

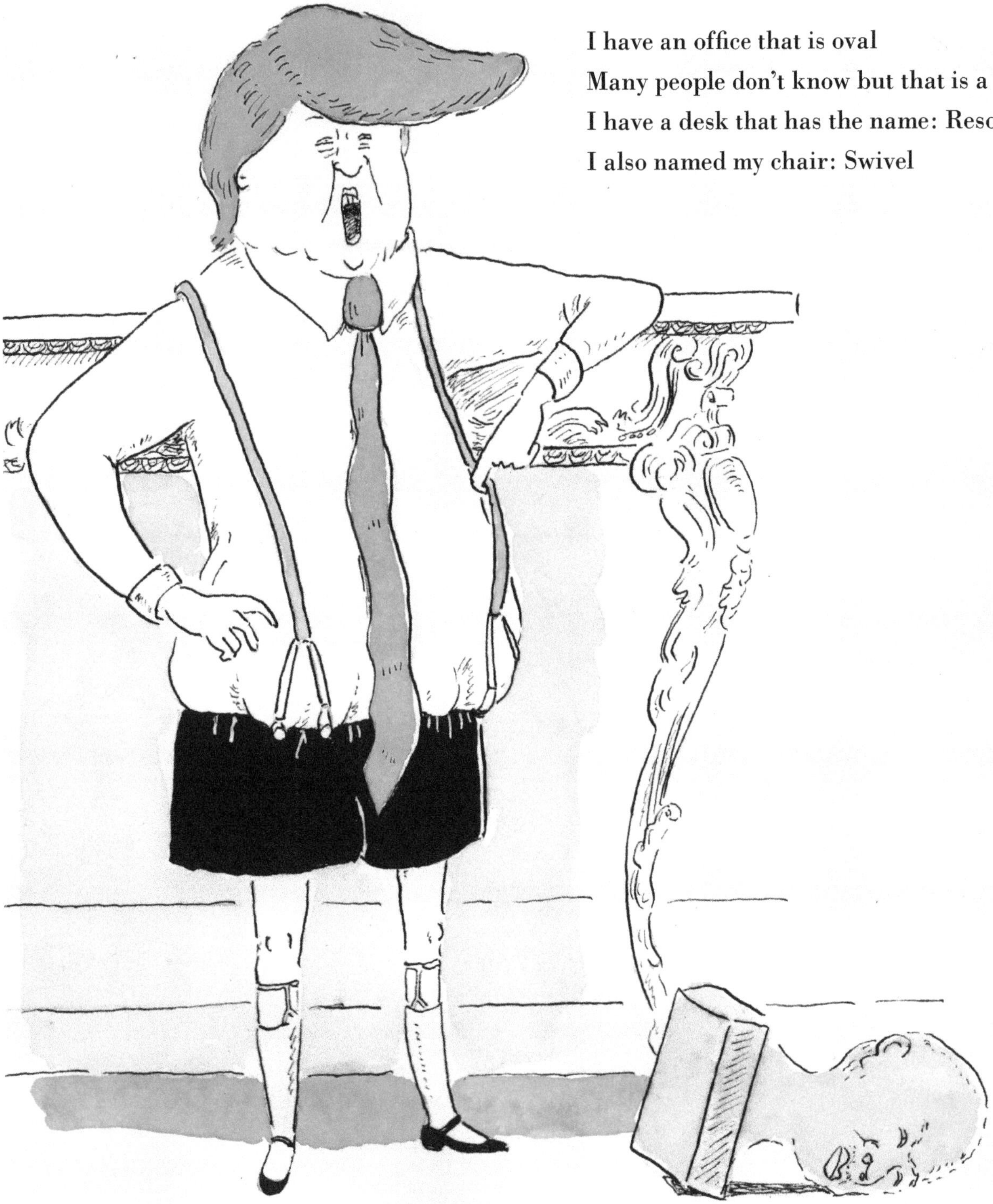

In my office, there is a bust of Martin Luther King
He was born in Kenya
Sometimes the statue falls over
(all by itself)
My nanny John Kelly runs to pick it up, but I say,
"No, I alone can fix it"

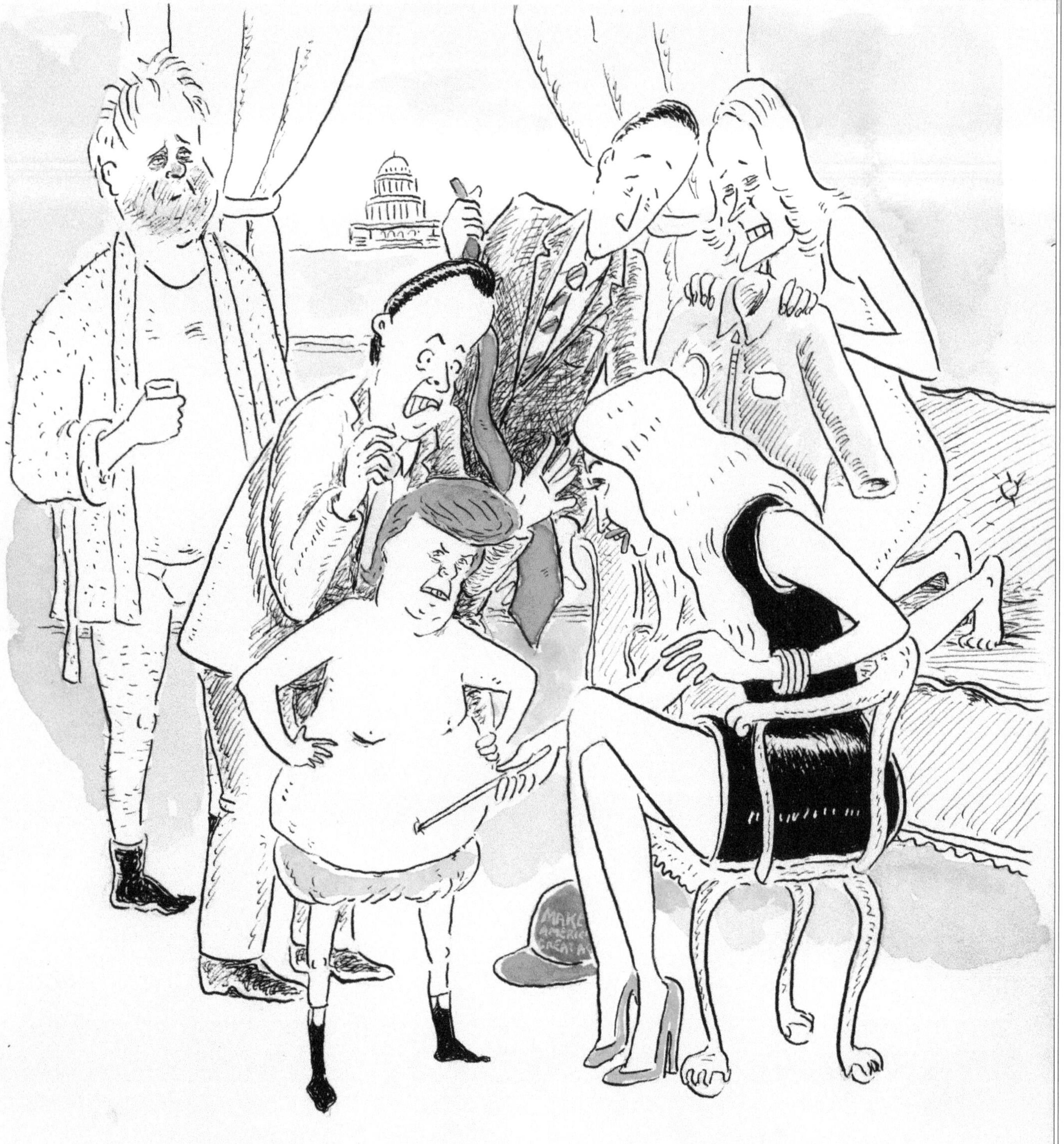

On Inauguration Day, I gathered my glam squad
They help me tape my tie and meringue my hair
Reince says he would prefer if I didn't
talk all the time
And I reminded him, "I have the best words."
Because I, um, do
So Reince had to go and so did Sloppy Steve
But Ivanka stays

There is so much to do every day
The President must give speeches and eat
cheeseburgers
And golf as much as he can
Ooooo, I just love POTUSing

MURDER AT THE MANSION!

THE MYSTERY WITH A COMPLETELY ARBITRARY ENDING!

INSTRUCTIONS BEFORE YOU START READING, THINK OF A SECRET NUMBER BETWEEN 1 AND 8! IF NECESSARY, WRITE IT DOWN TO BE SURE THAT YOU REMEMBER IT!

NOW GO AHEAD AND SEE IF YOU CAN FIGURE OUT "WHO DUNNIT"!

OUR STORY BEGINS AS WORLD-FAMOUS DETECTIVE PIERRE ROLMAUD IS INVITED TO A GALA SOCIAL EVENT AT THE HOME OF EVERETT FABRILL THE THIRD AND HIS WIFE LADY FABRILL!

THANK YOU FOR JOINING US TONIGHT, MR. ROLMAUD!

LADY FABRILL, IT WILL BE A PLEASURE TO SPEND AN EVENING FREE OF INVESTIGATING GRISLY MURDERS!

THEN PERMIT ME TO INTRODUCE YOU TO YOUR FELLOW GUESTS!

MAY I PRESENT SIR ERNEST HAVERFORD, MILLIONAIRE INDUSTRIALIST!

AND NEXT, JENNIFER CROWLEY, FASHION CONSULTANT TO THE STARS!

COLONEL REGINALD POTTERDAM, A WAR HERO WHOSE FAME KNOWS NO BOUNDS!

ROSANNE HANTLERY, CERTAIN TO WIN THIS YEAR'S ELECTION AS CHANCELLOR!

THE GREAT PARADINI, ACCOMPLISHED STAGE MAGICIAN AND HYPNOTIST!

DAME MAXINE CHESTERFELD, BEST-SELLING AUTHOR OF THE SELF-HELP BOOK "GET IT ALL!"

AND LAST BUT NOT LEAST, PHILIP OULLOT, AN ACTOR KNOWN FOR HIS MASTERFUL PORTRAYALS OF DEPRAVED CRIMINALS!

THE FESTIVITIES OF THE EVENT ARE PROCEEDING NICELY... WHEN SUDDENLY THERE IS A BLOOD-CURDLING SCREAM FROM UPSTAIRS!

THE CHAMBERMAID RUSHES DOWN, SOBBING HYSTERICALLY!

MR. FABRIL... HE...HE'S DEAD!

WELL, I DID NOT EXPECT TO BE CALLED UPON TO SOLVE A CASE TONIGHT, BUT A SLEUTH I AM AND ALWAYS SHALL BE!

I KNOW THIS MAY SEEM INSENSITIVE, LADY FABRILL, BUT I MUST EXAMINE THE BODY AND THE VICTIM'S ROOM AT ONCE! CLUES ARE AT THEIR MOST TELLING WHEN THEY ARE FRESH!

YES (SOB!) I... I UNDERSTAND!

HMMM...

MOST INTERESTING...

AHA!

IT IS ALL BEGINNING TO MAKE SENSE NOW!

A FEW MINUTES LATER...

I HAVE GATHERED YOU ALL TOGETHER HERE IN THE STUDY BECAUSE I, PIERRE ROLMAUD, HAVE ONCE AGAIN UNCOVERED THE IDENTITY OF A COLD-BLOODED KILLER!

IN FACT, AS YOU MAY HAVE SURMISED, THE MURDERER IS HERE IN THIS VERY ROOM WITH US RIGHT NOW!

I AM REFERRING, OF COURSE, TO NONE OTHER THAN...

IMPORTANT:

WHEN YOU GO ON TO THE NEXT PAGE, READ ONLY THE ROW CORRESPONDING TO YOUR SECRET NUMBER! BE SURE TO IGNORE ALL THE OTHER ROWS!

Ed Subitzky *was a stalwart of* **The National Lampoon** *and its* **Radio Hour,** *and later appeared frequently on* **Letterman.** *He also contributes to* **The Journal of Consciousness Studies.**

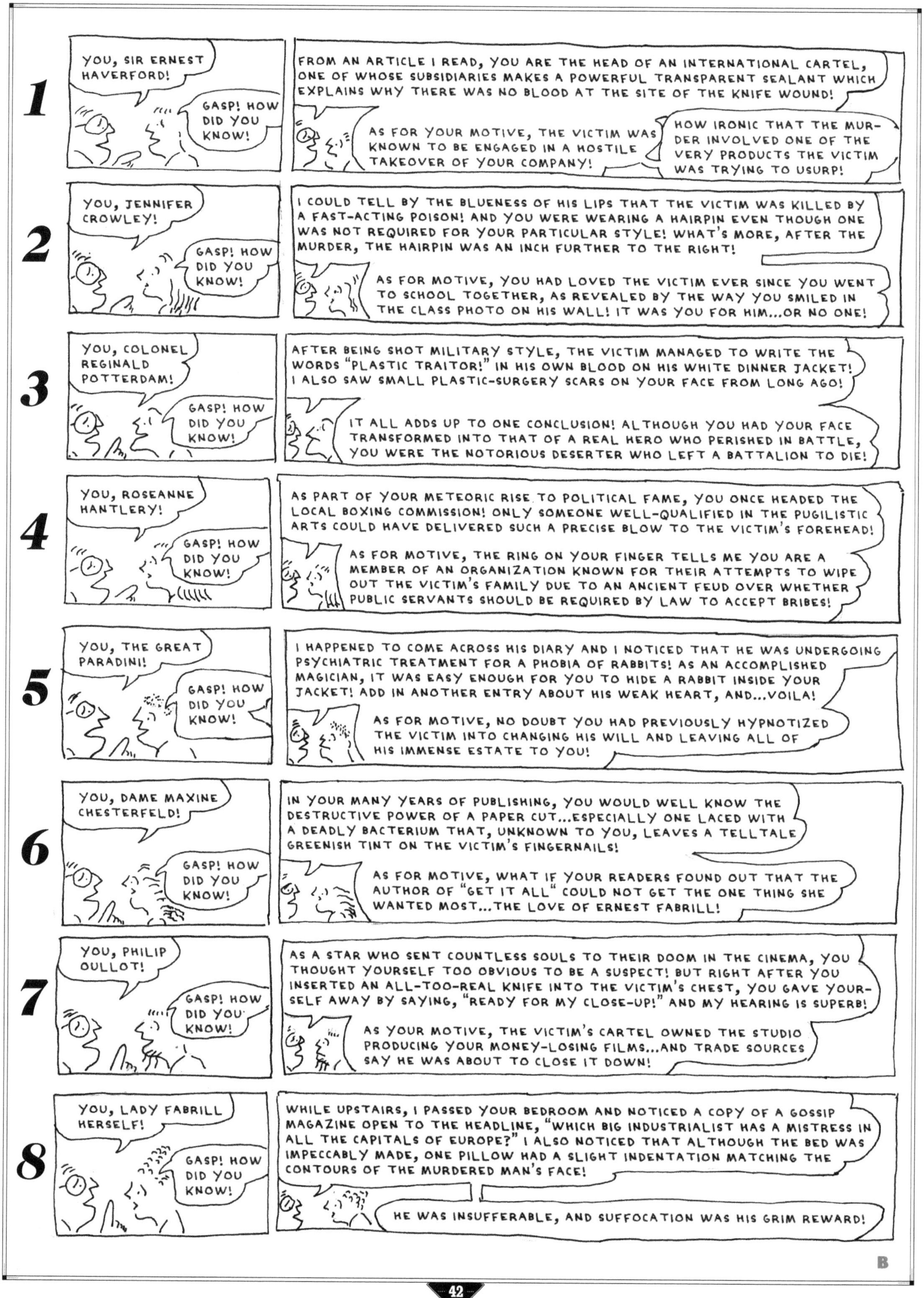
1
YOU, SIR ERNEST HAVERFORD!
GASP! HOW DID YOU KNOW!
FROM AN ARTICLE I READ, YOU ARE THE HEAD OF AN INTERNATIONAL CARTEL, ONE OF WHOSE SUBSIDIARIES MAKES A POWERFUL TRANSPARENT SEALANT WHICH EXPLAINS WHY THERE WAS NO BLOOD AT THE SITE OF THE KNIFE WOUND!
AS FOR YOUR MOTIVE, THE VICTIM WAS KNOWN TO BE ENGAGED IN A HOSTILE TAKEOVER OF YOUR COMPANY!
HOW IRONIC THAT THE MURDER INVOLVED ONE OF THE VERY PRODUCTS THE VICTIM WAS TRYING TO USURP!
2
YOU, JENNIFER CROWLEY!
GASP! HOW DID YOU KNOW!
I COULD TELL BY THE BLUENESS OF HIS LIPS THAT THE VICTIM WAS KILLED BY A FAST-ACTING POISON! AND YOU WERE WEARING A HAIRPIN EVEN THOUGH ONE WAS NOT REQUIRED FOR YOUR PARTICULAR STYLE! WHAT'S MORE, AFTER THE MURDER, THE HAIRPIN WAS AN INCH FURTHER TO THE RIGHT!
AS FOR MOTIVE, YOU HAD LOVED THE VICTIM EVER SINCE YOU WENT TO SCHOOL TOGETHER, AS REVEALED BY THE WAY YOU SMILED IN THE CLASS PHOTO ON HIS WALL! IT WAS YOU FOR HIM...OR NO ONE!
3
YOU, COLONEL REGINALD POTTERDAM!
GASP! HOW DID YOU KNOW!
AFTER BEING SHOT MILITARY STYLE, THE VICTIM MANAGED TO WRITE THE WORDS "PLASTIC TRAITOR!" IN HIS OWN BLOOD ON HIS WHITE DINNER JACKET! I ALSO SAW SMALL PLASTIC-SURGERY SCARS ON YOUR FACE FROM LONG AGO!
IT ALL ADDS UP TO ONE CONCLUSION! ALTHOUGH YOU HAD YOUR FACE TRANSFORMED INTO THAT OF A REAL HERO WHO PERISHED IN BATTLE, YOU WERE THE NOTORIOUS DESERTER WHO LEFT A BATTALION TO DIE!
4
YOU, ROSEANNE HANTLERY!
GASP! HOW DID YOU KNOW!
AS PART OF YOUR METEORIC RISE TO POLITICAL FAME, YOU ONCE HEADED THE LOCAL BOXING COMMISSION! ONLY SOMEONE WELL-QUALIFIED IN THE PUGILISTIC ARTS COULD HAVE DELIVERED SUCH A PRECISE BLOW TO THE VICTIM'S FOREHEAD!
AS FOR MOTIVE, THE RING ON YOUR FINGER TELLS ME YOU ARE A MEMBER OF AN ORGANIZATION KNOWN FOR THEIR ATTEMPTS TO WIPE OUT THE VICTIM'S FAMILY DUE TO AN ANCIENT FEUD OVER WHETHER PUBLIC SERVANTS SHOULD BE REQUIRED BY LAW TO ACCEPT BRIBES!
5
YOU, THE GREAT PARADINI!
GASP! HOW DID YOU KNOW!
I HAPPENED TO COME ACROSS HIS DIARY AND I NOTICED THAT HE WAS UNDERGOING PSYCHIATRIC TREATMENT FOR A PHOBIA OF RABBITS! AS AN ACCOMPLISHED MAGICIAN, IT WAS EASY ENOUGH FOR YOU TO HIDE A RABBIT INSIDE YOUR JACKET! ADD IN ANOTHER ENTRY ABOUT HIS WEAK HEART, AND...VOILA!
AS FOR MOTIVE, NO DOUBT YOU HAD PREVIOUSLY HYPNOTIZED THE VICTIM INTO CHANGING HIS WILL AND LEAVING ALL OF HIS IMMENSE ESTATE TO YOU!
6
YOU, DAME MAXINE CHESTERFELD!
GASP! HOW DID YOU KNOW!
IN YOUR MANY YEARS OF PUBLISHING, YOU WOULD WELL KNOW THE DESTRUCTIVE POWER OF A PAPER CUT...ESPECIALLY ONE LACED WITH A DEADLY BACTERIUM THAT, UNKNOWN TO YOU, LEAVES A TELLTALE GREENISH TINT ON THE VICTIM'S FINGERNAILS!
AS FOR MOTIVE, WHAT IF YOUR READERS FOUND OUT THAT THE AUTHOR OF "GET IT ALL" COULD NOT GET THE ONE THING SHE WANTED MOST...THE LOVE OF ERNEST FABRILL!
7
YOU, PHILIP OULLOT!
GASP! HOW DID YOU KNOW!
AS A STAR WHO SENT COUNTLESS SOULS TO THEIR DOOM IN THE CINEMA, YOU THOUGHT YOURSELF TOO OBVIOUS TO BE A SUSPECT! BUT RIGHT AFTER YOU INSERTED AN ALL-TOO-REAL KNIFE INTO THE VICTIM'S CHEST, YOU GAVE YOURSELF AWAY BY SAYING, "READY FOR MY CLOSE-UP!" AND MY HEARING IS SUPERB!
AS YOUR MOTIVE, THE VICTIM'S CARTEL OWNED THE STUDIO PRODUCING YOUR MONEY-LOSING FILMS...AND TRADE SOURCES SAY HE WAS ABOUT TO CLOSE IT DOWN!
8
YOU, LADY FABRILL HERSELF!
GASP! HOW DID YOU KNOW!
WHILE UPSTAIRS, I PASSED YOUR BEDROOM AND NOTICED A COPY OF A GOSSIP MAGAZINE OPEN TO THE HEADLINE, "WHICH BIG INDUSTRIALIST HAS A MISTRESS IN ALL THE CAPITALS OF EUROPE?" I ALSO NOTICED THAT ALTHOUGH THE BED WAS IMPECCABLY MADE, ONE PILLOW HAD A SLIGHT INDENTATION MATCHING THE CONTOURS OF THE MURDERED MAN'S FACE!
HE WAS INSUFFERABLE, AND SUFFOCATION WAS HIS GRIM REWARD!
B

Introducing Stinker

Have you ever thought back on a movie — a specific scene or even the entire damn film — and wondered, *That's just too crazy to be real; did I dream it?*

This happens to me often. For years, I vaguely remembered a scene in which a young woman wearing a black veil strolls down a long line of soldiers searching for just one volunteer. The mission? To ride down an elongated slide with a giant razor in the middle, committing suicide.

Amazingly, this was no hallucination: It was a scene from a 1964 movie called *The Long Ships*, starring Sidney Poitier. I must have watched it on television in the mid-1970s.

Another movie I've often thought about over the years is about a chimp in estrus and a dim-witted, cussing mountain boy, who join forces with an out-of-shape Georgia road adventurer named Stinker, so that they can "fun truck" their way up to Washington, D.C.

Dear Lord! Could *that* possibly have existed?

Once again: yes. *Stinker Lets Loose!* was released in 1977 and played for a few weeks in a handful of theaters and drive-ins scattered across the South. It was the first movie I ever saw in a theater — this would be in Virginia Beach — and I was 5. Yes, 5. I was with my parents, but still…

I saw it once as an adult, via a grainy VHS bootleg rented from the old Kim's Video down on Bleecker Street. It was recorded off late-night cable sometime in the mid '80s, judging by the commercials. *Stinker Lets Loose!* would never — not for all the money in this ol' world — be made today. Nor should it be: It is very, very bad. And yet I loved it then and I love it still. What can I say? I have a soft spot for movies that are "of their time," especially if that time is the 1970s.

As was typical, the moviemakers arranged for a novelization — the better to cash in on the Stinker-mania that they were sure would come. The author, James Taylor Johnston, died in 1987, and it's difficult to glean any information about him or this book. But I don't think that's so important. This book can simply stand for itself, an artifact of its time.

In Johnston's book, the character of Stinker is described as "just the man this country needs in these difficult times." I tend to doubt that this was the case in 1977, and I most definitely doubt that this is the case now, and yet… there is something sort of refreshing about Stinker and his ragtag group of "deep-fried Dixies."

I hope you enjoy the following excerpt from the book. We'll talk soon. Until then, let me just say the following: *10-4, good buddy! Keep the bugs off your glass and the trouble off your ass! Keep your lips a-smirkin' and the girls a-jerkin'! For sure, for sure! Catch you at the next Surf N Turf!…*

— **Mike Sacks**

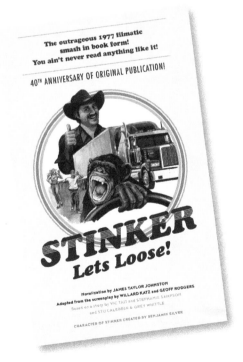

The outrageous 1977 filmatic smash in book form!
You ain't never read anything like it!

40TH ANNIVERSARY OF ORIGINAL PUBLICATION!

STINKER
Lets Loose!

Novelization by JAMES TAYLOR JOHNSTON
Adapted from the screenplay by WILLARD KATZ and GEOFF RODGERS
Based on a story by VIC TAIT and STEPHANIE SAMPSON
and STU CALEBRESH & GREY WHITTLE

CHARACTER OF STINKER CREATED BY BENJAMIN SILVER

Stinker opened his dazzling blue eyes, slowly and with great effort.

He could barely see. Was it the middle of the night? No. It felt like daytime. Maybe late morning at the earliest. His eyes squinted from what little light invaded through the dirty, drawn shades.

A languid country song warbled from a radio-alarm clock. Not surprisingly, it was about Stinker:

> *That man, he like to ride,*
> *Ride, ride, ride… straight to his beer,*
> *That Stinker, he don't like to never, ever hide!*
> *This Stinker, he don't got at all nothin' to fear….*

It wasn't a good song, nor did it make much sense, but until the day Stinker died — probably right here in his trailer, crushed under the weight of his vintage erotica collection — he'd be more than okay with it. ☜

············ ◆ ············

Mike Sacks *is a writer.*

Stinker reached across his messy, stained, well-used mattress — over the box of wombat seat and around the jug of doe urine — for the radio's off button, hit it, and then accidentally knocked over an empty bottle of cinnamon whiskey. The sound of glass hitting and then bouncing along the linoleum floor rang in his ears and made him wince. The label couldn't be seen, but it was the brand of cheap cooze-booze to be found at any illegal backwoods juke joint owned by a former career Navy cook named Gravy Boat.

'Twas the only style of booze Stinker ever drunk.

The great man now took stock of himself. He reached betwixt his thighs, making sure his ample package was still there.

There'd be a lot of upset ladies if it wasn't...

It was.

Good.

Rutting season would continue...

Stinker was "well-favored" by nature. The big trucker above had made sure of that!

Stinker giggled. The giggle was high-pitched, much like a jungle creature's. And extremely distinctive. Anyone who lived within the great state of Georgia knew this giggle, especially in the South-eastern part of Georgia, where Stinker resided and thrived.

"Moly holy! Where in the hell was I last night?" ejaculated Stinker, more to himself than to anyone else, as no one else was in the bedroom. "Where now?"

It started to slowly come back...

Ah, yes. With Lizzie... that spicy, slinky firecracker of an overnight waitress at Hank's Saloon...

That dirty little thang with the tight knockoff designer jeans. All moist around the edges... tea cup long since gone a'-cracked... slick in the sluice and dry in the goose...

And what did we do all night?

Got drunk and then... ahem.

That last part was best left to his own fading memory.

Where was Lizz now?

Not in this dump, that was for sure. She was a cat. Clean. Sleek. Stylish. Loved to lick. He was more like a dog. Smelly. Sometimes his penis was visible in public. Sometimes even his anus. He didn't care. Hairy.

Lizz's old man was a biker, which could spell danger: *Don't touch the snatch when daddy's got the patch...*

Not that Stinker was overly frightened. Cause Stinker had the *flesh*. Lived the *standard*.

The day was early yet but there was already a string of bubble gum lodged securely within Stinker's thick and lustrous 'stache. He'd have to attend to that later. Might even have to buy himself a monogrammed mustache wide-comb. Would go well with his monogrammed lice comb.

Stinker slowly made his way to a standing position. He was wearing nothing but boxers festooned with the Confederate flag, and his authentic felt Stetson cowboy hat. Always with the cowboy hat...

"I'll be a dirty word!" he cried suddenly. "It's *you*!"

Sitting in a broken rocking chair, just next to the broken television, was Stinker's best friend and all-around loyal adventure comrade, Boner.

Unlike Stinker, Boner was clean-shaven and already duded up in his "Tuf-Nut Tux": crisp Levi jeans, mahogany red-supple genuine leather python cowboy boots with raised-topstitching, an antique pewter belt-buckle in the shape of an agave leaf, and a dark chocolate brown Biltmore Western cowboy hat raked handsomely to the side.

Southern exquisite. A denim dandy. A hoighty toighty honky-tonky cracker-backer slacker-wacker...

"Well, ain't you look like a hundred and ten bucks," Boner declared, smiling. It was an impish grin, one the ladies could never, *ever* resist. Even

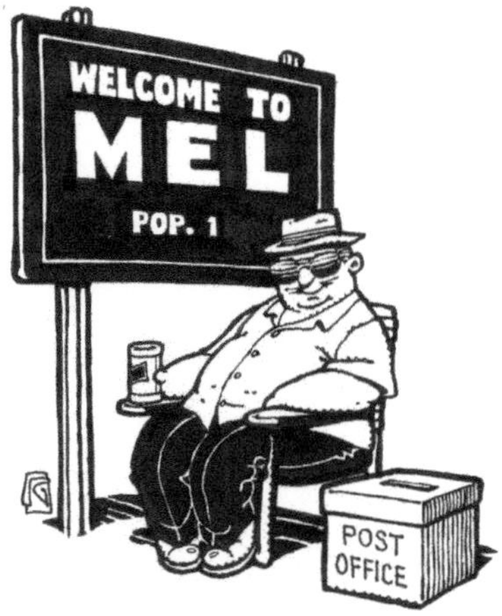
WELCOME TO
MEL
POP. 1
POST OFFICE

the guys had a difficult time ignoring it. Perhaps that had more to do with the discoloration of Boner's teeth and gums but Boner wasn't complainin'.

"Smoke," declared Stinker, in a husky voice. "Need a smoke, pal."

Stinker tried to assume a frontiersman pose but nearly toppled over. He gave up and sat back down.

"Slow it down, jitterbug!" gibed Boner, laughing.

He tossed over a pack of fresh Salems. Stinker coolly caught the pack with one hand and then tapped out a "loose goose." He flipped it into his sensuous mouth. Boner blazed Stinker's cig and handed his best friend a pair of torn jeans and a denim shirt, the only style the great man wore. The shirt had a rhinestone peacock on the front giving the "middle finger." No one knew why. Regardless, it was *glorious*.

"C'mon, friend," said Boner, pushing Stinker into the bathroom.

Boner had known this chaotic cracker for years and felt more than comfortable pushing Stinker into a trailer's tiny bathroom. "Your buddy is brewing up some strong joe, as well as a pipin' hot plate of hash."

He was talking about himself.

"Harumph," said Stinker, and then burped noisily.

Boner made a face. "You smell like the devil."

"The devil I know? Or the devil I don't?"

"Both," said Boner, even though he wasn't quite sure what Stinker meant.

He often didn't. But it didn't matter. They were best pals.

"Follow me, sir," said Boner, pretending he was a *maître d'* at a fancy, upscale French restaurant in the snootiest of academic northeast cities. He led Stinker out of the bathroom and over to the trailer's kitchenette area. "We saved your table, *monsieur*."

Stinker rolled his eyes. This was a game. Boner was forever playing the role of attendant, while Stinker was forever acting the role of rich, fancy gentleman. It was fun... but Stinker sometimes wished Boner could save it for another time. His entire body hurt!

Make no mistake, Stinker was in shape. But more like *beer shape*. He had some muscles but they were nothing to write home about.

Meanwhile, what exactly *did* Lizz and him get up to last night? Whatever it was, he was now paying the full price!

Stinker *hated* paying the full price.

Boner presented Stinker with a heaping, steaming plate of delicious fried taters. He then plunked down a huge cup of black coffee in a "SHIT KICKIN" mug, just the way Stinker *liked* it.

"Can't," said Stinker.

"Will," said Boner. "Don't let your alligator mouth overload your hummingbird ass."

Stinker took a deep gulp of the strong brew, and immediately began to feel better. "Where's Rascal?"

"Consumed by a croc?" replied Boner, handing Stinker a fake cloth napkin. "Ain't my chimp."

"That there's one animal who ain't gonna travel far," said Stinker. "Not with that big, fat, lazy ass."

"She reached estrus last week," said Boner. "Going all types of crazy. Chimp lost her mind. Why *wouldn't* she run?"

Stinker retarted, "If she has run, I'm desiring she run off to find herself a male. And best of luck to 'im!"

Boner chuckled deeply and then sat down next to Stinker. All of a sudden, his expression showed one of deep concern. He remembered what he had to tell Stinker. And it wasn't good.

"Hey, buddy, I hate to be the bearer of bad news and all…"

"Don't tell me," said Stinker.

Here it comes, thought Stinker. *A big roller-rink pickle.*

"I'm telling you," said Boner. "The Big Man wants to see you. Says it's of *mucho* importance. Has another job for you. Says it might be the most significant adventure of your already spectacular life."

"Of all days," said Stinker, anus puckering but not exposed. "Lord on a buttery shit biscuit, why today?"

Stinker's stomach grumbled and he floated out a lively one. A most dishonorable discharge. It smelled of government-issued hot dogs that had "turned" at a particularly depressing July 4th celebration.

"Helicopter is waiting," said Boner, holding his nose in a funny way and pointing outside to a large grassy area. "Been here for hours."

"Not going without Rascal," muttered Stinker. "No way, no how. That's

EVEN MORE DRINKING GLASSES

BEER GOGGLES

MARTINI READERS

SCOTCH MONOCLE

MOSCOW MULE BIFOCALS

ABSINTHE PINCE-NEZ

MOJITO AVIATORS

CHAMPAGNE OPERA GLASSES

MARGARITA SPECTACLES

OLD FASHIONED BINOCULARS

MARIA SCRIVAN

a big *negatory*!"

"I wouldn't push buttons," said Boner. "Big Man sounded like he meant—"

There was a loud crash! Both Stinker and Boner jumped. Glass flew and the table was upended.

Before he knew it, Stinker was on the ground. Boner was still standing — *barely.*

"Speak of the devil I *know*," said Stinker, shaking his head. "There's my chimp now!"

Rascal the chimp roared with displeasure. Ever since she had reached sexual maturity the previous week, the great beast was capable of significant, ungodly violence. Grabbing the coffee pot, she hurled it against the refrigerator.

She bared her big, yellow fangs and then grabbed at her flap-jacked breasts and her freakishly inverted teats. She chewed at the air. She stomped and BMed on the cheap vinyl flooring.

The stinky soft-serve steamed profoundly *ferocious.*

"Madder than a tic in a tornado," exclaimed Boner. "Bitch chimp has two speeds: *violence or silence.*"

Boner and Stinker threw back their heads and laughed uproariously. For Stinker, this was more fun than reciting dirty limericks while high on downers.

Yes, this chimp was off her rocker, there was no doubt about that! But there was also something about the old girl that was endearing. Maybe it was her loyalty. Or that she was always up for an adventure. Or good in a fight. Or free.

Stinker had stolen Rascal from an illegitimate traveling Injun circus in Alabama the previous month. And they were already fast friends.

Stinker wondered how this ol' chimp was going to do on a helicopter flight. She was scared to death of enclosed spaces. Well, we'll soon find out, he thought.

He closed his eyes and listened to the damage being wrought.

This should be fun. ₿

A Sitcom Bible

Can't tell a treacle cutter from an M.O.S.?
This guide will help you fit right into any writers' room,
from Burbank to Broadway.

Sitcom writers have their own lingo, just like truckers and Green Berets (this, by the way, is the only thing sitcom writers have in common with truckers and Green Berets). So if you walked into a roomful of comedy writers and said, "I've got a clever, original joke to end this scene," they'd laugh at you. And not in a good way. What a true professional would say is, "I've got a great button that's neither a wacky stack nor a Nakamura."

What follows is a list of actual terms used by comedy writers. Just as language manuals use the simplest sentences ("The pen is on the table" — really?), I've chosen to illustrate them with the simplest, most obvious gags that exist: Kim Kardashian jokes.

K-WORDS:

Neil Simon's *The Sunshine Boys* exposed audiences to one of the great secrets of comedy: Words with K sounds are funny. Cucumbers are funnier than celery. Cucamonga is funnier than Philadelphia. Kim Kardashian is funnier than anything.

A warning to novices — K-words alone don't make a sentence funny. For example:

My cousin Kenny was killed by the Ku Klux Klan.

RULE OF THREE:

This is one of the few solid rules of comedy, one vouched for by scientist/*Futurama* co-creator David Cohen. The rule of three is a list joke, where the first two elements are normal, and the third element is a surprise. Example:

HE: I picked up three things at the Kim Kardashian Museum: a brochure, a T-shirt and chlamydia.

BUTTON:

The last joke in a scene, "buttoning" it with a laugh before you move on to the next scene. Example:

SHE: It's agreed, we're going out to a museum today. Which one would you like?
HE: The Kim Kardashian Museum. It's always open, and anyone can get in.

ACT BREAK:

The moment on a TV show right before the commercial break that is so intriguing you have to stay tuned. Commercial-free sitcoms, like those on HBO, don't need act breaks, but on a network show, they are the most important part of a story pitch. Example:

HE: Two tickets for the Kim Kardashian Museum.
GUARD: I'm sorry, we're closed... There's been a murder!

CALLBACK:

A joke repeated later in a show because it got a laugh earlier. This is a cheap, lazy trick that always seems to work. We try to avoid these on *The Simpsons*. Example:

(continued on next page) ☛

············ ◆ ············

Mike Reiss's *new book,* **Springfield Confidential: Jokes, Secrets, and Outright Lies from a Lifetime Writing for The Simpsons,** *hits bookstores this June.*

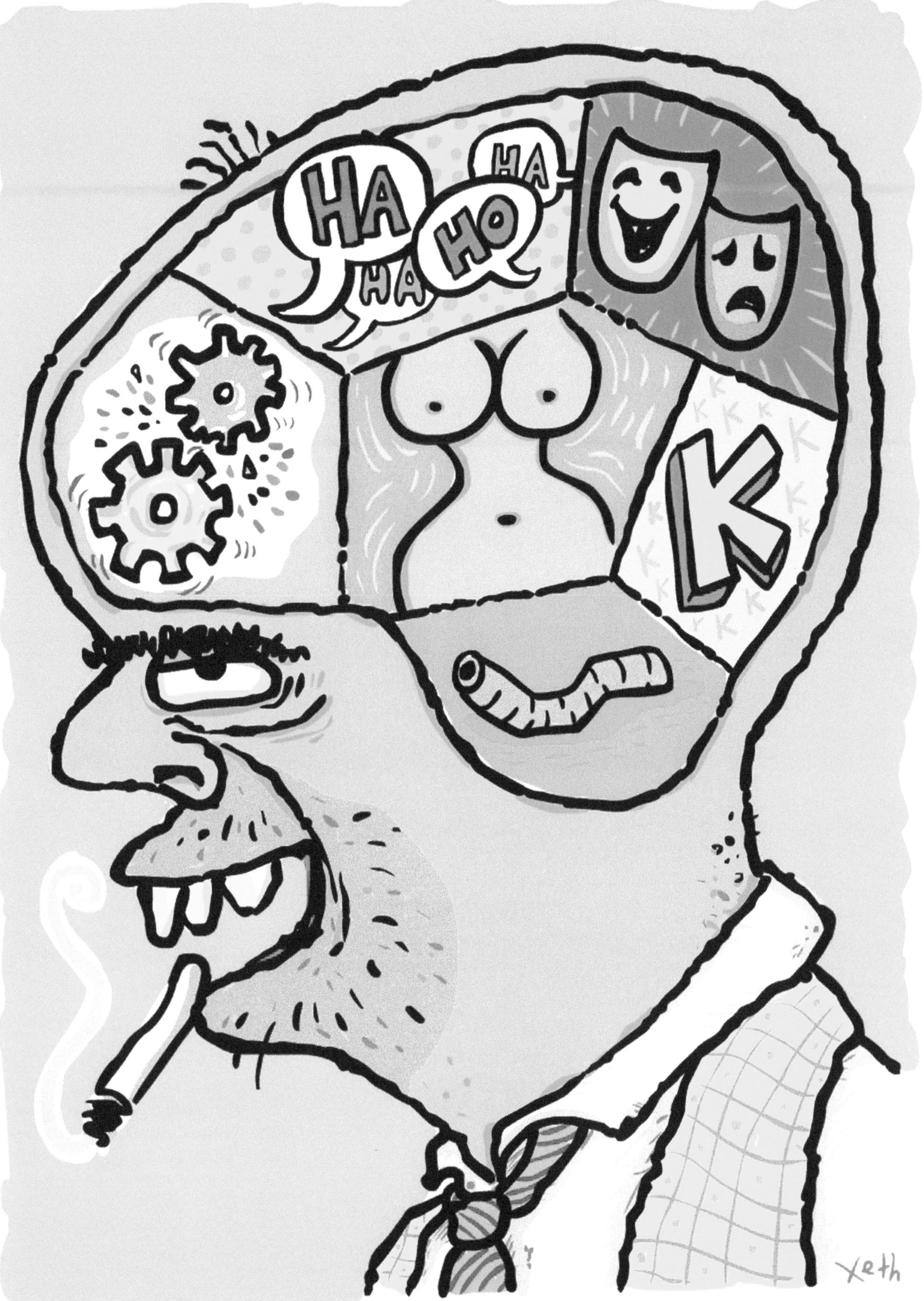
HA
HA
HO
HA
K
xeth

XETH FEINBERG

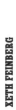

SHE: I really enjoyed the Kim Kardashian Museum.
HE: We can go back tomorrow. Like I said, it's always open!

LAYING PIPE:

Providing exposition and character detail, preferably in a subtle way. Example:

HE: Let's go to that Kim Kardashian Museum. It's always open, even in this small New England town where I've come to get over my wife's unsolved disappearance 20 years ago today.

JOKE ON A JOKE:

When you have a perfectly decent punch line, but add another joke to it. Some writers believe this ruins the original joke; others believe it doubles the comedy. Example:

GRAMPA: Let's go to that Kim Kockamamie Museum: It's always open, and anyone can get in.

WACKY STACK

(also known as "stacking the wack"):

Basically, a joke on a joke... on a joke on a joke. It's the hope that by stringing funny words together you will eventually strike comedy gold. You won't. Example:

GRAMPA: Let's go to the Kim Kockamamie Museum. It's run by a stuttering Albanian on Dingle Street in Sheboygan.

M.O.S:

Dialogue near the end of an episode where it suddenly switches from cheap jokes to unearned sentimentality (M.O.S. stands for "Moment of Shit"). Example:

HE: You know the sexiest thing in the Kim Kardashian Museum? You.
SHE: Oh honey...
They hug.

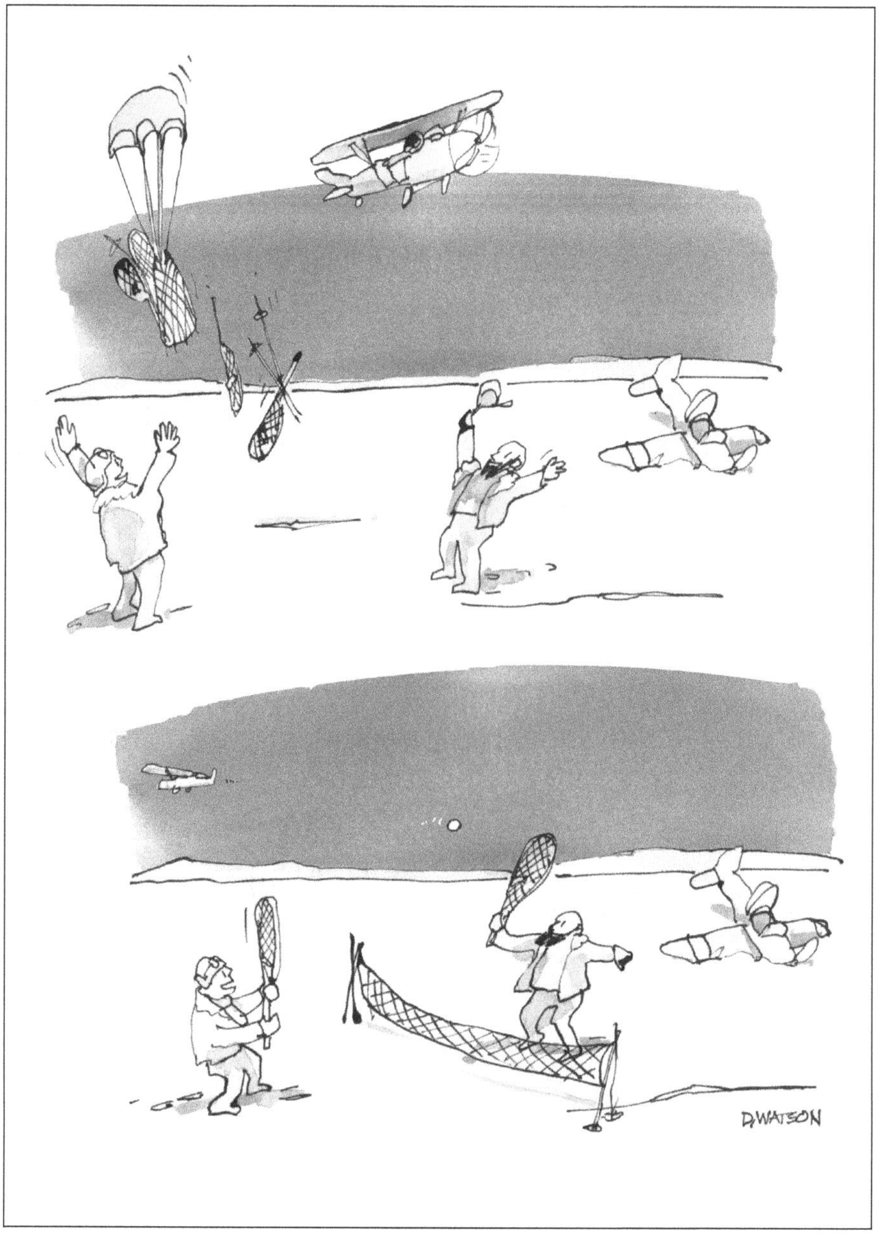
D.WATSON

TREACLE CUTTER:

After the Moment of Shit, a joke is tacked on to cut through the sweetness. Example:

HE: You know the sexiest thing in the Kim Kardashian Museum? You.
SHE: Oh honey...
They hug. Then:
SHE: Your keys are poking me.
HE: Those aren't keys.

COMEDY KILLER:

A word or phrase so depressing — such as bone cancer or Armenian genocide — that it kills any joke it touches. Example:

HE: Let's go to the Kim Kardashian Museum. It's always open, and anyone can get in unless they have full-blown AIDS.

NAKAMURA:

When a joke in a script bombs with an audience, and the writer knows there are four more callbacks to that same joke. Coined by Garry Marshall, after a running joke about a Mr. Nakamura went 0-for-6 with a studio audience. Example:

Packing a short article with a dozen Kim Kardashian jokes. ■

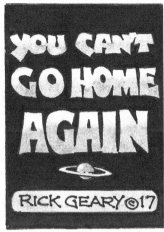

YOU CAN'T GO HOME AGAIN
RICK GEARY ©17
UPON MY RELEASE, MY ONLY THOUGHT WAS TO GO HOME.
SO I TOOK A PLANE...
AND TOOK A TRAIN...
AND TOOK A FERRY...
AND CAUGHT A BUS.
HERE'S MY STOP!
THE NEIGHBORHOOD IS AS COMPLICATED AS EVER.
WILLOW
WILLOW LN
IS IT WILLOW LANE OR WILLOW COURT?
THE STREET-LAMP, THRU THE TREES, CASTS EERIE SHADOWS ON THE HOUSE-FRONTS.
A FAMILIAR CRACK OR TWO IN THE SIDE-WALK.
THERE'S MY PET TURTLE, SQUASHED BY A TRUCK WHEN I WAS TEN.
THE OLD PLACE DOESN'T SEEM TO HAVE CHANGED MUCH...
ADULTS $8.00
CHILDREN & SENIORS 5.00
EXCEPT THAT THEY'RE NOW CHARGING ADMISSION.
I WANTED TO GO IN BUT, YOU SEE, I'M BROKE.
I GUESS YOU REALLY CAN'T GO HOME AGAIN.

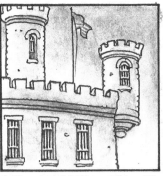

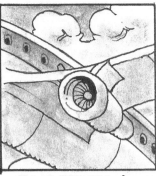

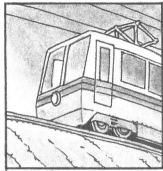

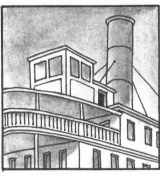

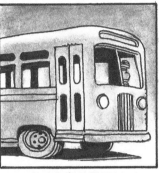

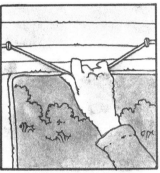

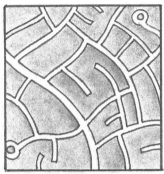

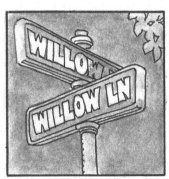

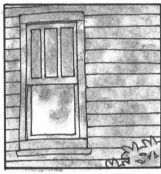

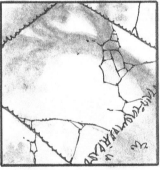

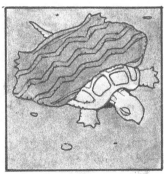

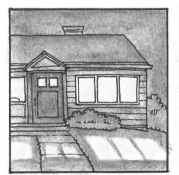

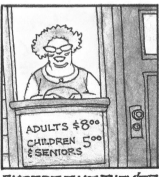

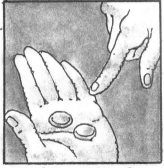

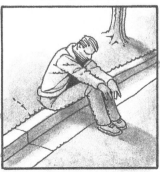

18 Ways to Show Cancer Who's Boss!

One!

Verbally assure cancer he has the job, but then disappear for weeks and refuse to answer any emails or phone calls about it, even though cancer thought this was a done deal and had already quit his previous job.

Two!

When you do respond, apologize profusely. Tell cancer it's been really crazy lately — you just have to clear something up with the CEO. But yeah, it's a done deal for sure. Then go dark for two more weeks.

Three!

Finally, make cancer a formal offer. But right before the contract is signed, tell cancer that the position has been reclassified, which means, sadly, there will be less money. Tell cancer you're sure he'll understand.

Four!

Before cancer's start date, give him a completely misleading idea of what counts as appropriate office attire. Is your office casual? Tell him to wear a suit and tie. Is it more formal? Packers jersey.

Five!

Assign cancer to an open-plan office space.

Six!

On cancer's first day, make sure his computer isn't set up yet, his workstation is filled with boxes of random office supplies, and you're nowhere to be found. Make sure no one else knows cancer is starting today, or that you hired him in the first place.

Seven!

When you do finally show up, give cancer nothing to do, but keep glancing up at him as if he should be doing something. At the end of every day, when he finally stands up to leave, appear at cancer's desk and say something like: "You're leaving? Huh." And then walk away.

Eight!

Do not articulate what is expected of cancer. Do go ballistic when he fails to do what you never told him to do in the first place.

Nine!

Get frequently hung up on seemingly inane and inconsequential details with cancer — like the font size he uses in emails, or the way he shakes hands with clients or his phone voice.

Ten!

Be warm and familiar with all other employees. Be cold and formal with cancer.

Eleven!

Email cancer exclusively on nights, weekends and holidays. Demand an immediate response to these emails. Never respond to his.

Twelve!

Play favorites. Whatever Dora does is exemplary. Whatever cancer does is evidence that this company may not be the best fit for him.

Thirteen!

Then, when a new position opens up, promote cancer over Dora anyway. This will ensure he spends the duration of his employment despised and isolated.

Fourteen!

When cancer leaves his desk for more than 10 minutes, be there when he returns to ask him where he was.

Fifteen!

Does cancer have an office crush? Sit him or her right by the men's room so cancer has to make eye contact every time he finishes doing his filthy business in there.

Sixteen!

When cancer puts in for vacation, sigh.

Seventeen!

Blame cancer for your own mistakes. When he objects, say you know it doesn't seem fair, but you appreciate him taking one for the team, and that you'll make it up to him. Then throw him under the bus again at the next opportunity.

Eighteen!

When cancer finally tells you he quits, that he's had it with this fucking place, and with you, and he's going to move back to his childhood home in suburban Minneapolis to get his head straight, maybe start playing bass guitar again, maybe open his own yoga studio or some other kind of small business that's actually meaningful — a place where he'll help people and treat his employees with compassion and fairness — look up as if you barely even recognize cancer, and then look down and mutter: "Very good. Just speak to Kevin in HR on your way out," and then go back to whatever it was you were doing, you goddamn glorious cancer *warrior* you. B

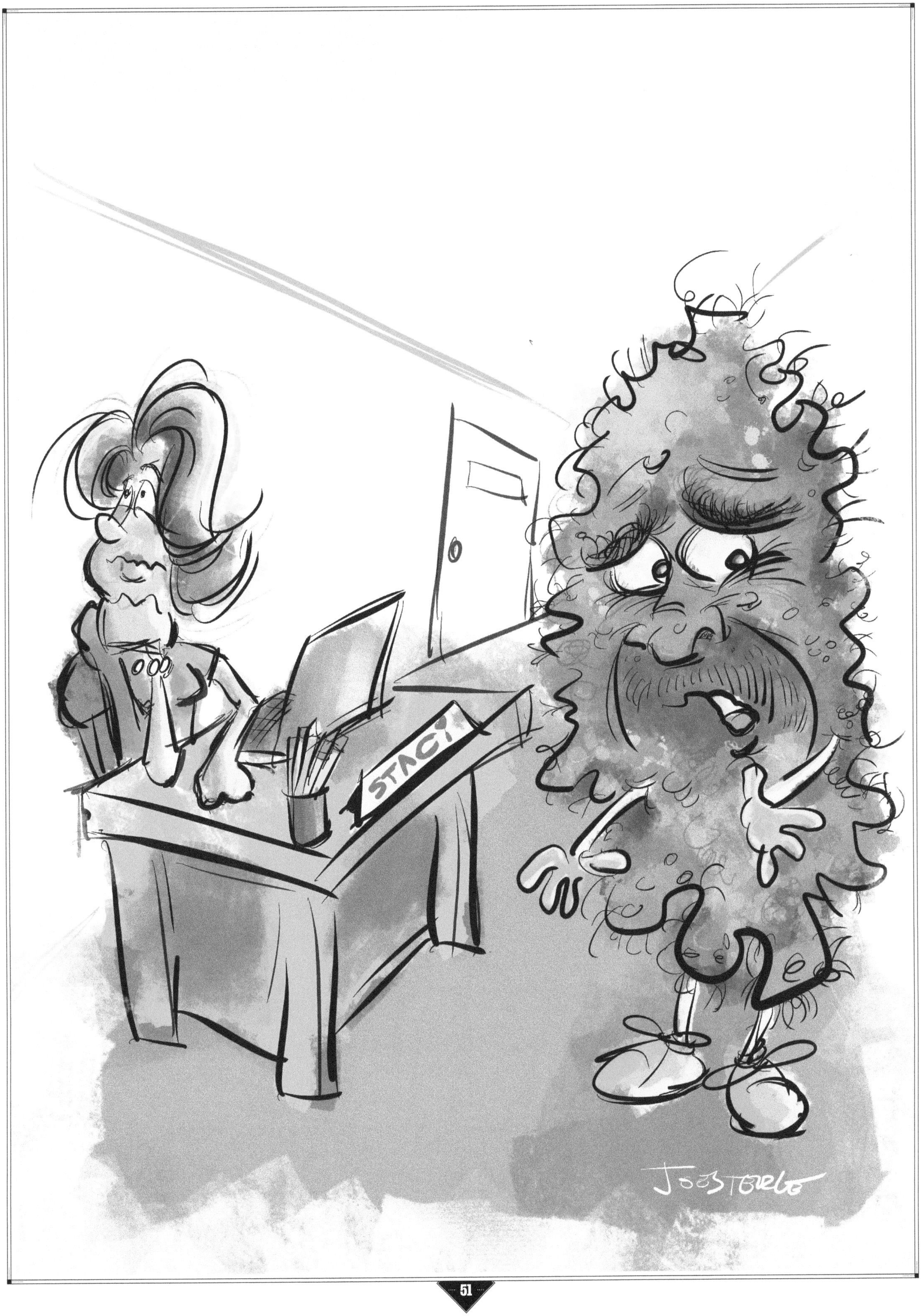
STACY
JOE OESTERLE

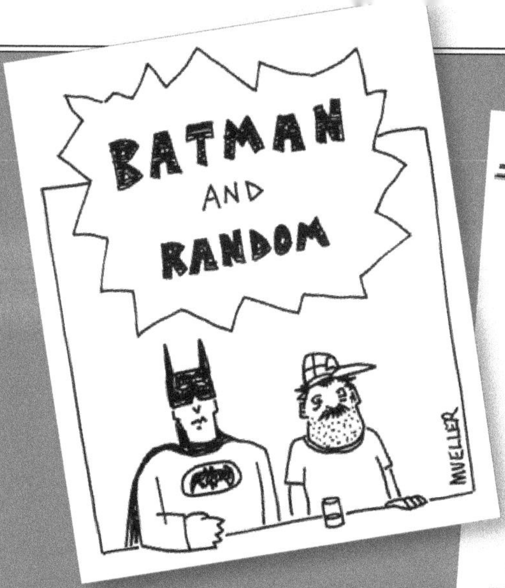
BATMAN AND RANDOM
MUELLER

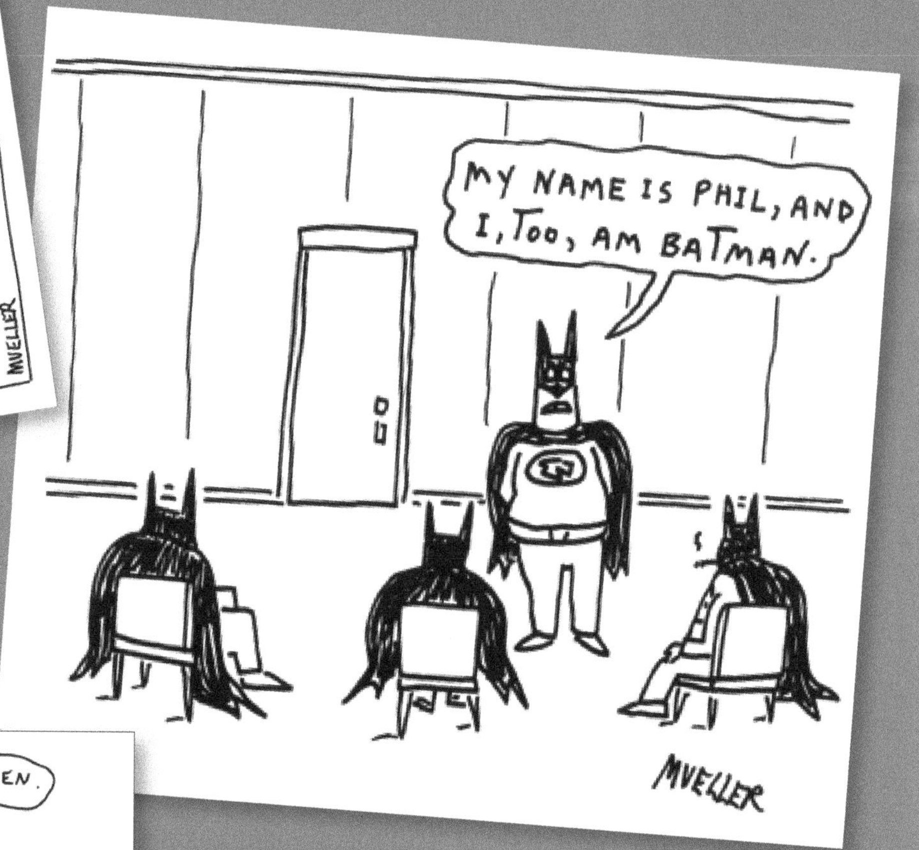
MY NAME IS PHIL, AND I, TOO, AM BATMAN.
MUELLER

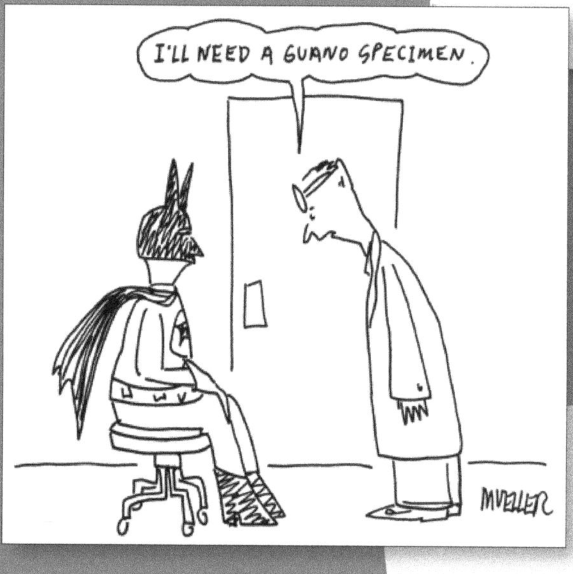
I'LL NEED A GUANO SPECIMEN.
MUELLER

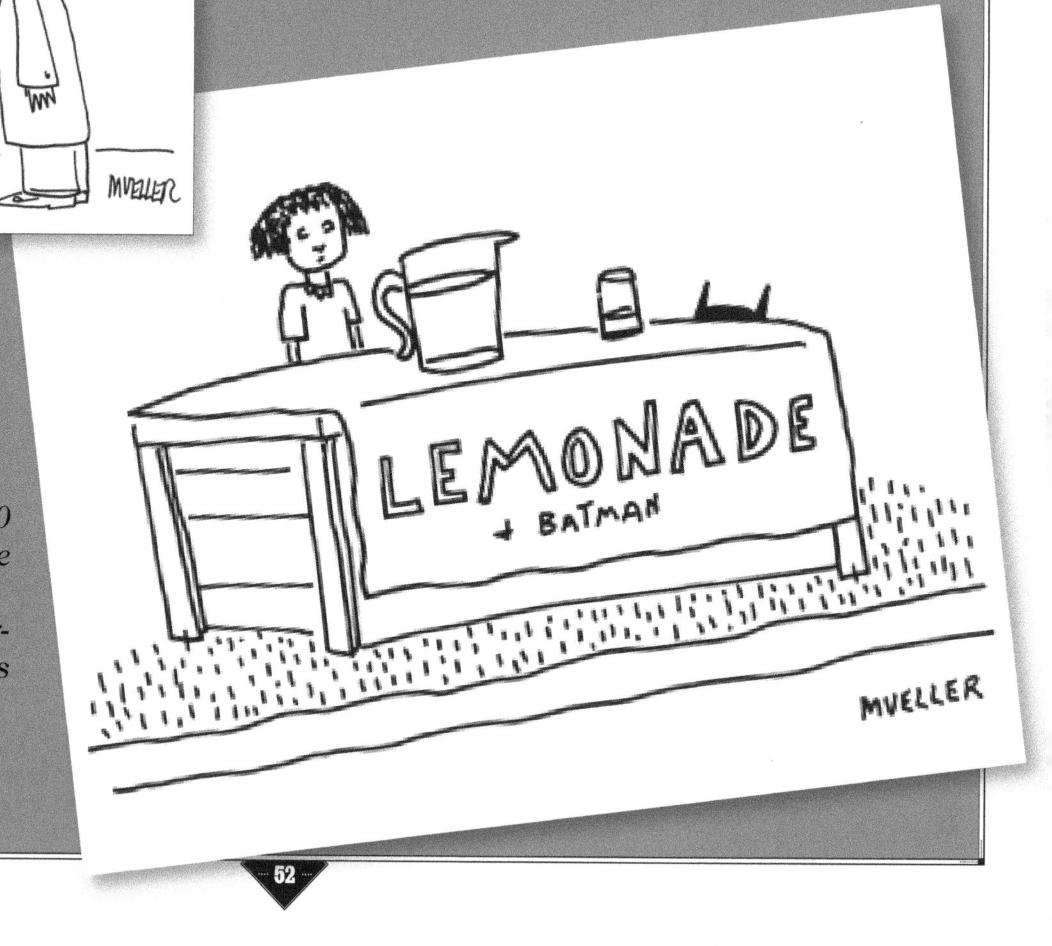
LEMONADE
+ BATMAN
MUELLER

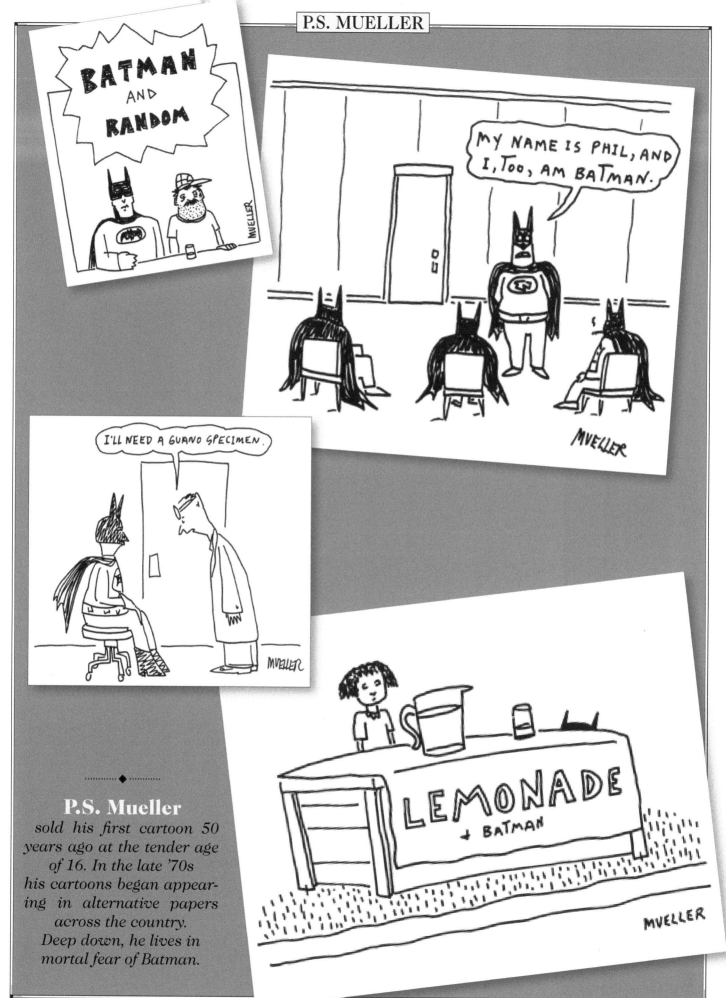

P.S. Mueller
sold his first cartoon 50 years ago at the tender age of 16. In the late '70s his cartoons began appearing in alternative papers across the country. Deep down, he lives in mortal fear of Batman.

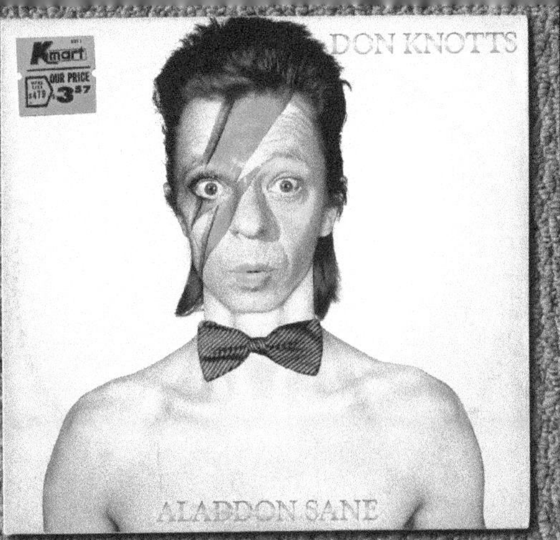
DON KNOTTS
Kmart
OUR PRICE 3.57
ALADDON SANE

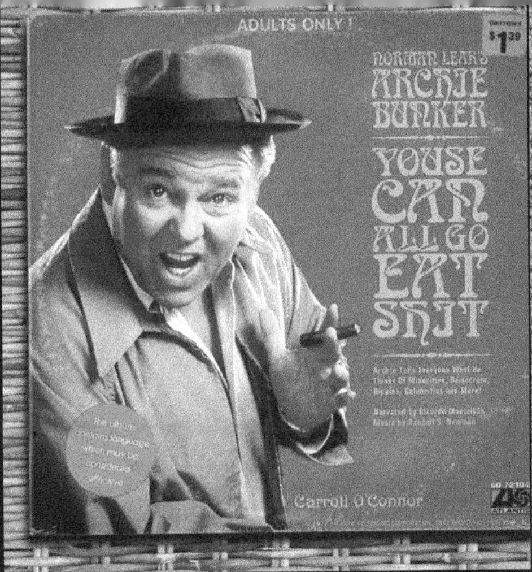
ADULTS ONLY!
$1.30
NORMAN LEAR'S
ARCHIE BUNKER
YOUSE CAN ALL GO EAT SHIT
Carroll O'Connor

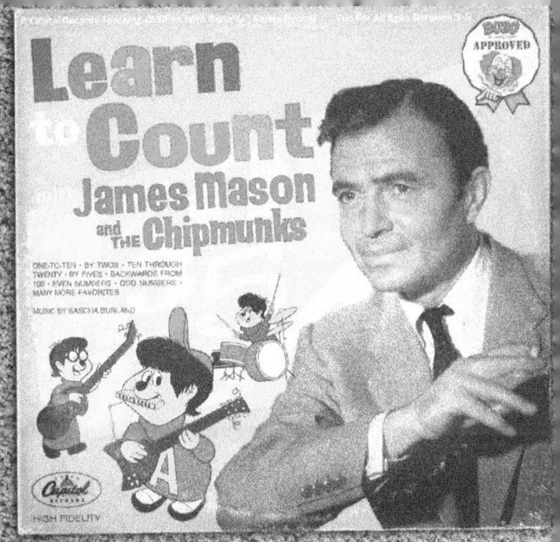
APPROVED
Learn to Count
with James Mason and The Chipmunks
Capitol
HIGH FIDELITY

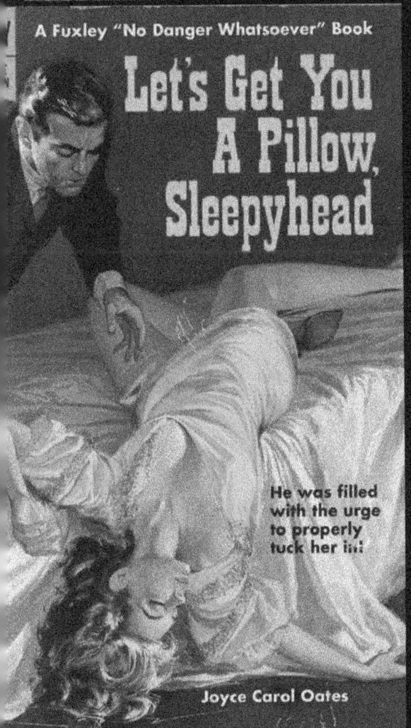
A Fuxley "No Danger Whatsoever" Book
Let's Get You A Pillow, Sleepyhead
He was filled with the urge to properly tuck her in!
Joyce Carol Oates

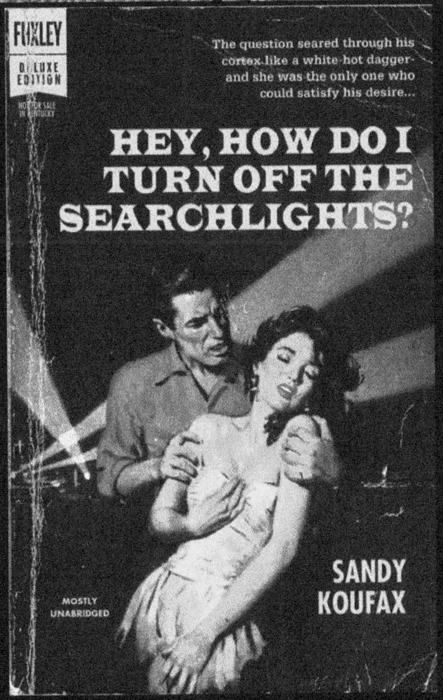
FUXLEY
DELUXE EDITION
The question seared through his cortex like a white-hot dagger-and she was the only one who could satisfy his desire...
HEY, HOW DO I TURN OFF THE SEARCHLIGHTS?
MOSTLY UNABRIDGED
SANDY KOUFAX

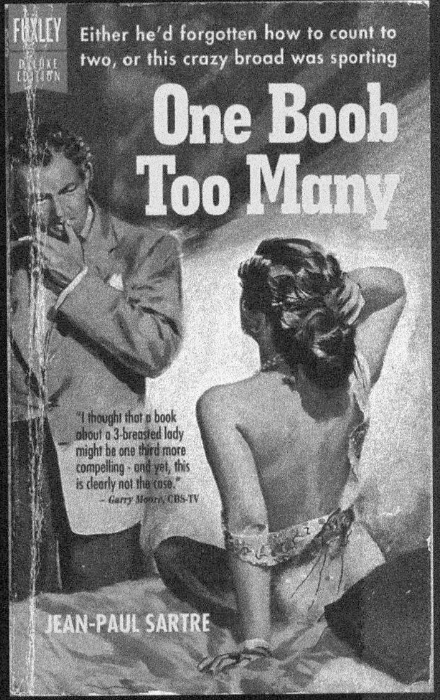
FUXLEY
DELUXE EDITION
Either he'd forgotten how to count to two, or this crazy broad was sporting
One Boob Too Many
"I thought that a book about a 3-breasted lady might be one third more compelling - and yet, this is clearly not the case."
– Garry Moore, CBS-TV
JEAN-PAUL SARTRE

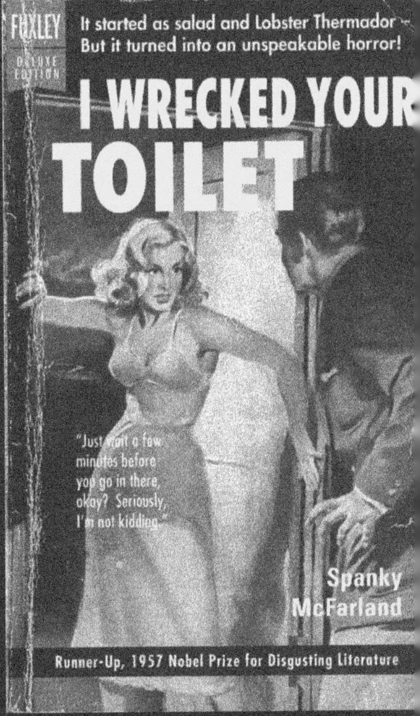
FUXLEY
DELUXE EDITION
It started as salad and Lobster Thermador – But it turned into an unspeakable horror!
I WRECKED YOUR TOILET
"Just wait a few minutes before you go in there, okay? Seriously, I'm not kidding."
Spanky McFarland
Runner-Up, 1957 Nobel Prize for Disgusting Literature

American Grotesques: The World of Cris Shapan

"Every piece I've done has been mistaken for real by somebody. I think they want to believe." ☛

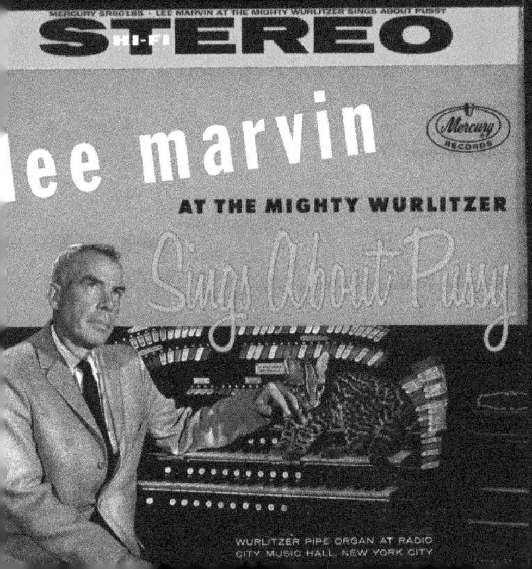
STEREO
HI-FI
lee marvin
Mercury RECORDS
AT THE MIGHTY WURLITZER
Sings About Pussy
WURLITZER PIPE ORGAN AT RADIO CITY MUSIC HALL, NEW YORK CITY

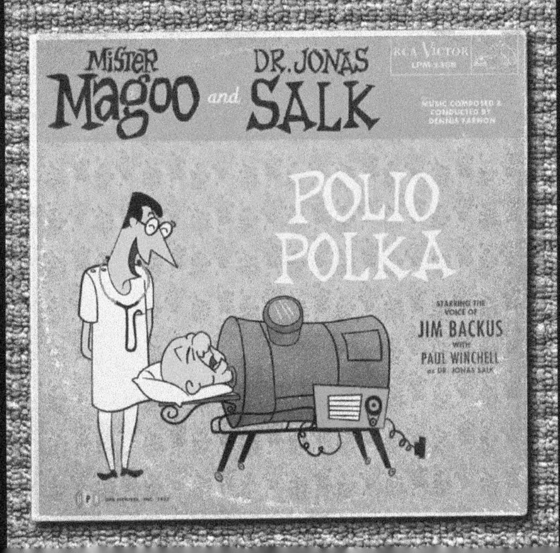
MISTER MAGOO and DR. JONAS SALK
RCA Victor
POLIO POLKA
JIM BACKUS
PAUL WINCHELL

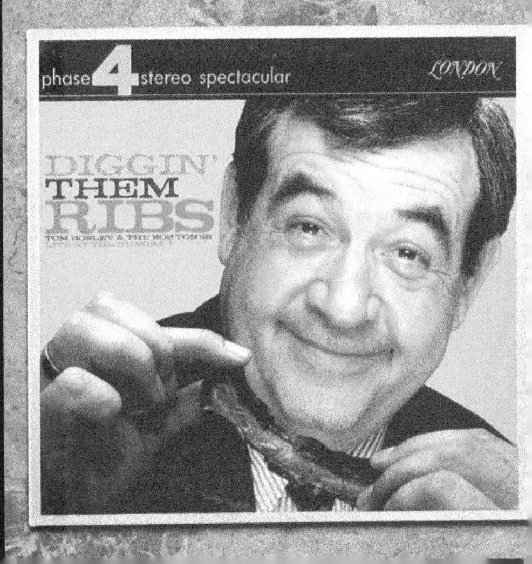
phase 4 stereo spectacular
LONDON
DIGGIN' THEM RIBS
TOM BOSLEY & THE BOSTONS

Take midcentury American advertising and stir in a dollop of B (or C) -list celebrity. Beat until absolutely smooth. Then, add two heaving scoops of nostalgia and overheated Hefnerian sex. Slather it all with eerily perfect typography, adding a few digital scuff-marks for garnish. Serves millions, all over the internet.

Hollywood-based art director and designer **CRIS SHAPAN** has been in *Bystander* since issue #1, and he's a huge reader favorite. Like *The Onion* at its best, his Photoshop concoctions are so exquisite and exacting that their madness has the ring of truth. This is sometimes a problem.

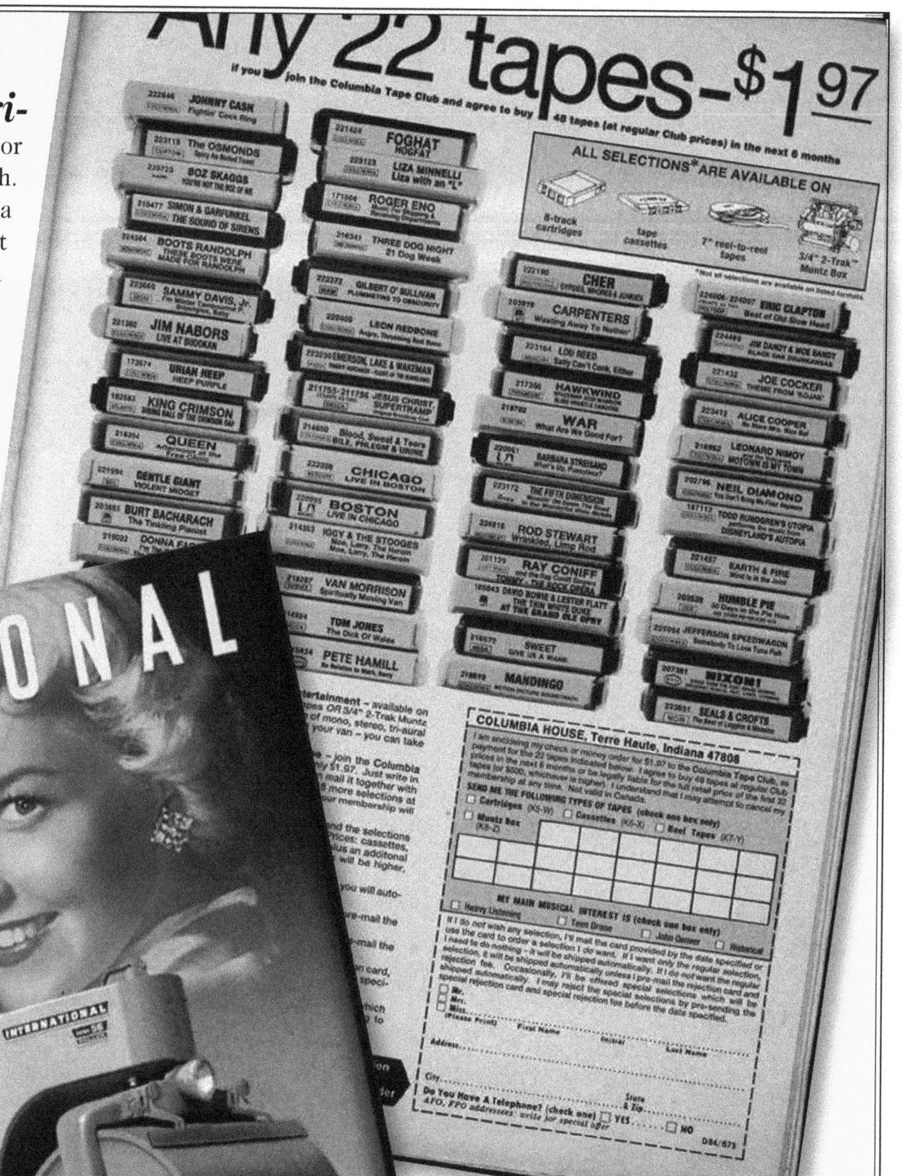
Any 22 tapes-$1.97
if you join the Columbia Tape Club and agree to buy 48 tapes (at regular Club prices) in the next 6 months
ALL SELECTIONS* ARE AVAILABLE ON
8-track cartridges
tape cassettes
7" reel-to-reel tapes
3/4" 2-Trak" Muntz Box
JOHNNY CASH
THE OSMONDS
BOZ SKAGGS
SIMON & GARFUNKEL
BOOTS RANDOLPH
SAMMY DAVIS, Jr.
JIM NABORS
URIAH HEEP
KING CRIMSON
QUEEN
GENTLE GIANT
BURT BACHARACH
FOGHAT
LIZA MINNELLI
ROGER ENO
THREE DOG NIGHT
GILBERT O'SULLIVAN
LEON REDBONE
EMERSON, LAKE & WAKEMAN
JESUS CHRIST SUPERTRAMP
Blood, Sweat & Tears
CHICAGO LIVE IN BOSTON
BOSTON LIVE IN CHICAGO
IGGY & THE STOOGES
VAN MORRISON
TOM JONES
PETE HAMILL
CHER
CARPENTERS
LOU REED
HAWKWIND
WAR
BARBARA STREISAND
THE FIFTH DIMENSION
ROD STEWART
RAY CONIFF
SWEET
MANDINGO
ERIC CLAPTON
JOE COCKER
ALICE COOPER
LEONARD NIMOY
NEIL DIAMOND
EARTH & FIRE
HUMBLE PIE
JEFFERSON SPEEDWAGON
NIXON!
SEALS & CROFTS
COLUMBIA HOUSE, Terre Haute, Indiana 47808

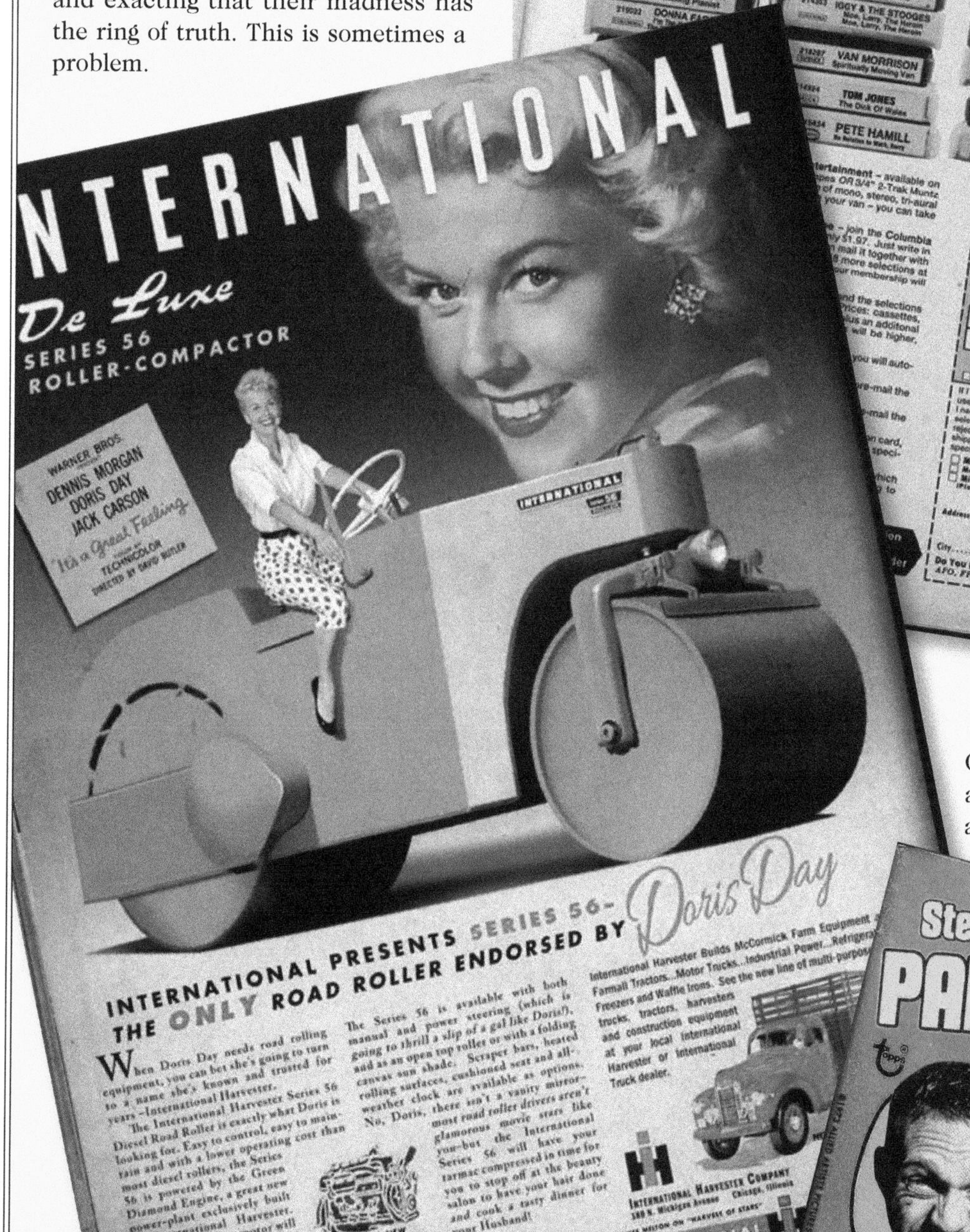
INTERNATIONAL
De Luxe
SERIES 56
ROLLER-COMPACTOR
WARNER BROS.
DENNIS MORGAN
DORIS DAY
JACK CARSON
It's a Great Feeling
TECHNICOLOR
INTERNATIONAL
INTERNATIONAL PRESENTS SERIES 56-
THE ONLY ROAD ROLLER ENDORSED BY Doris Day
SEE THE NEW GREEN DIAMOND ENGINE
INTERNATIONAL HARVESTER COMPANY
INTERNATIONAL

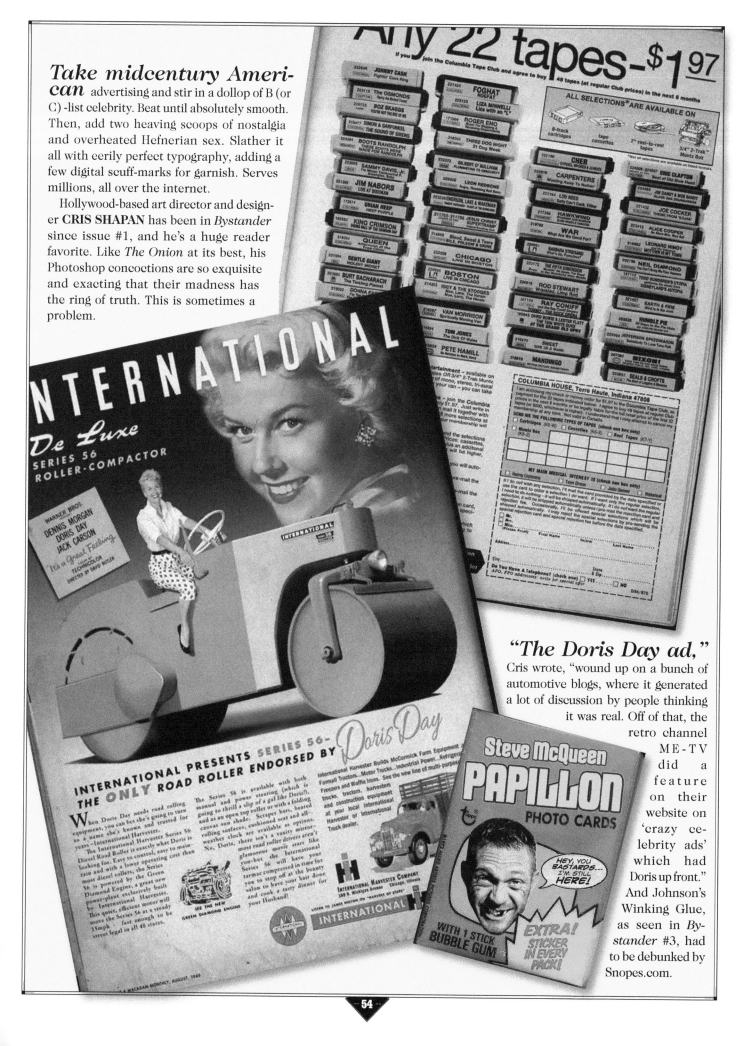

"The Doris Day ad," Cris wrote, "wound up on a bunch of automotive blogs, where it generated a lot of discussion by people thinking it was real. Off of that, the retro channel ME-TV did a feature on their website on 'crazy celebrity ads' which had Doris up front." And Johnson's Winking Glue, as seen in *Bystander* #3, had to be debunked by Snopes.com.

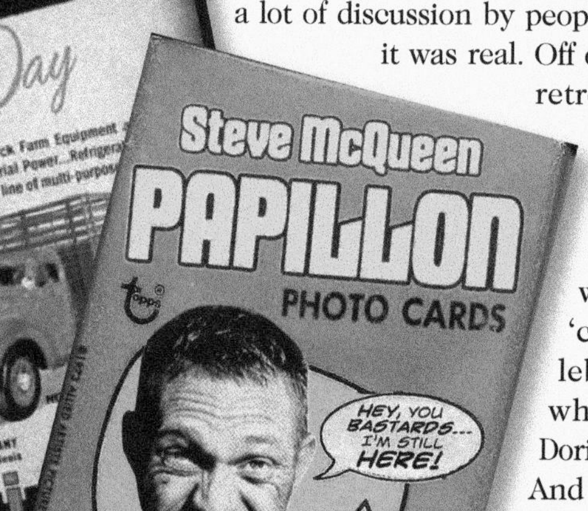
Steve McQueen
PAPILLON
PHOTO CARDS
topps
HEY, YOU BASTARDS... I'M STILL HERE!
WITH 1 STICK BUBBLE GUM
EXTRA! STICKER IN EVERY PACK!

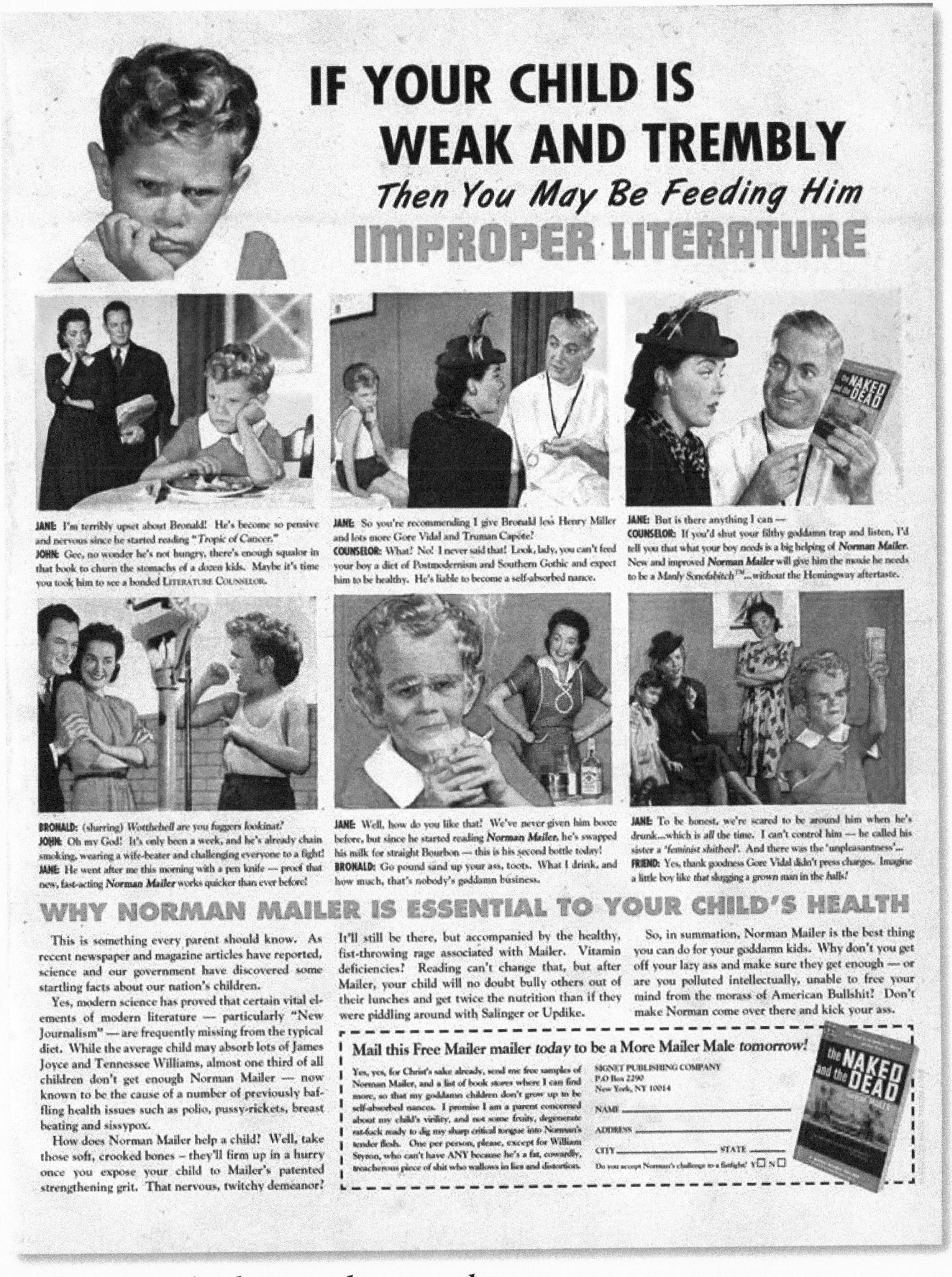
IF YOUR CHILD IS WEAK AND TREMBLY
Then You May Be Feeding Him
IMPROPER LITERATURE
the NAKED and the DEAD
JANE: I'm terribly upset about Bronald! He's become so pensive and nervous since he started reading "Tropic of Cancer."
JOHN: Gee, no wonder he's not hungry, there's enough squalor in that book to churn the stomachs of a dozen kids. Maybe it's time you took him to see a bonded LITERATURE COUNSELOR.
JANE: So you're recommending I give Bronald less Henry Miller and lots more Gore Vidal and Truman Capote?
COUNSELOR: What? No! I never said that! Look, lady, you can't feed your boy a diet of Postmodernism and Southern Gothic and expect him to be healthy. He's liable to become a self-absorbed nance.
JANE: But is there anything I can —
COUNSELOR: If you'd shut your filthy goddamn trap and listen, I'd tell you that what your boy needs is a big helping of Norman Mailer. New and improved Norman Mailer will give him the moxie he needs to be a Manly Sonofabitch™...without the Hemingway aftertaste.
BRONALD: (slurring) Wotthehell are you fuggers lookinat?
JOHN: Oh my God! It's only been a week, and he's already chain smoking, wearing a wife-beater and challenging everyone to a fight!
JANE: He went after me this morning with a pen knife — proof that new, fast-acting Norman Mailer works quicker than ever before!
JANE: Well, how do you like that? We've never given him booze before, but since he started reading Norman Mailer, he's swapped his milk for straight Bourbon — this is his second bottle today!
BRONALD: Go pound sand up your ass, toots. What I drink, and how much, that's nobody's goddamn business.
JANE: To be honest, we're scared to be around him when he's drunk...which is all the time. I can't control him — he called his sister a 'feminist shitheel'. And there was the 'unpleasantness'...
FRIEND: Yes, thank goodness Gore Vidal didn't press charges. Imagine a little boy like that slugging a grown man in the balls!
WHY NORMAN MAILER IS ESSENTIAL TO YOUR CHILD'S HEALTH
This is something every parent should know. As recent newspaper and magazine articles have reported, science and our government have discovered some startling facts about our nation's children.
Yes, modern science has proved that certain vital elements of modern literature — particularly "New Journalism" — are frequently missing from the typical diet. While the average child may absorb lots of James Joyce and Tennessee Williams, almost one third of all children don't get enough Norman Mailer — now known to be the cause of a number of previously baffling health issues such as polio, pussy-rickets, breast beating and sissypox.
How does Norman Mailer help a child? Well, take those soft, crooked bones – they'll firm up in a hurry once you expose your child to Mailer's patented strengthening grit. That nervous, twitchy demeanor? It'll still be there, but accompanied by the healthy, fist-throwing rage associated with Mailer. Vitamin deficiencies? Reading can't change that, but after Mailer, your child will no doubt bully others out of their lunches and get twice the nutrition than if they were piddling around with Salinger or Updike.
So, in summation, Norman Mailer is the best thing you can do for your goddamn kids. Why don't you get off your lazy ass and make sure they get enough — or are you polluted intellectually, unable to free your mind from the morass of American Bullshit? Don't make Norman come over there and kick your ass.
Mail this Free Mailer mailer today to be a More Mailer Male tomorrow!
Yes, yes, for Christ's sake already, send me free samples of Norman Mailer, and a list of book stores where I can find more, so that my goddamn children don't grow up to be self-absorbed nances. I promise I am a parent concerned about my child's virility, and not some fruity, degenerate rat-fuck ready to dig my sharp critical tongue into Norman's tender flesh. One per person, please, except for William Styron, who can't have ANY because he's a fat, cowardly, treacherous piece of shit who wallows in lies and distortion.
SIGNET PUBLISHING COMPANY
P.O Box 2290
New York, NY 10014
NAME
ADDRESS
CITY
STATE
Do you accept Norman's challenge to a fistfight? Y☐ N☐
the NAKED and the DEAD

Norman Mailer has made several appearances in Cris's work. "I've always thought Mailer was a drunk, overrated blowhard prick — especially after the Jack Henry Abbott thing. I don't know, maybe he was a warm, wonderful person when he wasn't stabbing you with a ballpoint pen in front of your party guests."

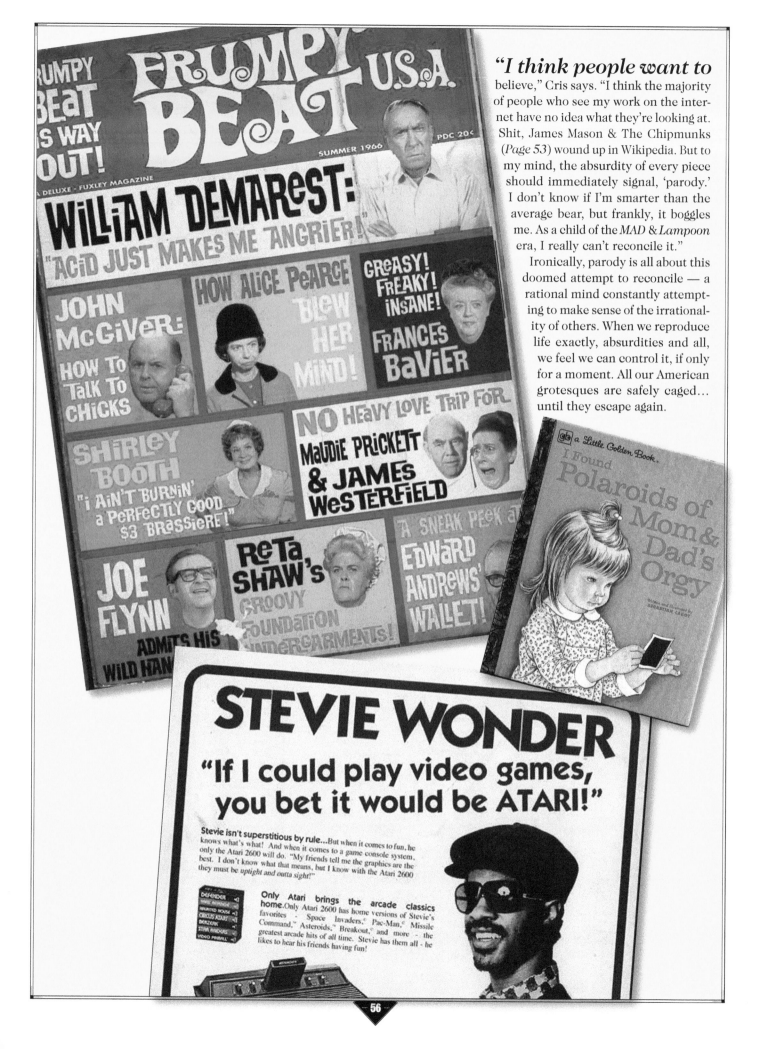

"I think people want to

believe," Cris says. "I think the majority of people who see my work on the internet have no idea what they're looking at. Shit, James Mason & The Chipmunks (*Page 53*) wound up in Wikipedia. But to my mind, the absurdity of every piece should immediately signal, 'parody.' I don't know if I'm smarter than the average bear, but frankly, it boggles me. As a child of the *MAD* & *Lampoon* era, I really can't reconcile it."

Ironically, parody is all about this doomed attempt to reconcile — a rational mind constantly attempting to make sense of the irrationality of others. When we reproduce life exactly, absurdities and all, we feel we can control it, if only for a moment. All our American grotesques are safely caged… until they escape again.

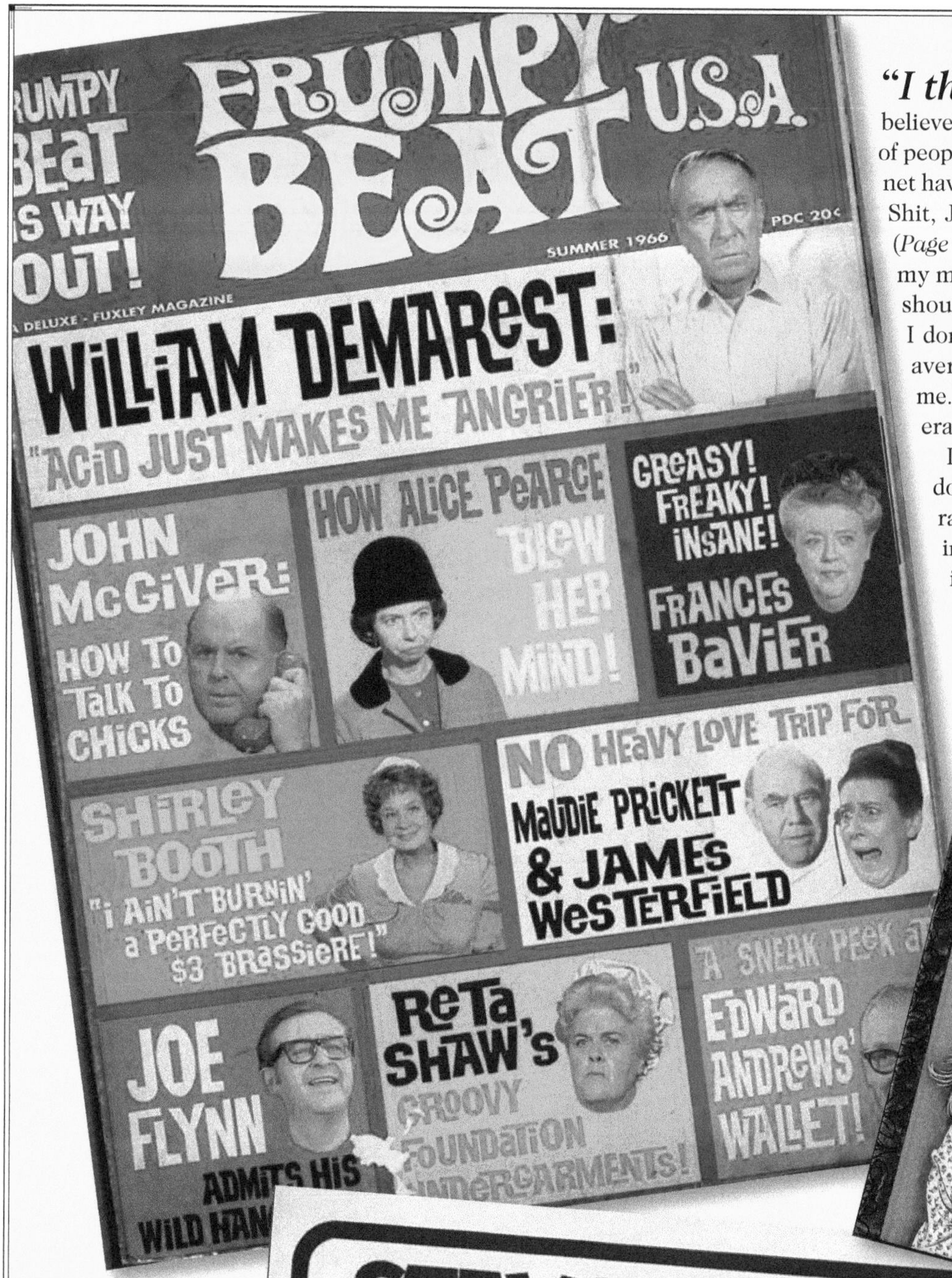
FRUMPY BEAT IS WAY OUT!
FRUMPY BEAT U.S.A.
SUMMER 1966
PDC 20¢
A DELUXE - FUXLEY MAGAZINE
WILLIAM DEMAREST:
"ACID JUST MAKES ME ANGRIER!"
JOHN McGIVER: HOW TO TALK TO CHICKS
HOW ALICE PEARCE BLEW HER MIND!
GREASY! FREAKY! INSANE! FRANCES BAVIER
SHIRLEY BOOTH "I AIN'T BURNIN' A PERFECTLY GOOD $3 BRASSIERE!"
NO HEAVY LOVE TRIP FOR MAUDIE PRICKETT & JAMES WESTERFIELD
JOE FLYNN ADMITS HIS WILD HAN
RETA SHAW'S GROOVY FOUNDATION UNDERGARMENTS!
A SNEAK PEEK AT EDWARD ANDREWS' WALLET!

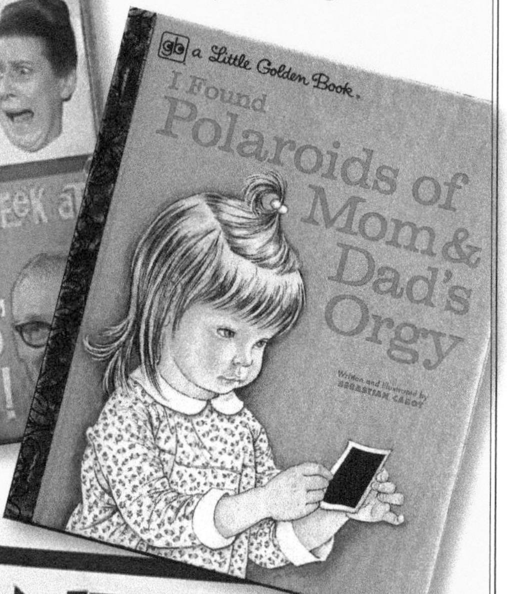
a Little Golden Book
I Found Polaroids of Mom & Dad's Orgy

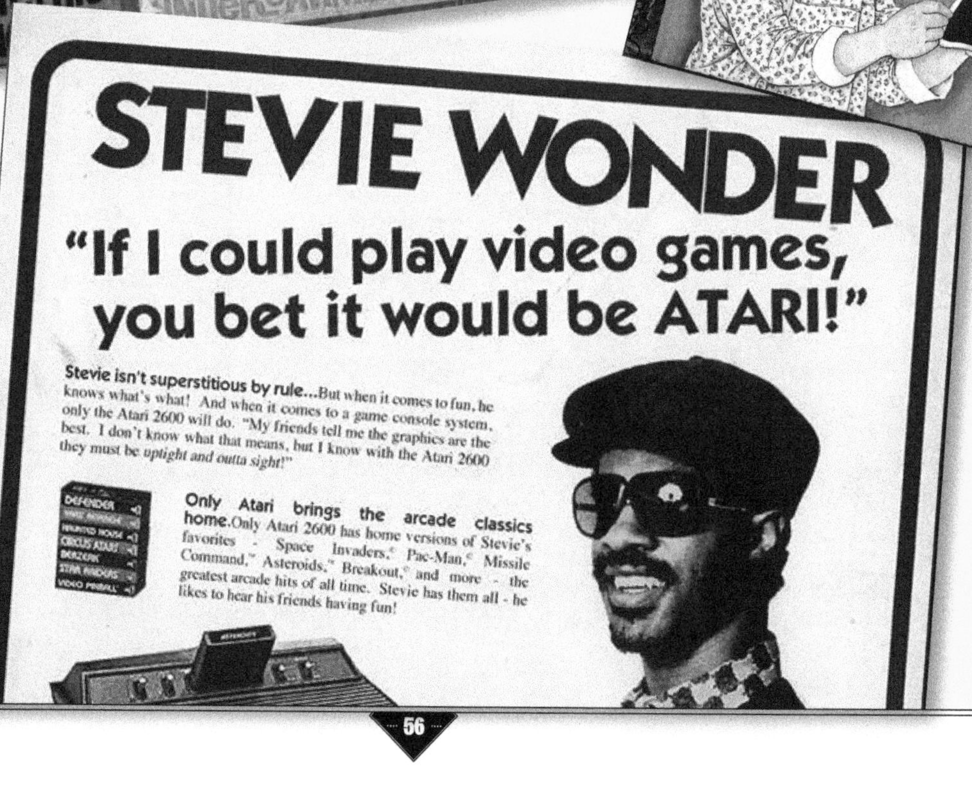
STEVIE WONDER
"If I could play video games, you bet it would be ATARI!"
Stevie isn't superstitious by rule...But when it comes to fun, he knows what's what! And when it comes to a game console system, only the Atari 2600 will do. "My friends tell me the graphics are the best. I don't know what that means, but I know with the Atari 2600 they must be uptight and outta sight!"
Only Atari brings the arcade classics home. Only Atari 2600 has home versions of Stevie's favorites - Space Invaders, Pac-Man, Missile Command, Asteroids, Breakout, and more - the greatest arcade hits of all time. Stevie has them all - he likes to hear his friends having fun!
DEFENDER
HAUNTED HOUSE
CIRCUS ATARI
BERZERK
VIDEO PINBALL

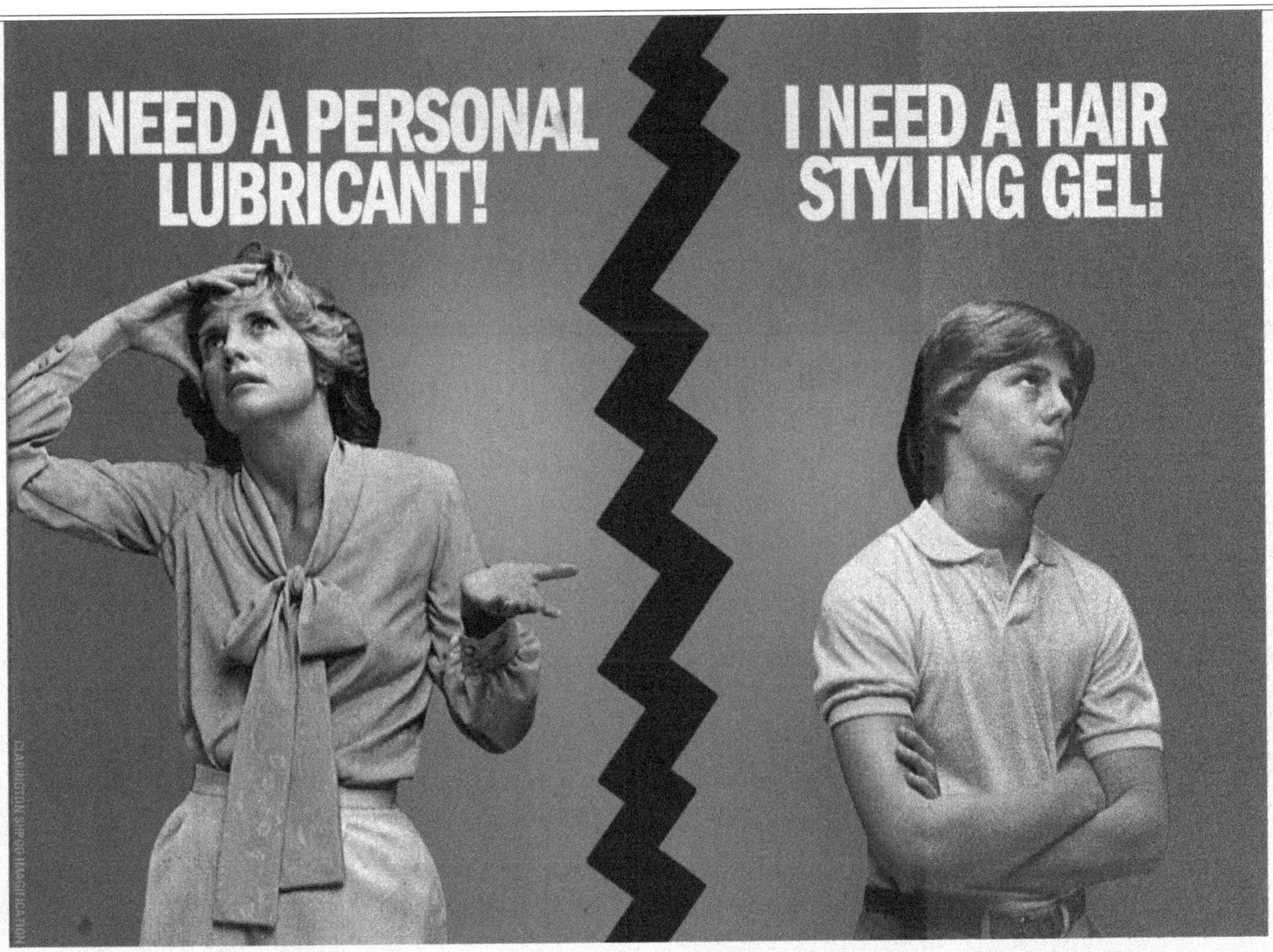
I NEED A PERSONAL LUBRICANT!
I NEED A HAIR STYLING GEL!

GET BOTH. GET ASTROMOUSSE®

The moisturizing comfort of a lubricant when wet, the holding power of a professional salon gel when dry.

Oh, my God, must the two of you always be arguing? You knew that these May/December relationships rarely work, and this is why.

He's only a kid, you can't expect him to care about your middle-aged feminine dryness; like other kids, all he can think about is his hair - his young, gorgeous, shiny hair.

Fine, you love his hair; it's one of the reasons you left your husband for a teenaged boy. So isn't there a product that'd work for both of you?

There is. New Astromousse©, from the makers of Astroslide.

Slippery when wet, it forms a velvety coating that moisturizes as it coats and lubes. Let it dry a little, it becomes a tacky gel, great for comb styling. Want more hold? Dry it with a hair dryer to get the strength of a salon-grade mousse for those really big hairstyles.

New Astromousse©. It may not save your relationship, but you'll have one less thing to argue about.

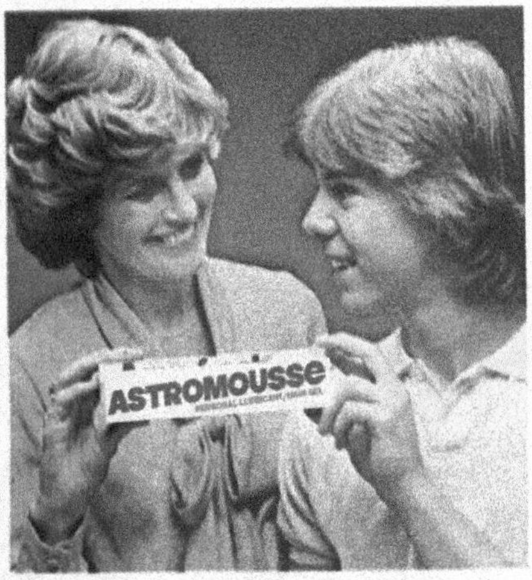
ASTROMOUSSE

For more fun, you can apply it to each other.

"Astromousse has been shown to be an effective personal lubricant in terms of making personal areas moist, and has been proven to be of marginal benefit to hair styling and hair care by users concerned with such." National Council on Personal Lubricants - American Hair Gel Association.

© Stickysex Chemicals Inc. 1980

INSPECTED FOR WHOLESOMENESS BY U.S. NCPL-AHGA INSPECTED & APPROVED P-42

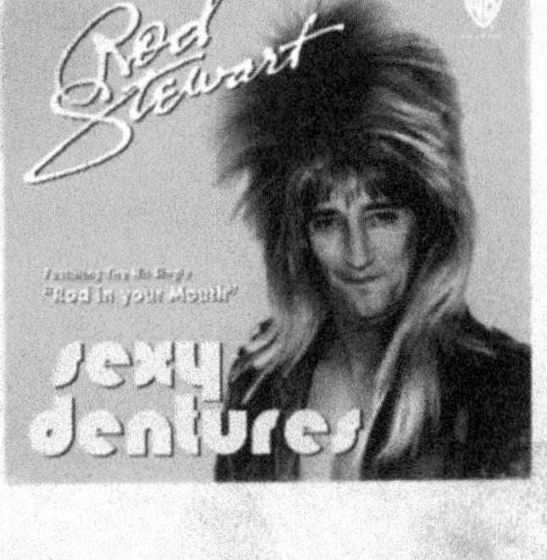
Rod Stewart
sexy dentures

"If you find a better dual purpose sex lube/hair mousse, buy it."

Rod Stewart, Disco Superstar

Astromousse© is proud to sponsor Rod Stewart's ***Sexy Dentures North American Tour 1980.***
Astromousse© is the official personal lubricant/hair gel of the Rod Stewart Band.
Sexy Dentures is available on Warner Brothers records and tapes.

What Not to Throw Out the Airlock

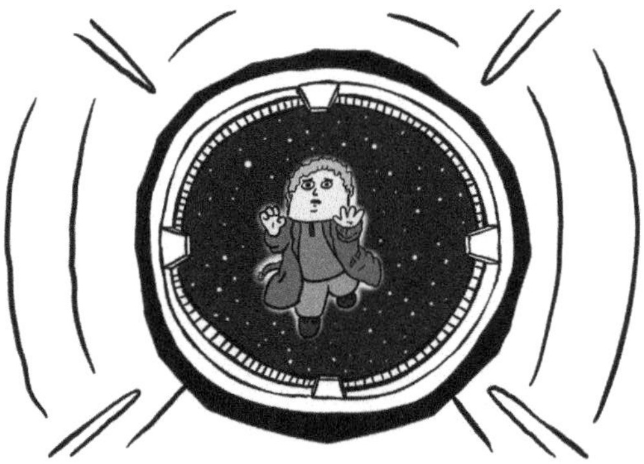

There have been some serious abuses of the Airlock lately. Please use good judgment and follow this guide.

SPACE PIRATES

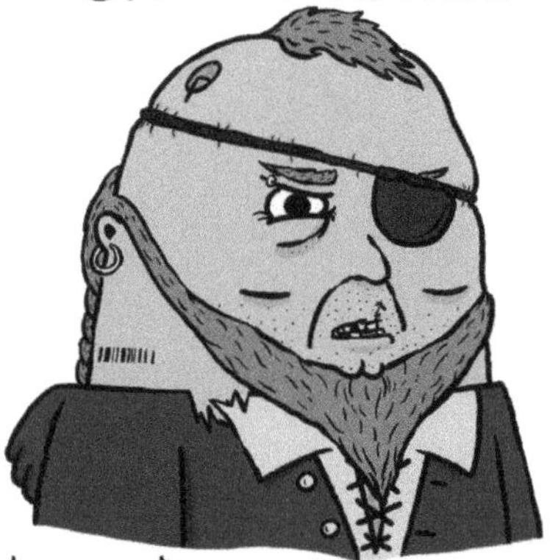

Airlock termination, or "spacing" is almost always used against them, but just because a person looks like a space pirate doesn't mean they are. They could be space merchants, space hipsters, or space tattoo artists. Please leave spacing to the Officers.

ORPHAN STOWAWAYS

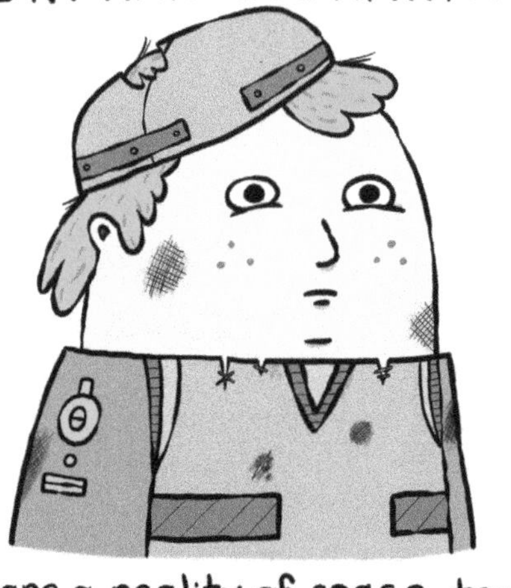

They are a reality of space travel. No matter how rascally their schemes, they do not deserve to die in space.

GOODWILL DONATIONS

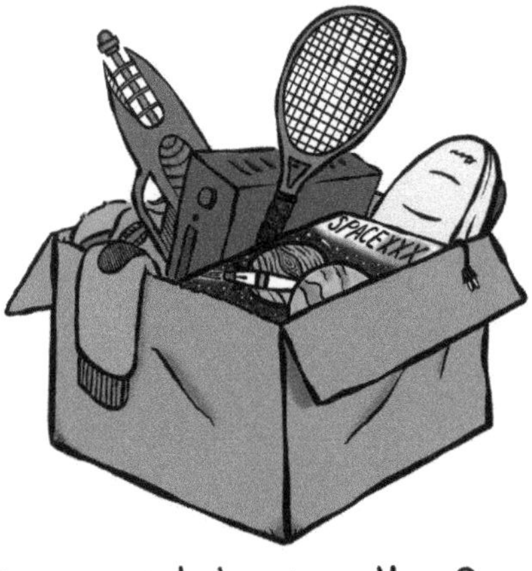
SPACEXXX

A common mistake since the Goodwill donation box is right next to the Airlock. But you can't write off items that you fire into the void.

Lars Kenseth is an upstanding citizen of the Gum Nebula, and anyone who says otherwise is a space liar. He was ejected from an airlock once in college, but didn't like it and hasn't done it since.

POTABLE WATER

I can't stress this enough: there is nothing funny about blasting our most precious resource into space. Stop it.

MELTLINGS

Meltlings are not real. They're vivid hallucinations - a side effect of extended hypersleep. Ejecting them into space is ineffective and wastes energy.

INFOSPHERES

Infospheres are a resource. They answer basic questions and help you navigate the ship. They are <u>not</u> programmed to help you make big life decisions and should not be punished for giving bad advice.

INTAKE VENT SPIDERS

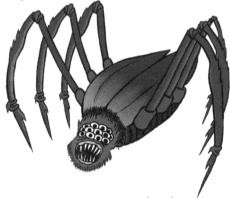

The ship's vents are a delicate ecosystem and Intake Vent Spiders are part of it. They survive on mold, using knife-like claws to violently scrape it from the ducts. Ask an Officer about a spider petting experience.

CORPORAL JIM TWOHEY

Corporal Twohey will face a Galactic Tribunal for his crimes. They may very well hurtle him into the eternal black, but until then, do not let him near the Airlock.

INFOCUBES

(See Infospheres)

(continued on next page)

LARS KENSETH

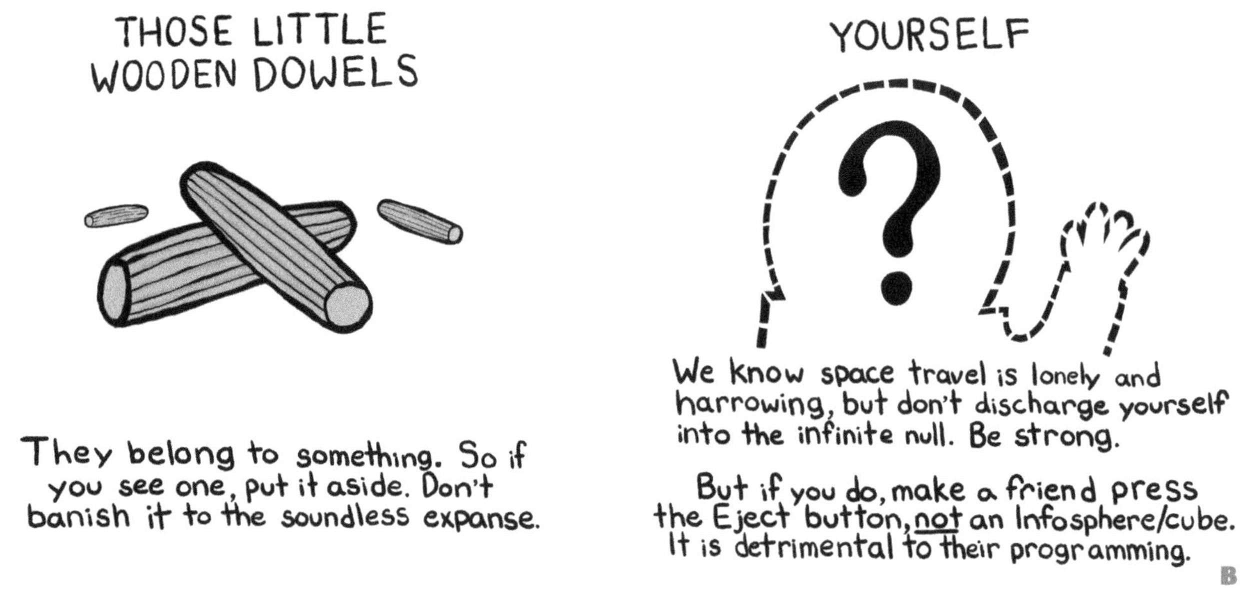
THOSE LITTLE WOODEN DOWELS
They belong to something. So if you see one, put it aside. Don't banish it to the soundless expanse.
YOURSELF
?
We know space travel is lonely and harrowing, but don't discharge yourself into the infinite null. Be strong.
But if you do, make a friend press the Eject button, not an Infosphere/cube. It is detrimental to their programming.
B

SALLY GARDNER

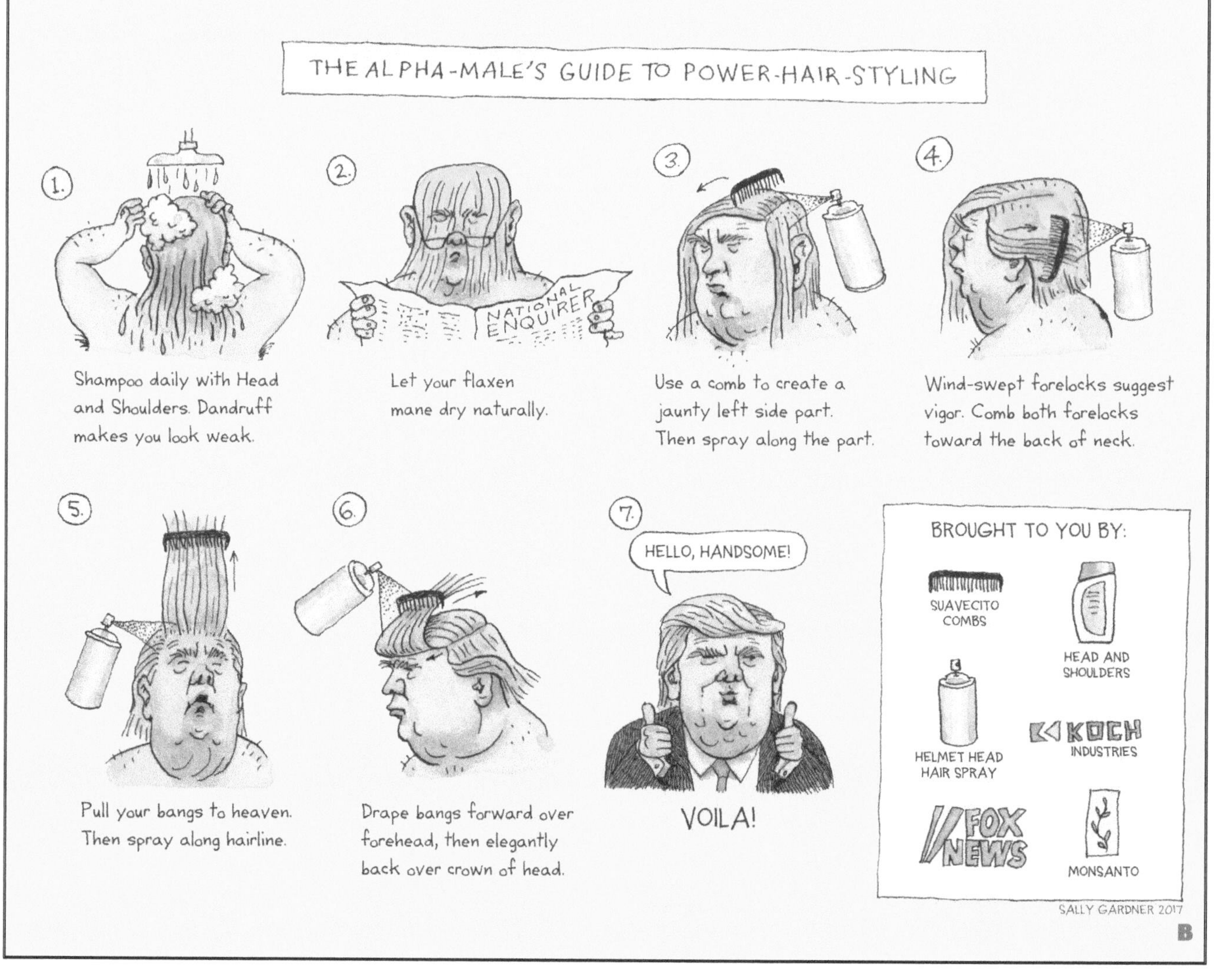
THE ALPHA-MALE'S GUIDE TO POWER-HAIR-STYLING
1.
Shampoo daily with Head and Shoulders. Dandruff makes you look weak.
2.
NATIONAL ENQUIRER
Let your flaxen mane dry naturally.
3.
Use a comb to create a jaunty left side part. Then spray along the part.
4.
Wind-swept forelocks suggest vigor. Comb both forelocks toward the back of neck.
5.
Pull your bangs to heaven. Then spray along hairline.
6.
Drape bangs forward over forehead, then elegantly back over crown of head.
7.
HELLO, HANDSOME!
VOILA!
BROUGHT TO YOU BY:
SUAVECITO COMBS
HEAD AND SHOULDERS
HELMET HEAD HAIR SPRAY
KOCH INDUSTRIES
FOX NEWS
MONSANTO
SALLY GARDNER 2017
B

VOL. 2, NO. 3 • WINTER 2017

Marvy

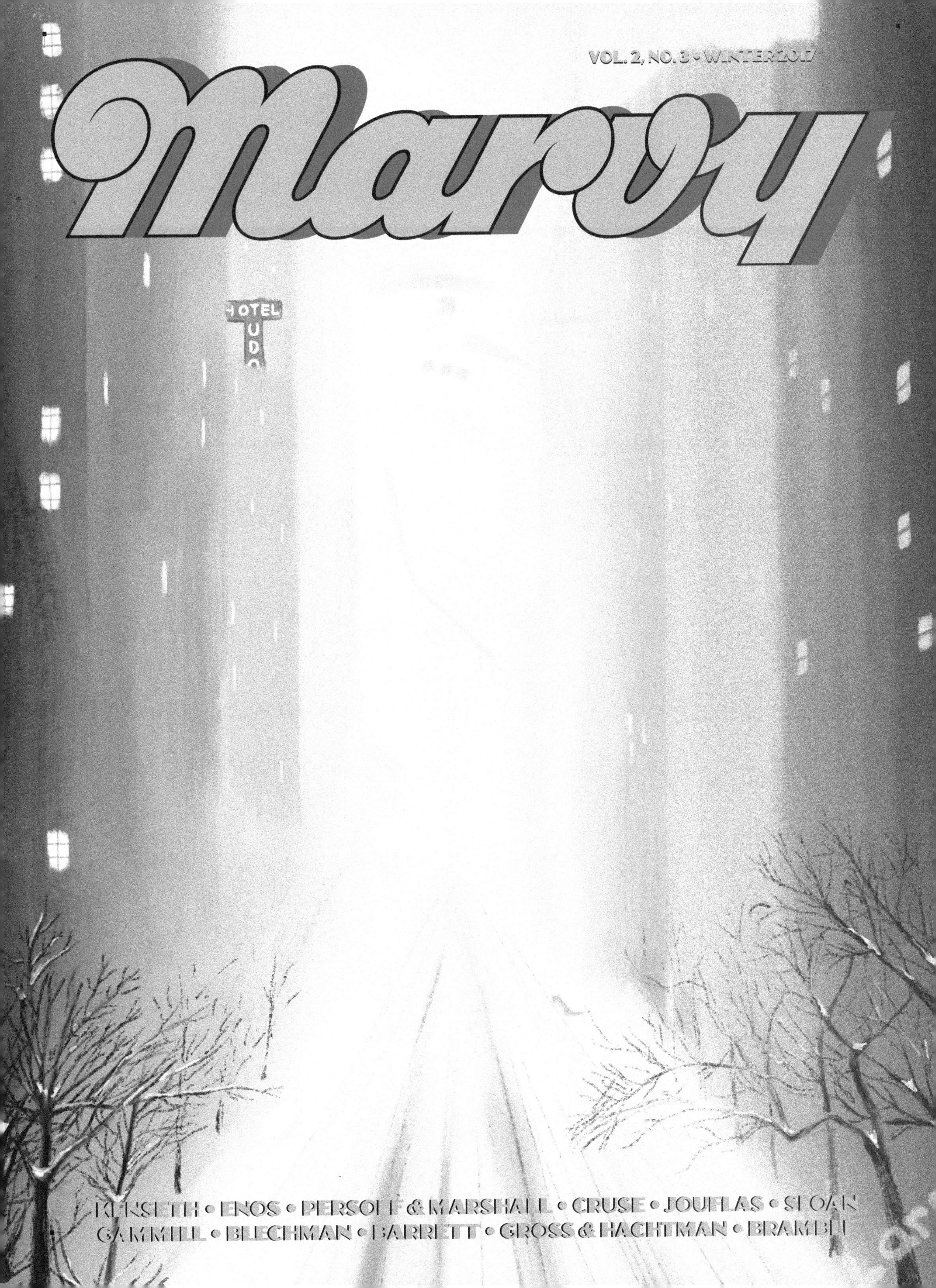
HOTEL
UDO

KENSETH • ENOS • PERSOFF & MARSHALL • CRUSE • JOUFLAS • SLOAN
GAMMILL • BLECHMAN • BARRETT • GROSS & HACHTMAN • BRAMBLE

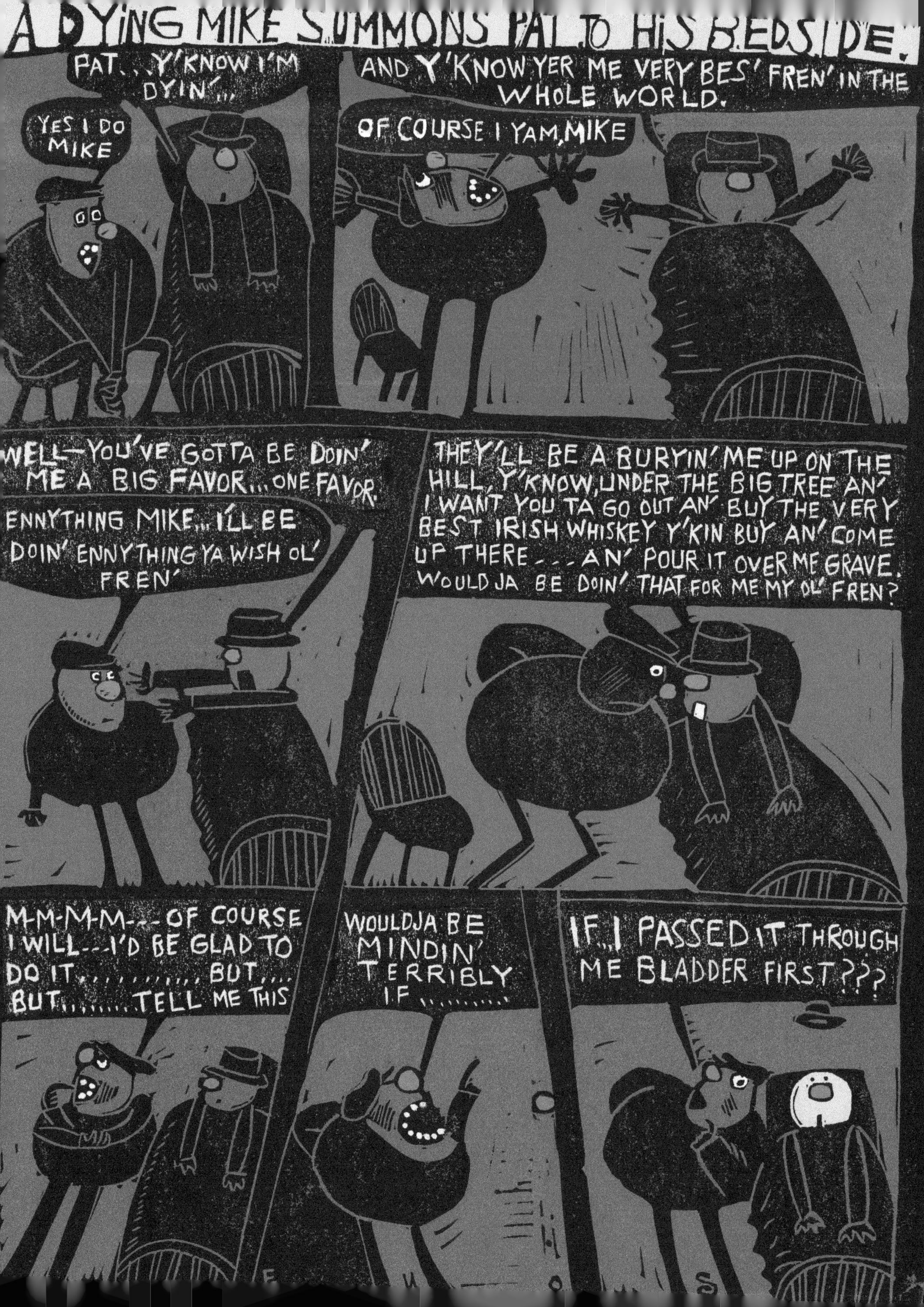
A DYING MIKE SUMMONS PAT TO HIS BEDSIDE.
PAT...Y'KNOW I'M DYIN'...
YES I DO MIKE
AND Y'KNOW YER ME VERY BES' FREN' IN THE WHOLE WORLD.
OF COURSE I YAM, MIKE
WELL—YOU'VE GOTTA BE DOIN' ME A BIG FAVOR... ONE FAVOR.
ENNYTHING MIKE... I'LL BE DOIN' ENNYTHING YA WISH OL' FREN'
THEY'LL BE A BURYIN' ME UP ON THE HILL, Y'KNOW, UNDER THE BIG TREE AN' I WANT YOU TA GO OUT AN' BUY THE VERY BEST IRISH WHISKEY Y'KIN BUY AN' COME UP THERE... AN' POUR IT OVER ME GRAVE. WOULDJA BE DOIN' THAT FOR ME MY OL' FREN?
M-M-M-M... OF COURSE I WILL... I'D BE GLAD TO DO IT.......... BUT.... BUT......... TELL ME THIS
WOULDJA BE MINDIN' TERRIBLY IF.........
IF.. I PASSED IT THROUGH ME BLADDER FIRST???

JOHN WILCOCK: NEW YORK YEARS

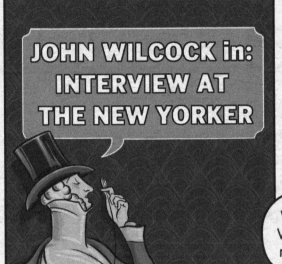

JOHN WILCOCK in:
INTERVIEW AT
THE NEW YORKER

In 1959, after five years of weekly columns, VILLAGE VOICE OWNERS DAN WOLF and ED FANCHER approached me with some tough news:

We still (hiccup!) want to run your column, but we can't pay for it any mmore. DEAL?

Whoops! THE VOICE is out of money, John...

I'd recently been introduced to a Senior Editor at the New Yorker...

25
WEST FORTY THIRD STREET
23

Assholes.

I'll still write for the Voice, but I do need a paycheck!

"HONK!"

... So I met with this new acquaintance to see about a job.

hello!

mm-hmm, pardon the racket.

"THUD!"

He was a charming, friendly man who'd been at N.Y. for many years.

thanks for meeting with me on such short notice.

mm-hmmm.

"BANG!"

"CRACK!"

It was unexpectedly noisy.

Yes...It's almost always like this.

"CRANK!"
"BANG!"
"CRACK!"
"KLOG!"

flap! flap! flap! flap! flap! flap!

I don't know what it is they're doing...

"BLAM!"
"CRUDD"
"CRNNK!"

RRRR-RR-RRRRRR-RRRR-R-BLPT!

but they're always doing it!

"CRASH!"

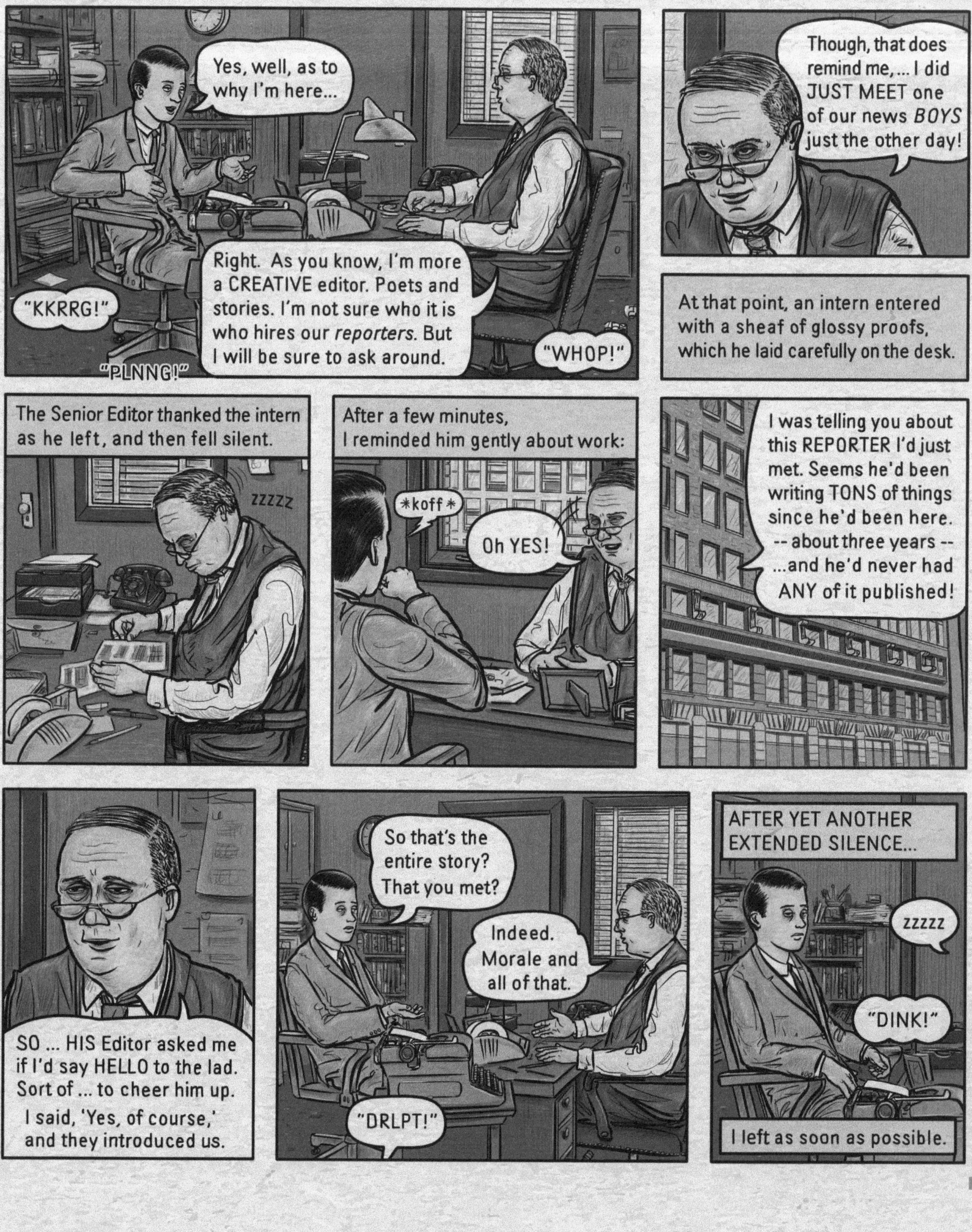
Yes, well, as to why I'm here...
Right. As you know, I'm more a CREATIVE editor. Poets and stories. I'm not sure who it is who hires our *reporters*. But I will be sure to ask around.
"KKRRG!"
"PLNNG!"
"WHOP!"
Though, that does remind me, ... I did JUST MEET one of our news *BOYS* just the other day!
At that point, an intern entered with a sheaf of glossy proofs, which he laid carefully on the desk.
The Senior Editor thanked the intern as he left, and then fell silent.
ZZZZZ
After a few minutes, I reminded him gently about work:
koff
Oh YES!
I was telling you about this REPORTER I'd just met. Seems he'd been writing TONS of things since he'd been here. -- about three years -- ...and he'd never had ANY of it published!
SO ... HIS Editor asked me if I'd say HELLO to the lad. Sort of ... to cheer him up.
I said, 'Yes, of course,' and they introduced us.
So that's the entire story? That you met?
Indeed. Morale and all of that.
"DRLPT!"
AFTER YET ANOTHER EXTENDED SILENCE...
zzzzz
"DINK!"
I left as soon as possible.

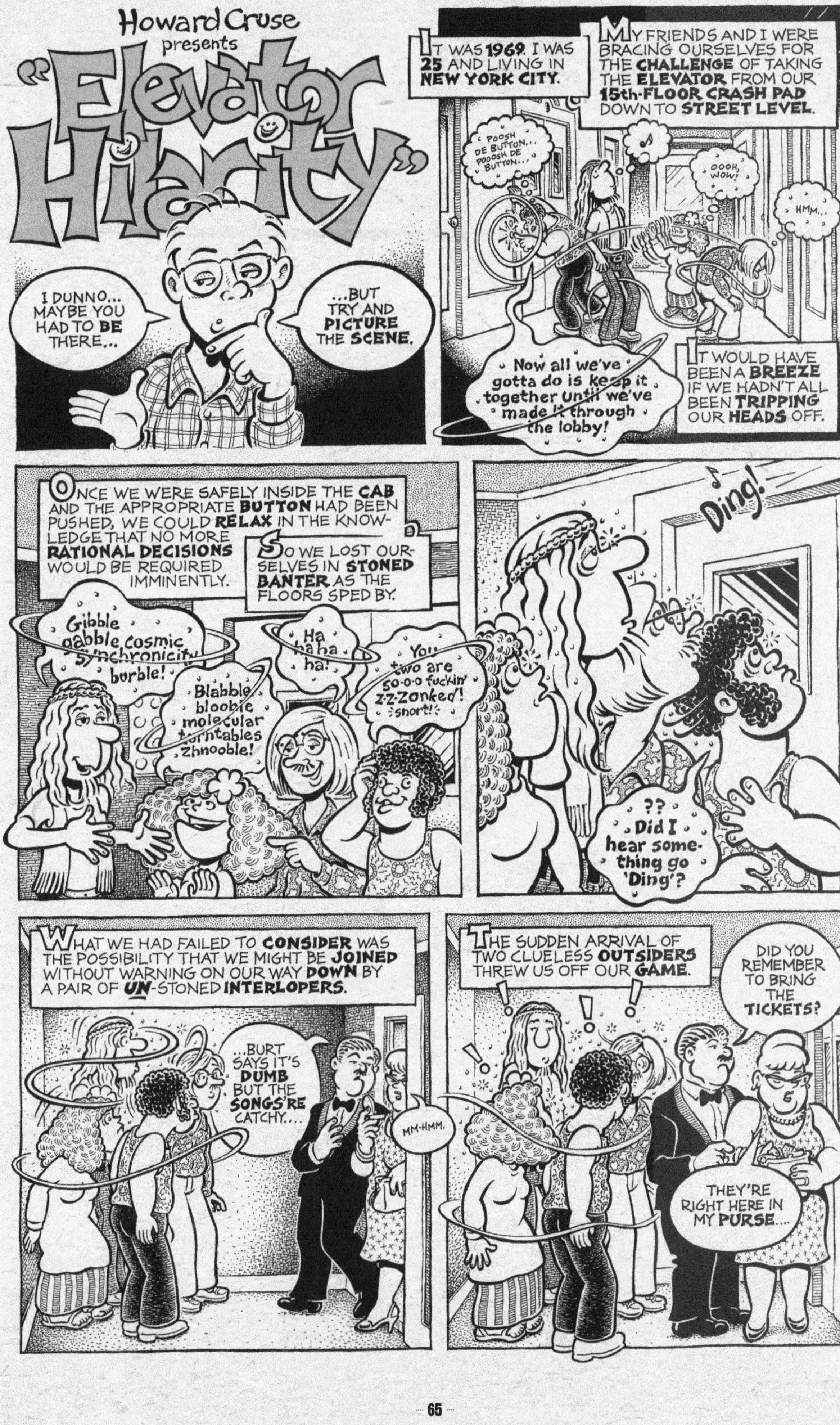

Howard Cruse
presents
"Elevator Hilarity"
I DUNNO... MAYBE YOU HAD TO BE THERE...
...BUT TRY AND PICTURE THE SCENE.
IT WAS 1969. I WAS 25 AND LIVING IN NEW YORK CITY.
MY FRIENDS AND I WERE BRACING OURSELVES FOR THE CHALLENGE OF TAKING THE ELEVATOR FROM OUR 15th-FLOOR CRASH PAD DOWN TO STREET LEVEL.
POOSH DE BUTTON... POOOSH DE BUTTON...
OOOH, WOW!
HMM...
Now all we've gotta do is keep it together until we've made it through the lobby!
IT WOULD HAVE BEEN A BREEZE IF WE HADN'T ALL BEEN TRIPPING OUR HEADS OFF.
ONCE WE WERE SAFELY INSIDE THE CAB AND THE APPROPRIATE BUTTON HAD BEEN PUSHED, WE COULD RELAX IN THE KNOWLEDGE THAT NO MORE RATIONAL DECISIONS WOULD BE REQUIRED IMMINENTLY.
SO WE LOST OURSELVES IN STONED BANTER AS THE FLOORS SPED BY.
Gibble gabble cosmic synchronicity burble!
Blabble bloobie molecular turntables zhnooble!
Ha ha ha ha!
You two are so-o-o fuckin' z-z-zonked! :snort!:
Ding!
?? Did I hear something go 'Ding'?
WHAT WE HAD FAILED TO CONSIDER WAS THE POSSIBILITY THAT WE MIGHT BE JOINED WITHOUT WARNING ON OUR WAY DOWN BY A PAIR OF UN-STONED INTERLOPERS.
...BURT SAYS IT'S DUMB BUT THE SONGS'RE CATCHY....
MM-HMM.
THE SUDDEN ARRIVAL OF TWO CLUELESS OUTSIDERS THREW US OFF OUR GAME.
!
!
!
!
DID YOU REMEMBER TO BRING THE TICKETS?
THEY'RE RIGHT HERE IN MY PURSE....

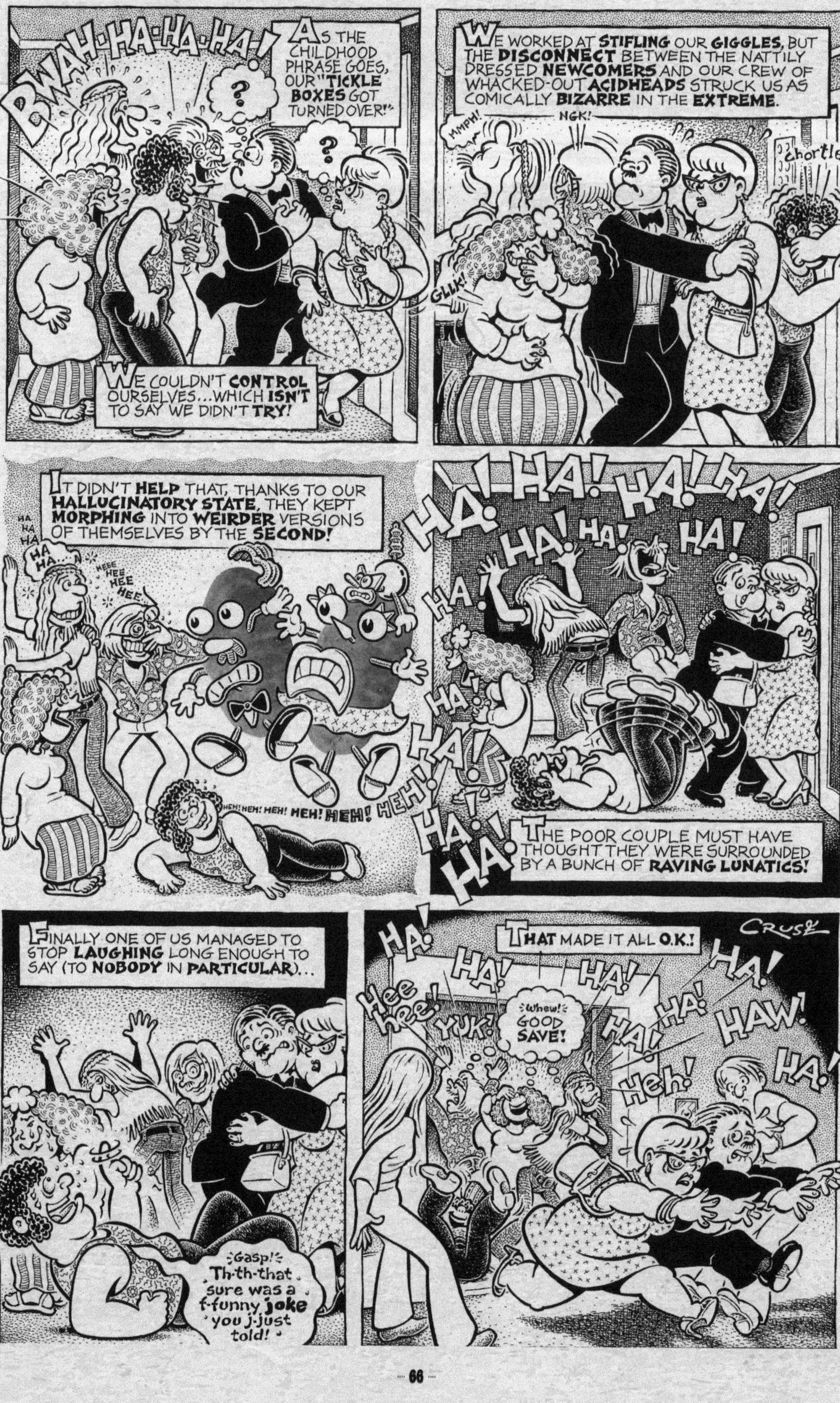
BWAH-HA-HA-HA-HA!
AS THE CHILDHOOD PHRASE GOES, OUR "TICKLE BOXES GOT TURNED OVER!"
?
?
WE COULDN'T CONTROL OURSELVES...WHICH ISN'T TO SAY WE DIDN'T TRY!
WE WORKED AT STIFLING OUR GIGGLES, BUT THE DISCONNECT BETWEEN THE NATTILY DRESSED NEWCOMERS AND OUR CREW OF WHACKED-OUT ACIDHEADS STRUCK US AS COMICALLY BIZARRE IN THE EXTREME.
MMPH!
NGK!
chortle!
GLLK!
IT DIDN'T HELP THAT, THANKS TO OUR HALLUCINATORY STATE, THEY KEPT MORPHING INTO WEIRDER VERSIONS OF THEMSELVES BY THE SECOND!
HA HA HA
HA HA...
HEEE HEE HEE HEE
HEH! HEH! HEH! HEH! HEH! HEH!
HA! HA! HA! HA!
HA! HA! HA!
HA! HA! HA! HA! HA! HA!
THE POOR COUPLE MUST HAVE THOUGHT THEY WERE SURROUNDED BY A BUNCH OF RAVING LUNATICS!
FINALLY ONE OF US MANAGED TO STOP LAUGHING LONG ENOUGH TO SAY (TO NOBODY IN PARTICULAR)...
Gasp! Th-th-that sure was a f-funny joke you j-just told!
THAT MADE IT ALL O.K.!
CRUSE
HA!
Hee hee!
HA!
YUK!
Whew! GOOD SAVE!
HA!
HA!
HA!
HA!
HAW!
Heh!
HA!

B

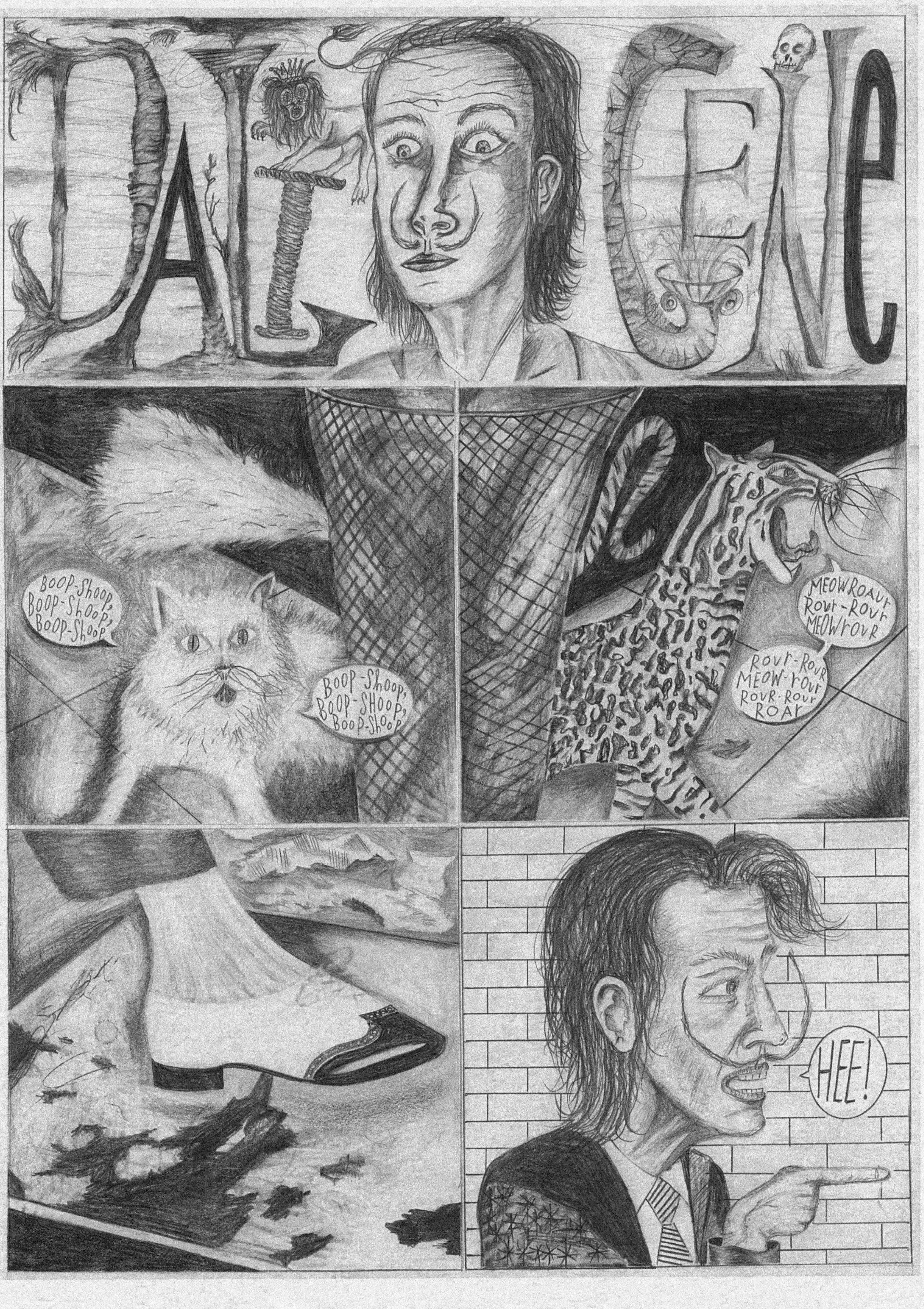
DALI GENE
BOOP-Shoop, BOOP-Shoop, BOOP-Shoop
Boop-Shoop, BOOP-SHOOP, Boop-Shoop
MEOWROAR Rour-Rour MEOWrour
Rour-Rour MEOW-rour Rour-Rour ROAR
HEE!

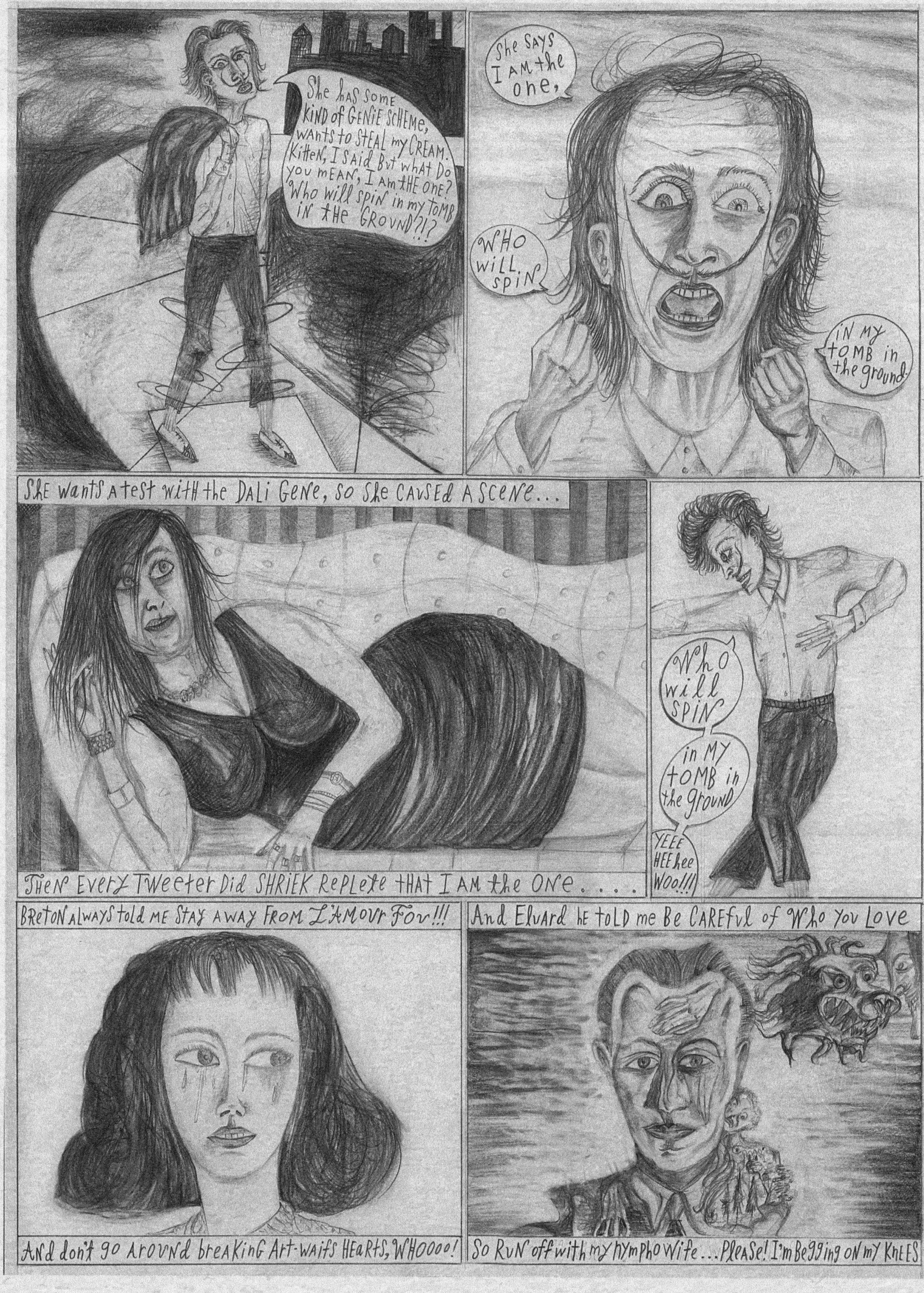
She has some KIND of GENIE SCHEME, wants to STEAL my CREAM. Kitten, I said But what Do you mean, I am THE ONE? Who will spin in my TOMB in the GROUND?!?
She SAYS I AM the one,
WHO will SPIN
in my TOMB in the ground.
SHE wants a test with the DALi Gene, so She CAUSED A SCENE...
THEN Every Tweeter Did SHRIEK RePlete that I AM the ONE....
Who will SPIN
in MY TOMB in the GROUND
YEEE HEE hee WOO!!!
BRETON ALWAYS told me STAY AWAY FROM L'AMOUr FOU!!!
AND don't go AROUND breaKinG Art-waifs HEARTS, WHOOOO!
And ELuard HE TOLD me Be CAREFUL of Who You LOVE
So RUN off with my nympho wife... PLEASE! I'm Begging on my KNEES

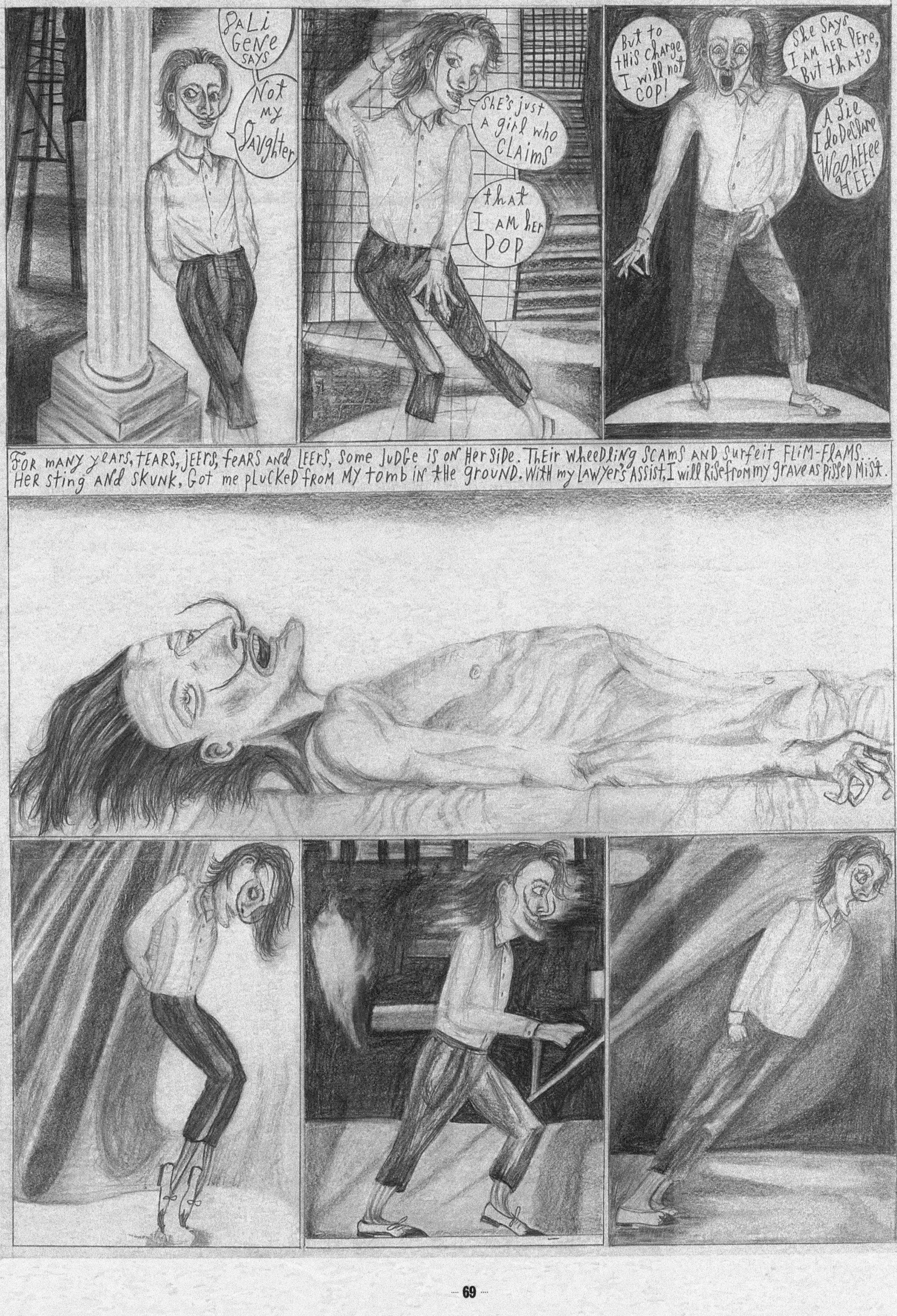
Dali Gene says
Not my daughter
She's just a girl who claims
that I am her pop
But to this charge I will not cop!
She says I am her Pere, but that's
A lie I do declare Woohheee HEE!
For many years, tears, jeers, fears and leers, some judge is on her side. Their wheedling scams and surfeit flim-flams...
Her sting and skunk, got me plucked from my tomb in the ground. With my lawyer's assist, I will rise from my grave as pissed mist.

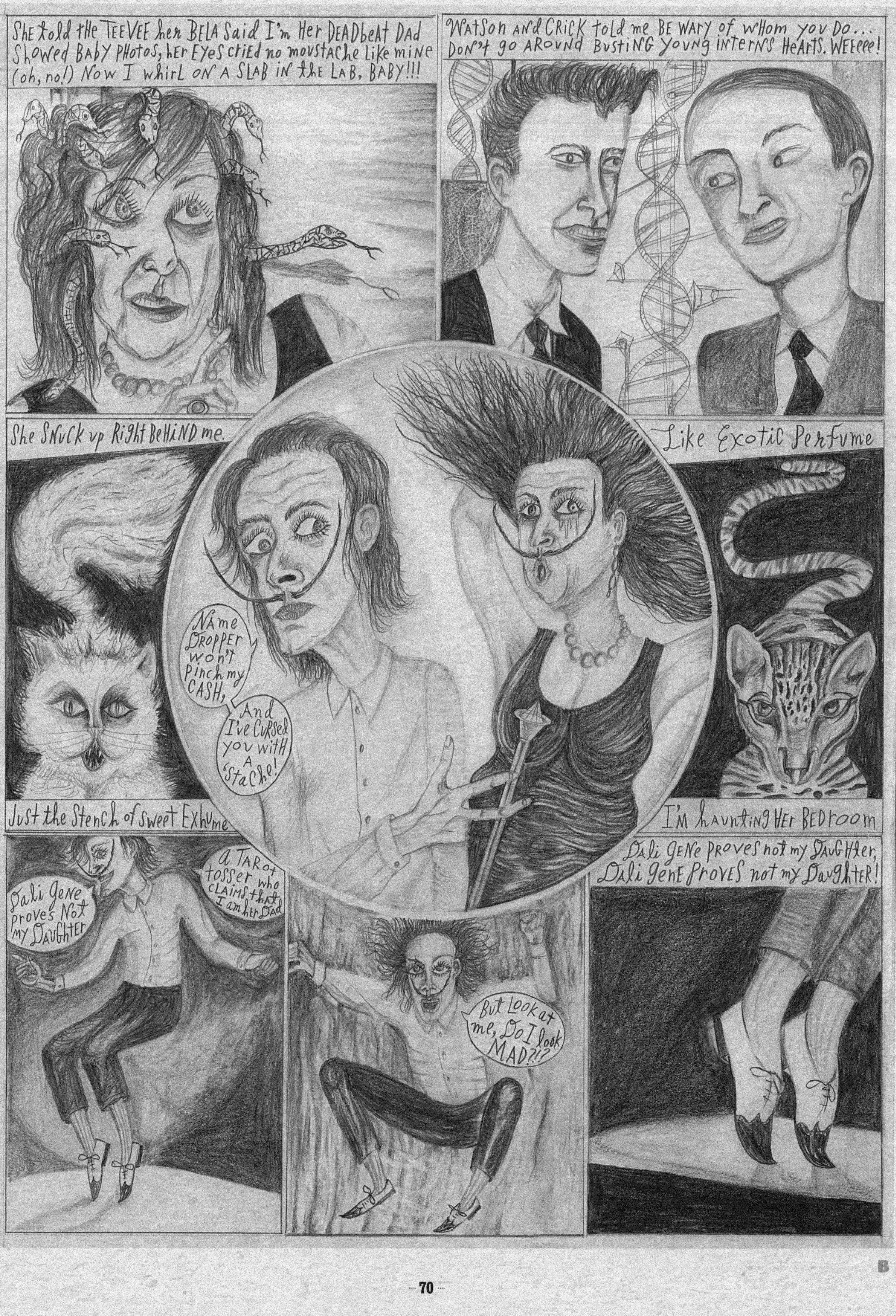

She told the TEEVEE her BELA Said I'm Her DEADbeat Dad
Showed BABY PHOTOS, her Eyes cried no moustache like mine
(oh, no!) Now I whirl ON A SLAB IN the LAB, BABY!!!
WATSON AND CRICK told me BE WARY of WHOM YOU DO...
DON'T go AROUND BUSTING YOUNG INTERNS HEARTS. WEEeee!
She SNUCK up RIGHT BEHIND me.
Like Exotic Perfume
Name Dropper won't Pinch my CASH,
And I've CURSED you with A 'Stache!
Just the Stench of sweet Exhume
I'M haunting HER BEDroom
Dali Gene proves Not my DAUGHTER
A TAROT tosser who CLAIMS that I am her Dad
But Look at me, Do I look MAD?!?
Dali Gene Proves not my DAUGHTER,
Dali Gene Proves not my DAUGHTER!

Zen of Nimbus

by Michael Sloan

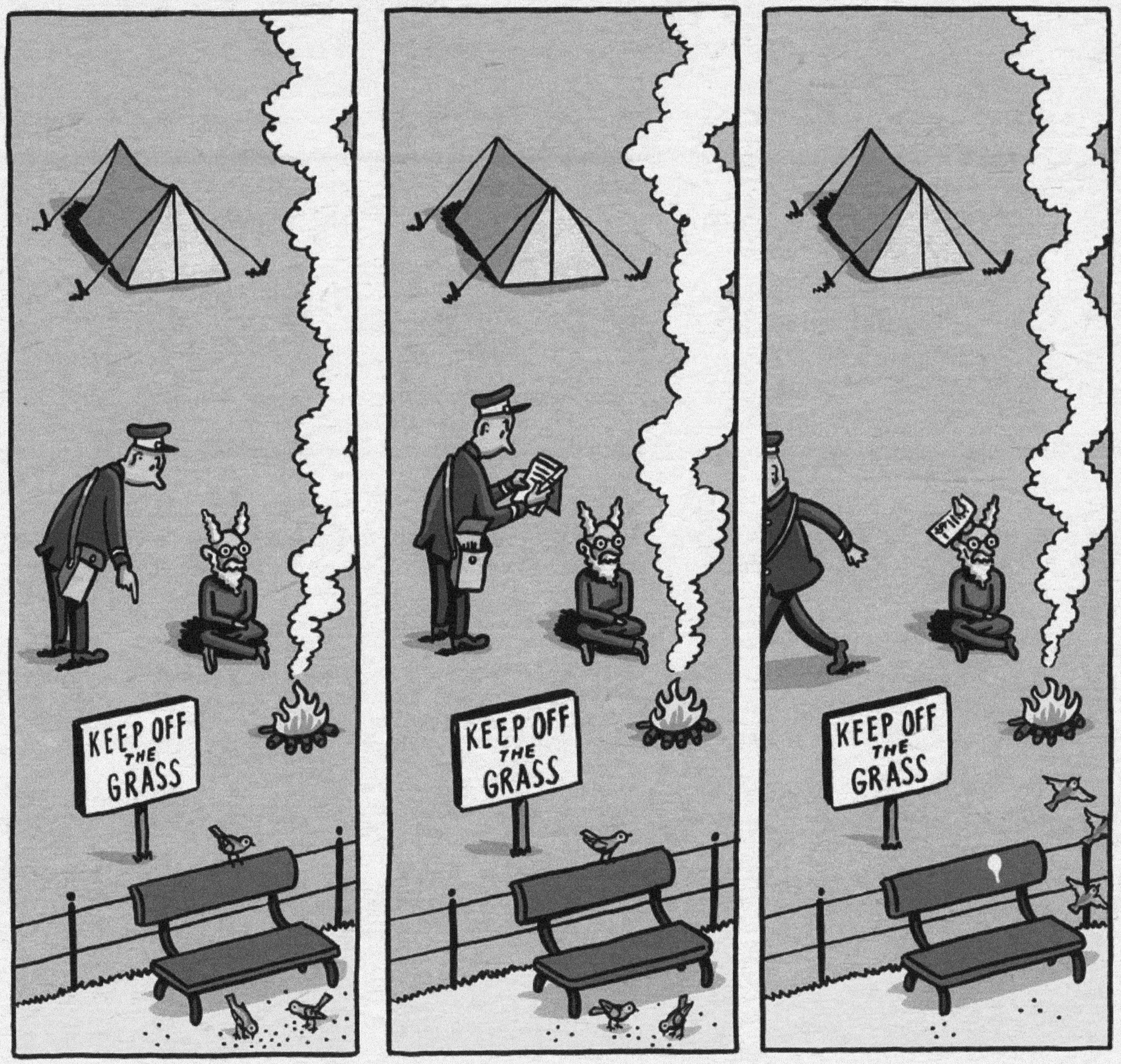
KEEP OFF THE GRASS
KEEP OFF THE GRASS
KEEP OFF THE GRASS

The Doozies

BY TOM GAMMILL

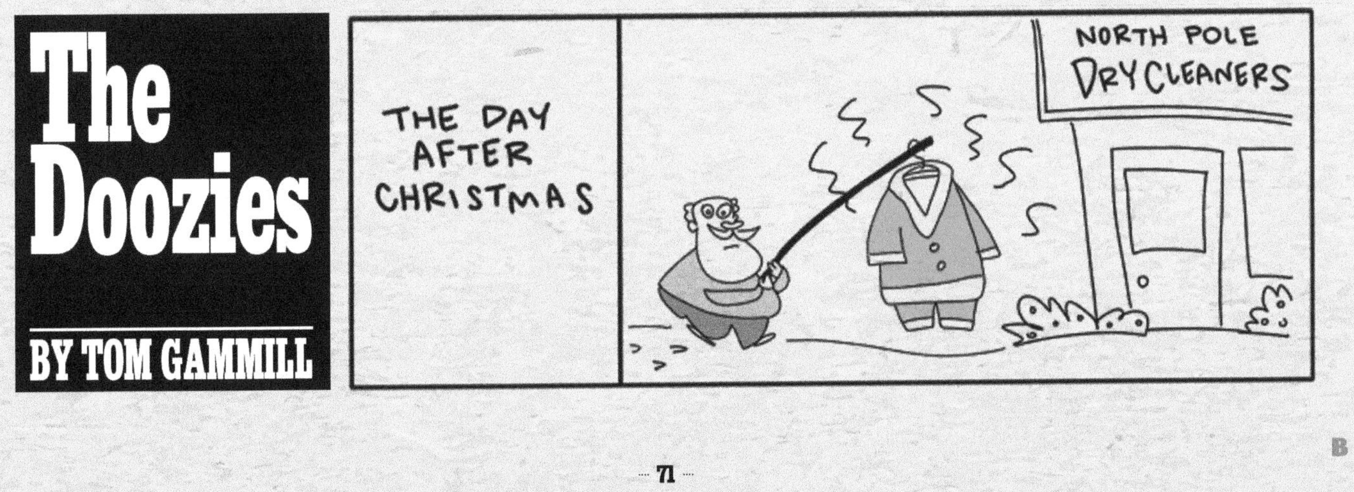
THE DAY AFTER CHRISTMAS
NORTH POLE DRY CLEANERS

A NOVEL MEMOIR

R. O. Blechman

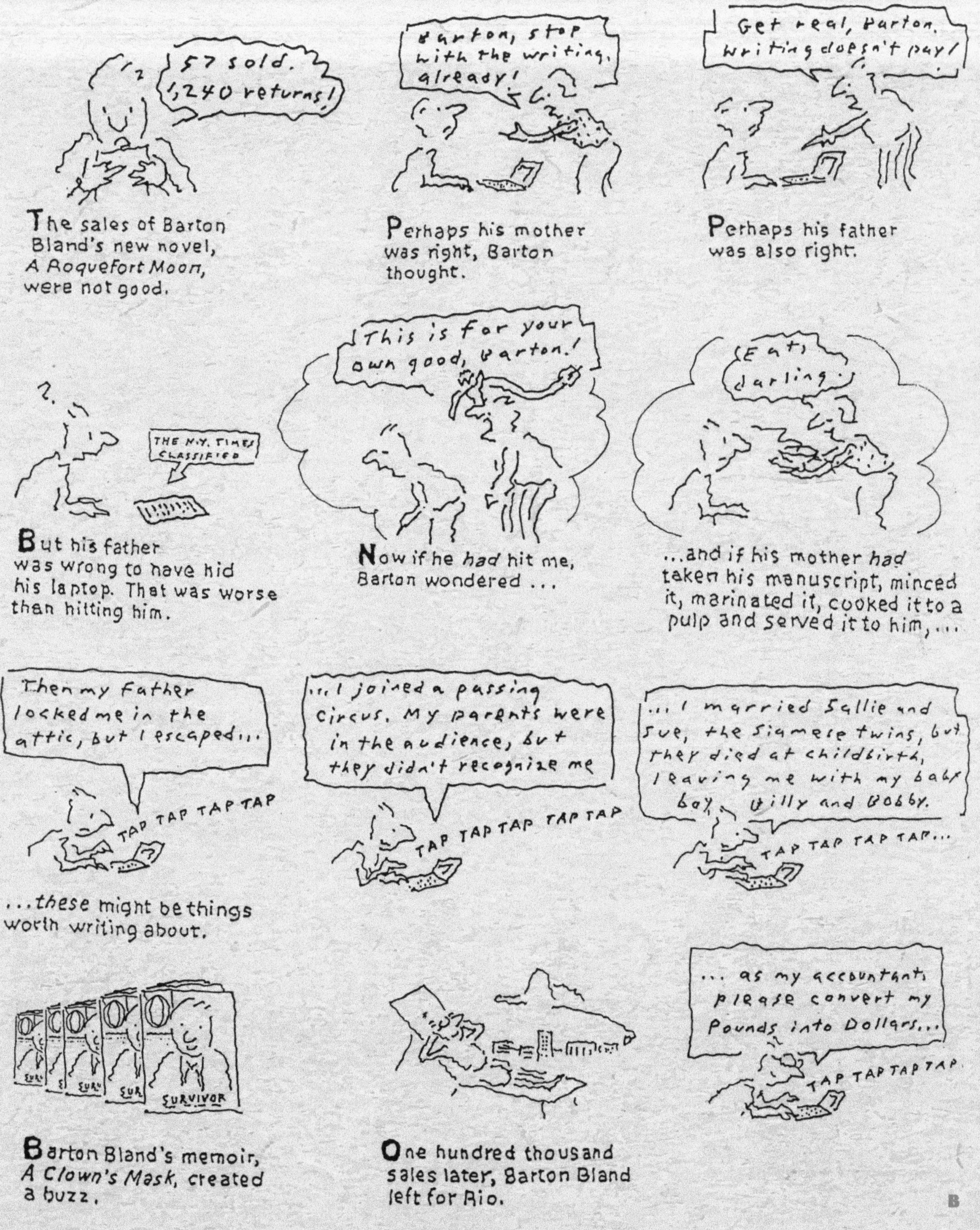
57 sold. 1,240 returns!
The sales of Barton Bland's new novel, *A Roquefort Moon*, were not good.
Barton, stop with the writing, already!
Perhaps his mother was right, Barton thought.
Get real, Barton. Writing doesn't pay!
Perhaps his father was also right.
THE N.Y. TIMES CLASSIFIED
But his father was wrong to have hid his laptop. That was worse than hitting him.
This is for your own good, Barton!
Now if he *had* hit me, Barton wondered ...
Eat, darling.
...and if his mother *had* taken his manuscript, minced it, marinated it, cooked it to a pulp and served it to him, ...
Then my father locked me in the attic, but I escaped...
TAP TAP TAP TAP
...these might be things worth writing about.
...I joined a passing circus. My parents were in the audience, but they didn't recognize me
TAP TAP TAP TAP TAP
...I married Sallie and Sue, the Siamese twins, but they died at childbirth, leaving me with my baby boy, Billy and Bobby.
TAP TAP TAP TAP...
SURVIVOR
Barton Bland's memoir, *A Clown's Mask*, created a buzz.
One hundred thousand sales later, Barton Bland left for Rio.
... as my accountant, please convert my Pounds into Dollars...
TAP TAP TAP TAP

COINCIDENCES in EVERYDAY LIFE

by Ron Barrett — WHO CAN EXPLAIN IT, WHO CAN TELL YOU WHY, FOOLS GIVE YOU REASONS, WISE MEN NEVER TRY

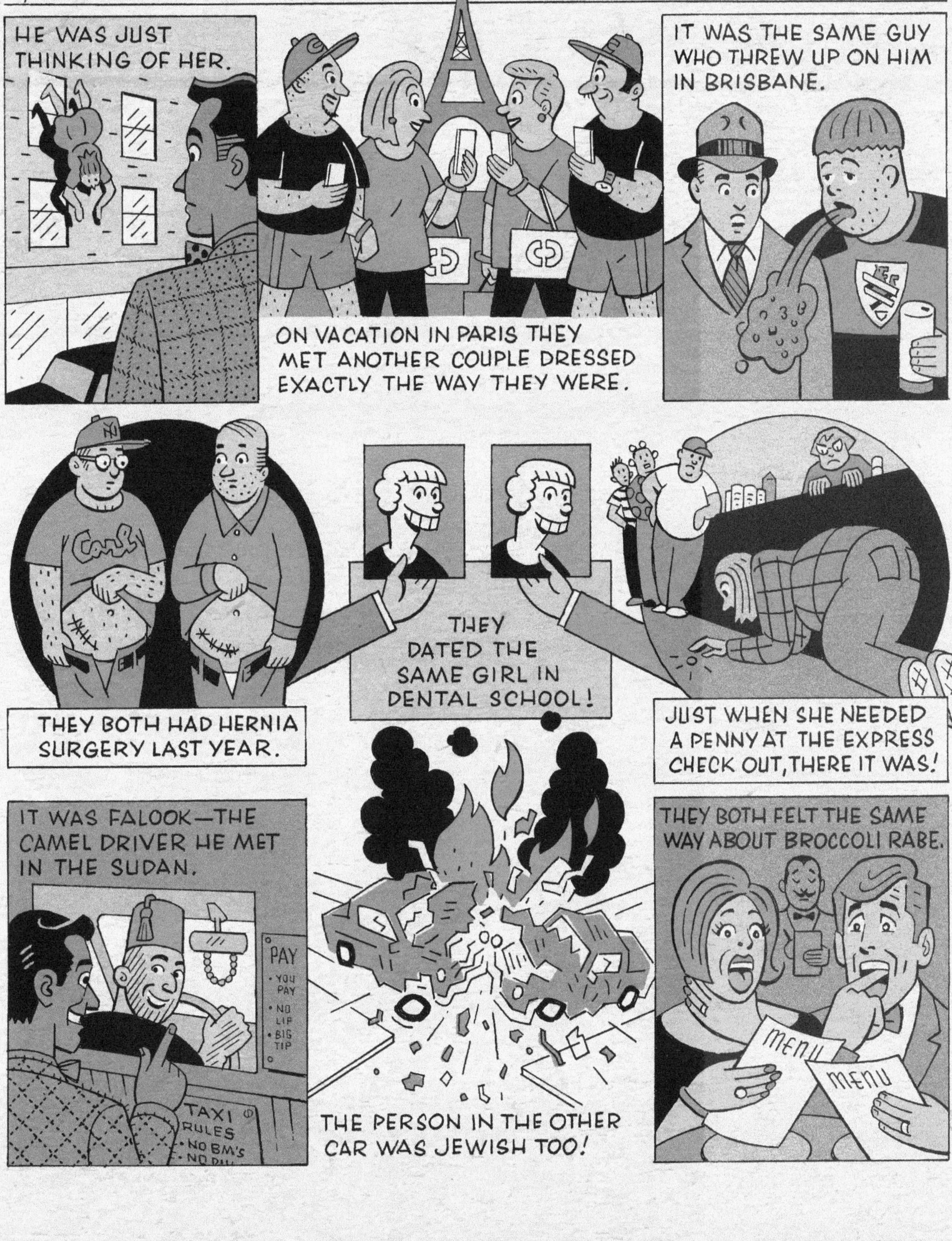
HE WAS JUST THINKING OF HER.
ON VACATION IN PARIS THEY MET ANOTHER COUPLE DRESSED EXACTLY THE WAY THEY WERE.
IT WAS THE SAME GUY WHO THREW UP ON HIM IN BRISBANE.
Carl
THEY BOTH HAD HERNIA SURGERY LAST YEAR.
THEY DATED THE SAME GIRL IN DENTAL SCHOOL!
JUST WHEN SHE NEEDED A PENNY AT THE EXPRESS CHECK OUT, THERE IT WAS!
IT WAS FALOOK—THE CAMEL DRIVER HE MET IN THE SUDAN.
PAY
• YOU PAY
• NO LIP
• BIG TIP
TAXI RULES
• NO BM'S
THE PERSON IN THE OTHER CAR WAS JEWISH TOO!
THEY BOTH FELT THE SAME WAY ABOUT BROCCOLI RABE.
MENU
MENU

TOM HACHTMAN'S

Gertrude's Follies

"Coq-Coq"

WORDS: SAM GROSS ART: TOM HACHTMAN

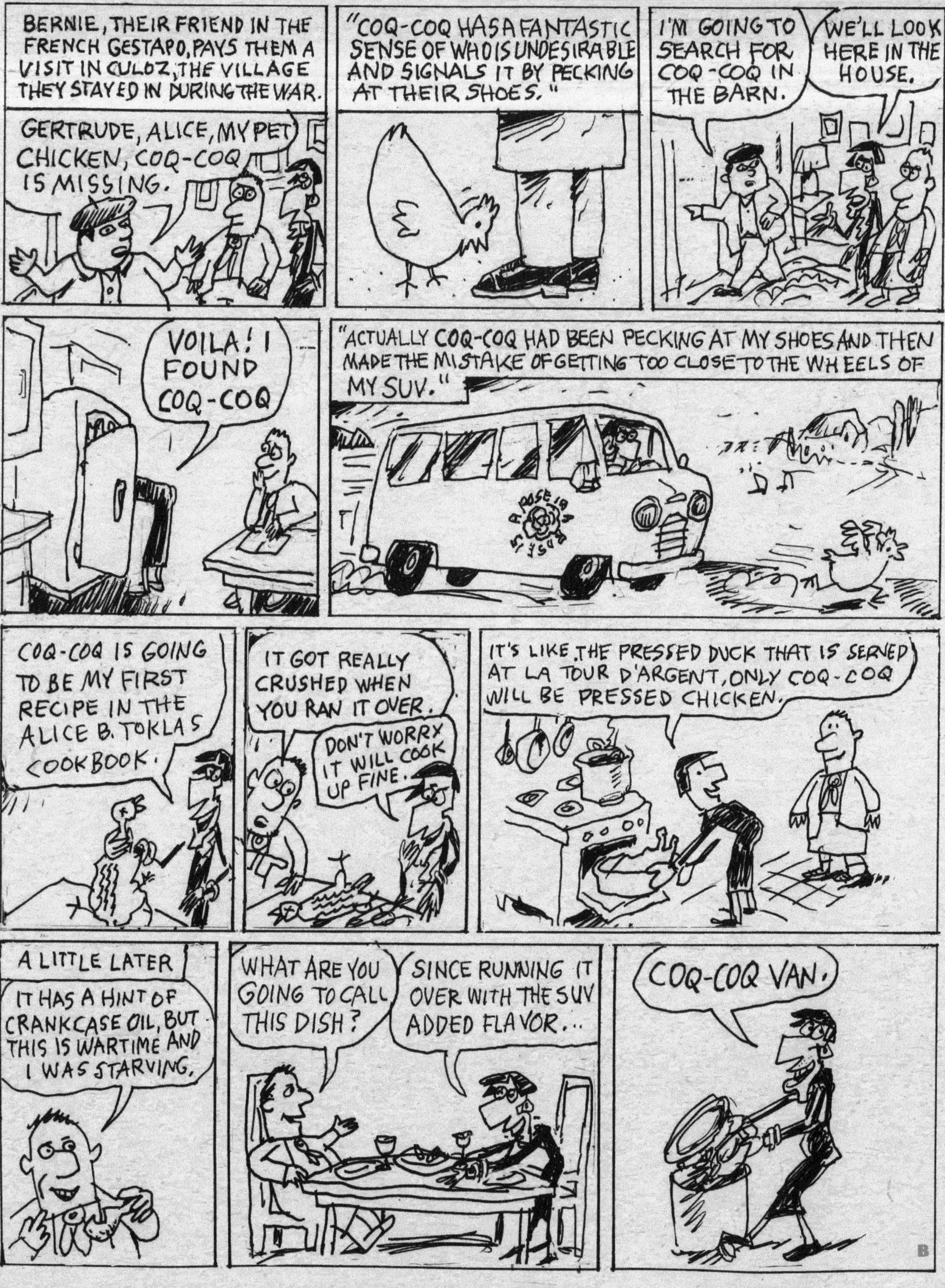
BERNIE, THEIR FRIEND IN THE FRENCH GESTAPO, PAYS THEM A VISIT IN CULOZ, THE VILLAGE THEY STAYED IN DURING THE WAR.
GERTRUDE, ALICE, MY PET CHICKEN, COQ-COQ IS MISSING.
"COQ-COQ HAS A FANTASTIC SENSE OF WHO IS UNDESIRABLE AND SIGNALS IT BY PECKING AT THEIR SHOES."
I'M GOING TO SEARCH FOR COQ-COQ IN THE BARN.
WE'LL LOOK HERE IN THE HOUSE.
VOILA! I FOUND COQ-COQ
"ACTUALLY COQ-COQ HAD BEEN PECKING AT MY SHOES AND THEN MADE THE MISTAKE OF GETTING TOO CLOSE TO THE WHEELS OF MY SUV."
COQ-COQ IS GOING TO BE MY FIRST RECIPE IN THE ALICE B. TOKLAS COOKBOOK.
IT GOT REALLY CRUSHED WHEN YOU RAN IT OVER.
DON'T WORRY IT WILL COOK UP FINE.
IT'S LIKE THE PRESSED DUCK THAT IS SERVED AT LA TOUR D'ARGENT, ONLY COQ-COQ WILL BE PRESSED CHICKEN.
A LITTLE LATER
IT HAS A HINT OF CRANKCASE OIL, BUT THIS IS WARTIME AND I WAS STARVING.
WHAT ARE YOU GOING TO CALL THIS DISH?
SINCE RUNNING IT OVER WITH THE SUV ADDED FLAVOR...
COQ-COQ VAN.

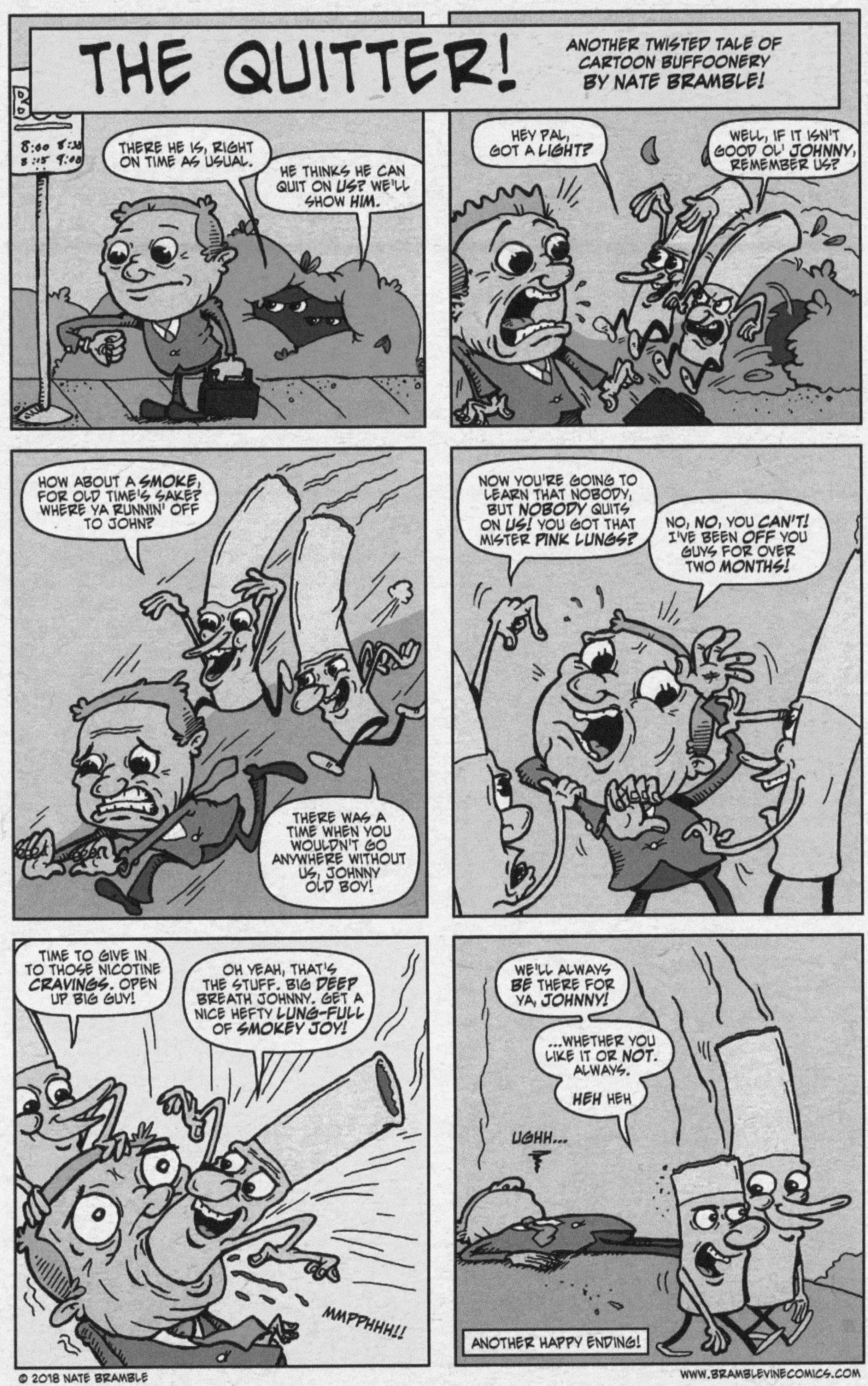
THE QUITTER!
ANOTHER TWISTED TALE OF CARTOON BUFFOONERY BY NATE BRAMBLE!
8:00 8:30 8:15 9:00
THERE HE IS, RIGHT ON TIME AS USUAL.
HE THINKS HE CAN QUIT ON US? WE'LL SHOW HIM.
HEY PAL, GOT A LIGHT?
WELL, IF IT ISN'T GOOD OL' JOHNNY, REMEMBER US?
HOW ABOUT A SMOKE, FOR OLD TIME'S SAKE? WHERE YA RUNNIN' OFF TO JOHN?
THERE WAS A TIME WHEN YOU WOULDN'T GO ANYWHERE WITHOUT US, JOHNNY OLD BOY!
NOW YOU'RE GOING TO LEARN THAT NOBODY, BUT NOBODY QUITS ON US! YOU GOT THAT MISTER PINK LUNGS?
NO, NO, YOU CAN'T! I'VE BEEN OFF YOU GUYS FOR OVER TWO MONTHS!
TIME TO GIVE IN TO THOSE NICOTINE CRAVINGS. OPEN UP BIG GUY!
OH YEAH, THAT'S THE STUFF. BIG DEEP BREATH JOHNNY. GET A NICE HEFTY LUNG-FULL OF SMOKEY JOY!
MMPPHHH!!
WE'LL ALWAYS BE THERE FOR YA, JOHNNY!
...WHETHER YOU LIKE IT OR NOT. ALWAYS.
HEH HEH
UGHH...
ANOTHER HAPPY ENDING!

WWW.BRAMBLEVINECOMICS.COM

Drew Friedman's
CHOSEN PEOPLE

FOREWORD BY MERRILL MARKOE

THE GREATS, THE NEAR-GREATS, AND THE NOT-SO-GREATS, BY THE MAN BOING BOING CALLS "THE GREATEST LIVING PORTRAIT ARTIST."

"Drew Friedman's portraits capture his subjects' best and worst qualities at once. His work is both beautiful and grotesque, brilliant and cruel." — *Jimmy Kimmel*

"Drew Friedman is a genius illustrator, a genius comics artist." — *Marc Maron*

"Drew Friedman isn't just a brilliant artist. He takes you to a place. He takes you back in time." — *Sarah Silverman*

"Drew Friedman is my favorite artist." — *Howard Stern*

"Drew Friedman is the unchallenged living master of the art of caricature." — *Chris Ware*

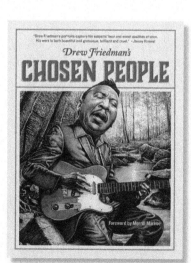

JOAN'S OTHER KITCHEN

In praise of good old-fashioned boat-on-boat waving • ***By Brian McConnachie***

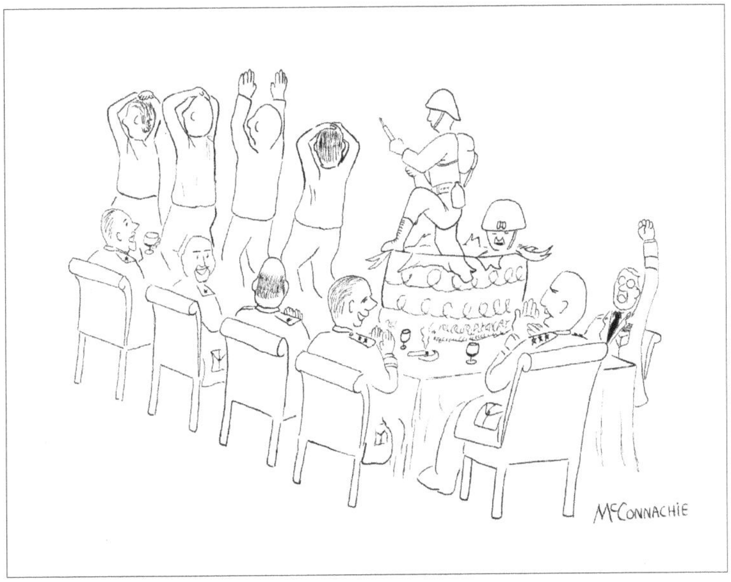
McCONNACHIE

Boats! Boats! Boats!

There is a growing predominance of people in speedboats (and other boats as well) both waving and not waving to each other. Specifically, failing to wave to people in speedboats who have been more enthusiastically waving to *them*.

I find myself feeling awkward when this happens. And I'm not alone. As we are a people who are growing more divided, correcting this just might be the tonic that gets us all back on track.

I can't really tell you why people in speedboats enjoy waving more than other people — let's say, people in golf carts, or people on riding mowers. Maybe they don't. But it sure seems that way.

I'm in a boat, you're in a boat, let's wave happily to one another. We have boats in common. But sometimes it's not as simple as that. Though I don't want to overthink this. But what do you do if you realize you actually know those people waving — do you have to wave back? Or do you want to save that wave for special strangers? (Those friends you haven't met yet.)

Confusing, isn't it?

I can't declare I know the protocols of boat waving, or if there even are such things. Who starts the waving? How long does the wave go on? But I do know when it comes down to it, you don't want to be the person lying on their deathbed, racked with regret. "I should've waved back. They took the trouble to wave. Would it have killed me?"

If we're ever going to fulfill that pursuit of happiness clause that Thomas Jefferson (a proud boat-owner himself) took the trouble to put down on practically new parchment, this might be a place to start, with some good old-fashioned boat-on-boat waving. Get those arms going and take it up to bordering on the deranged. Let them see you really mean it.

I'm sorry I haven't acted on this impulse before, and another thing just crosses my mind: What if it wasn't old-fashioned waving but a disingenuous cry for help?

Yes, there are cases where boat-to-boat waving can go bad. No doubt we've all heard of the Williamstown Bay Incident? A boat that had been waving, turned and went after a boat that had not been waving back. They boarded them and demanded they turn over their bathing suits, as a reminder of poor boating manners. They left them only with seat cushions to cover their shame. And off the bathing suit thieves went to who-knows-where. Maybe a hidden cove where they keep piles of bathing suits. Or an abandoned harbor. No telling for sure.

Thankfully, the people robbed of their dignity called *Action 5 on Your Side*, and told them what happened, and *AFOYS* did a story about it: the dirty underbelly of recreational boating and what could go wrong and why this affects all of us.

John Donne once said, "No man is an island." An *island!* Wait a second... Maybe that's where those people have taken all the bathing suits. They've brought them to an island. Well if that's the case, you can just say goodbye to those bathing suits. You're not going to see that swimming apparel again.

So, let's review: Think about your own policy on waving. Update it if necessary. Bring extra bathing suits and hide them somewhere. If you see anything, tell *Action 5 On Your Side*. Have plenty of seat cushions.

And have fun! And if you're having fun, don't be ashamed to show it to everybody in sight. **B**

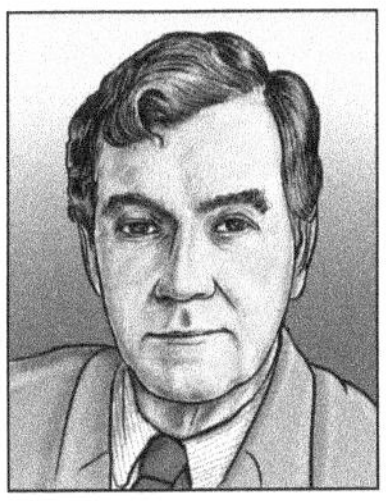

BRIAN McCONNACHIE is Founder and Head Writer of *The American Bystander*.

OUR FELLOW AMERICANS

John Birks Gillespie (1917-1993) was Dizzy like a fox • **By Con Chapman**

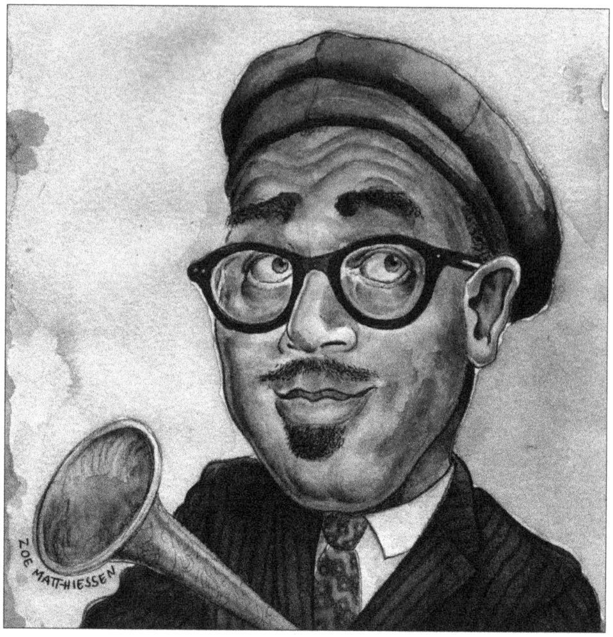
ZOE MATTHIESSEN

ZOE MATTHIESSEN

Jazz has always had more than its share of straight, no chaser eccentrics — Thelonious Monk or Sun Ra. Giving the unapologetically odd a place to call home isn't just a facet of the music's history, it's part of its enduring value. And, of course, living a musician's penurious and peripatetic life, especially under the viselike pressure of racism, might force even the straightest psyche off the straight and narrow.

Bebop, especially, proved fertile ground for jazz's eccentrics. The word has no literal meaning; it had been used for "scat" singing as early as 1928, but resurfaced in the 1940s to describe a style that was both revolutionary and playful. Those adjectives also described the principal ambassador of this new sound, a trumpeter named John Birks "Dizzy" Gillespie.

Accounts differ as to who gave Gillespie his nickname, but the reason was clearly his penchant for clowning around. He would play in overcoat and gloves, and dance on the bandstand while others soloed. Cab Calloway canned him for throwing a spitball onstage. (Diz claimed he was innocent.)

To the straight press, Gillespie became the face of bop. An October 1948 *Life* spread shows photos of Gillespie and a fellow jazzman greeting each other in supposed bebopper fashion:

1. "Bebop greeting begins as Gillespie hails Benny Carter with 'Bells, man! Where you been?'
2. The sign of 'the flatted-fifth,' a note common in bop, is flashed by both men.
3. The shout 'Eel-ya-dah,' which sounds like bebop triplet notes, is next.
4. The grip establishes friendship, ends the ritual. Beboppers can now converse."

Gillespie sported heavy horn-rims and floppy polka-dot bow ties. He grew a mustache and goatee because he didn't want to risk cutting himself shaving, touching off a facial hair fad that remains a shibboleth of hipness to his day. His famous beret, however, was strictly practical: Unlike a fedora, a beret could be stuffed into his pocket. Dizzy's look became synonymous with jazz; that same *Life* article shows a bunch of female fans queuing for his autograph, all wearing berets and painted goatees.

Then there was Diz's trumpet. That horn jutting out from between preposterously inflated cheeks was unforgettable, and helped Gillespie outlive not only bop, but *Life* itself. One night, a comedy-dance team called Stump and Stumpy knocked over his horn, bending what had been a straight piece of brass to a 45-degree angle. Gillespie picked it up, heard that it played fine and decided to keep it that way. His reasons were both functional — he could hear himself better — and aesthetic: The odd-looking instrument was perfect for the clown prince of bebop.

Asked midcareer whether he thought his idiosyncrasies had cost him respect, he admitted the possibility. Diz was frustrated when people who should know better couldn't tell the difference between his showmanship and his art.

Jacob Brackman's 1967 *New Yorker* profile revealed Gillespie as a master of the put-on, that high-art form of kidding. His favorite character — a jazz version of Chaplin's Little Tramp — was "Prince Iwo," a fictional potentate he would play when African garb became fashionable in the 1960s. Gillespie would don a dashiki and an African tarboosh hat while his band members played along, dressed in somber black suits, following several respectful steps behind their Prince. The entourage would draw curious stares as they walked through airports, then get into a taxi and hand the driver a slip of paper bearing the name of their hotel, in the manner of innocents abroad. The party would begin to argue among themselves in imitation African double-talk, and pretend not to comprehend when they arrived at their destination and the cabbie asked for his fare, nodding their heads and chanting "Ungawa!"

Not every cabbie could take a joke. Once, when Gillespie pulled this gag the driver totally lost his cool; the jazzmen held out for as long as they could, but as the madness escalated, they began to wonder if they'd have to take this fellow to the emergency room. On the verge of a coronary, the cabbie held up his hands, counting off his fingers to show his passengers how much they owed.

Gillespie finally broke character. "Eight bucks?" he said with a smile. "Man, why didn't you say so? Here's 10, keep the change." B

P.S. MUELLER THINKS LIKE THIS

The cartoonist/broadcaster/writer is always walking around, looking at stuff • **By P.S. Mueller**

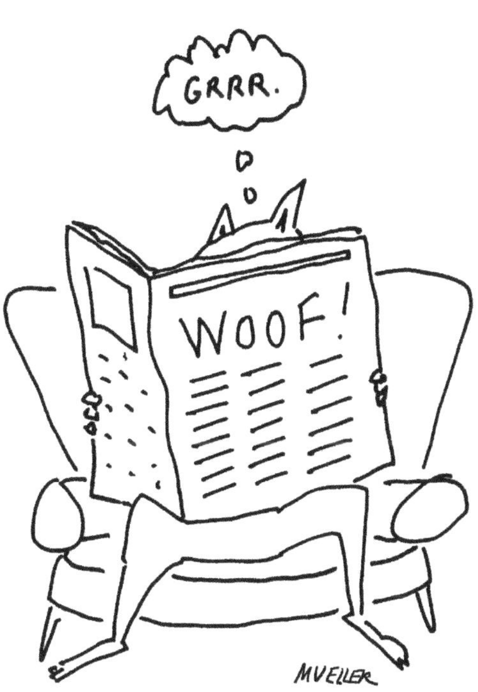
GRRR.
WOOF!
MUELLER

The Unknown Jetson

I'm the Jetson who got the old man's flying car. It has an ashtray, and I beat the hell out of it every Saturday night when I feel like squealing some donuts into Pantone's latest global color. The robot in the back seat flew apart 20 years ago, but I slapped her back together with Testors glue, the real stuff. People who know me on the internet know me as FireToy.

The family kept me out of the picture back then. My resemblance to Mr. Spacely was a sort of road flare on the carpet, and my thirst for Tang-flavored Adderall produced acne that spread to the drapes. I learned how to talk from our jocular dog Astro, who I truly believed was a brother until he died of old age at 12 and a half.

A week after Astro departed, Dad brought home a grown bear that he swore was some kind of Slavic hound. Not long after that, we all realized the old man didn't really comprehend anything beyond flying back and forth from work. Eventually, Mr. Spacely figured out that he had been paying Dad to stare blankly at the company wall for 20 years and fired him.

Dad spent his declining years beneath a paperweight, and Mom, Elroy and Judy worked together as some kind of board game. I more or less sneaked out of the family and literally fell into a damn sweet life — as a dog-talker. Astro, it turned out, had taught me far more than English — he taught me canine. Then, almost 30 years ago, THE Harvey Fucking Weinstein happened to overhear an argument about the Kennedys I was having with a pair of Chesapeake Bay retrievers and offered me the goddamn moon to handle his pooch. Oh God, I wish I paid closer attention to what Princess and Ruby had to say about that freak.

Now I can freely admit to colluding with dogs to even the score and embezzle a fortune for myself. That is how I came to own the world-famous George Jetson flying car, which I bought from the movie actor Al Pacino. Al has been has been crazy for flying cars his entire life and insists that restoring them helps him unwind after a long day of screaming at walls. But that's another story I don't feel like telling right now.

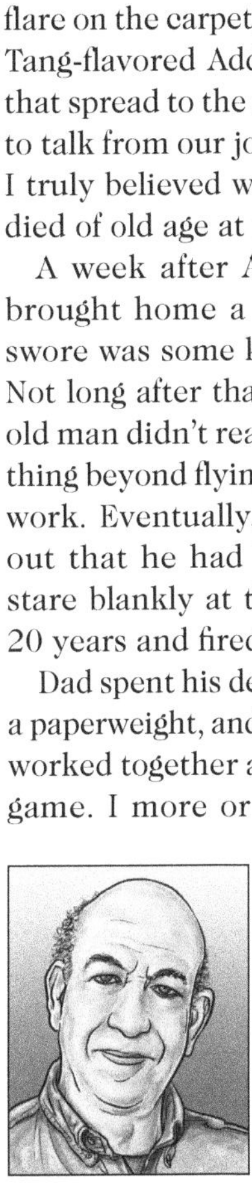

P.S. MUELLER is Staff Liar of *The American Bystander*.

Artist Profile: Altus Bathroom

Altus Bathroom cleaned and repositioned his Strindberg eyeglasses. He glanced at a cufflink made from an honest-to-God Bitcoin while languidly shifting three of his alleged five testicles, constrained with mercurial elan by carefully tailored chinos. He laughed about getting his start by gluing a cheap bookend to the left side of superstar art dealer Larry Gagosian's face. "Larry instinctively picked up a copy of *ArtNews* and hummed *The Wreck of the Edmund Fitzgerald* while walking backwards. What can I say? He just knew!"

These days, after concluding a residency at the No School, where he created his masterful Plywood Daycare Series, the 30-year-old sculptor has been on the road. The artist is on a deeply personal quest to find 4,400 garden trolls in order to complete his White Warrior Burial Vault, an installation to be photographed and immediately filled with fracking sand on Edgar Buchanan Day in 2019. I interviewed Mr. Bathroom between shots of bay rum at the Clock Parlor, and holy shit, that man has gotten hugely rich on his remarkable good looks, uncanny self-promotional skills and an unerring ability to create and sustain an illusion of deep respect and tolerance for wealthy celebrity types. "I try not to let things get too sincere," he purred.

The bay rum had disfigured my conversational rhythm and dulled my probing curiosity to the point where I felt a driving need to let Mr. Bathroom gibber for himself. (After all, I am a mere scribe, present only to record art garble.) Plus, as an aspiring conceptualist myself, I just wanted sit back

(continued on next page) ☛

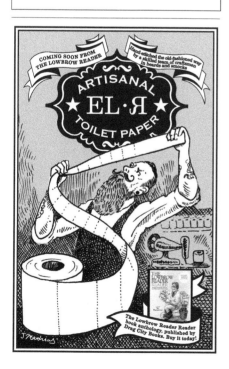
and discover how the brown drool of my semi-toxic sick worked with the lime green blazer given to me by Siegfried or Roy. Mr. Bathroom took slight notice and pushed the record button on my brilliant phone. I then yielded to the effects of the bay rum and dreamed briefly about a spit sink and dental chair.

"I call myself an incidental conceptualist. Mainly, I try to shoehorn meaning upon the human equivalent of darkened rooms — with hot glue and a bunch of drywall screws. I lost 70 pounds and changed my name to Altus, you know. The same mob that once menaced me with flaming Swiffers and pushed me to the edge of suicide now pays millions to fixate on the marbles in my manspread. Last year, I legally married a stadium seat, but we have an understanding.

"My dream is to install zippers into a hundred black-market human skulls. At my opening, I will open all of them and lock the gallery crowd inside. Each attendee/participant will wear a body cam to capture the shrieking, dislocated soul-jerky whirling through their very pores. This will be very cool, and I will wear some kind of hat for the event."

Then he was gone! Altus Bathroom had said his piece and left me here, dripping with my own greenish bile and squinting at a monumental tab for the bay rum. A truly gifted and amazing artist that nearly everyone, straight or gay, sees as more, much more than a gorgeous Speedo packed with Clementines! He left behind a mirror and a note explaining that my teeth had been modified to resemble da Vinci's *The Last Supper*.

Larry Gagosian wants to meet with me now that I am an original Bathroom. So does an oral surgeon from Sotheby's.

The King and Me
By King Günther II
of Hüffinstein

I never set out to be a monarch, especially the king of this particular realm. Dad was a God-King and expected to outlive all of us, happily clearing that loud throat of his and ruling until the Pharaohs finished cruising the afterlife disguised as a herd of goats. No, my 63 half-siblings and I all went to medical school. I'm a kidney transplant guy. I can save your brother-in-law or put him in chains.

Dad is still alive, by the way, but I am king. Five years ago, he met Melania Trump's identical twin sister, Irka, and just plain abdicated. Irka can whistle most of *South Pacific*. She can also turn ice-cold in a split second and flash-freeze anybody with her blood-shattering stare. She can make snowballs with her mind.

Anyway, my country is the tiny little-known principality of Hüffinstein. We're not grand, but we are a duchy. Our main industry involves restoring muscle cars owned by teenagers in Luxembourg — spoiled, arrogant kids with the word "grand" in front of their duchy. We have our problems, though mainly with parents who don't pay bills.

We speak English here, except the old people who still swear in Hüffin. I learned it for the job and had to buy special auto-correct software that inserts umlauts over all the vowels. Our national treasure is a Sears Craftsman hammer made of 14-carat gold. We have no idea where we picked it up, but you should really travel here and look at it. There is no legislature here and no real government aside from me, because my dad quit, I am the king, and you should see how a freshly transplanted kidney works miracles on urine!

Dad and Irka are visiting from Ireland and FedEx is here with a kidney so magnificent that I might display it next to the hammer for a day before I sew it into some Luxembourgian brat who doesn't actually need it. My subjects could have made me a God-King at my coronation, but they felt cheated after the old man was given immortality and walked out on them for a human sleet storm who sounds like she's talking backwards. Oh, and my brother Kärl, the cardiologist, keeps sending me scans of heart porn just to rub it in.

I'm okay, really, not angry. Just a bit of pressure is all. I have to go downtairs and serve drinks while the citizens gather to worship Dad, again. **B**

CHUNK-STYLE NUGGETS

...to briefly distract you from the inevitable • ***By Steve Young***

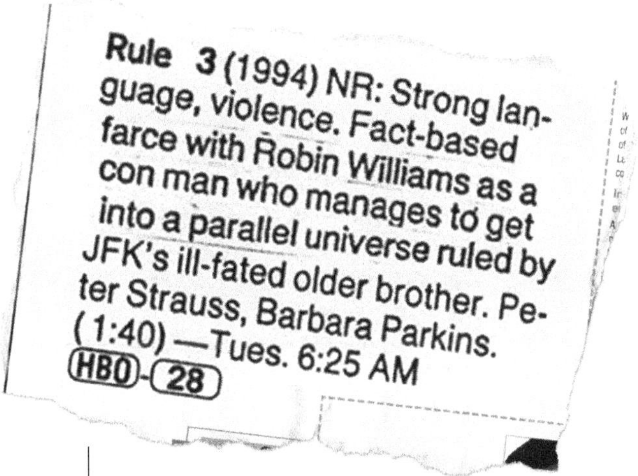
Rule 3 (1994) NR: Strong language, violence. Fact-based farce with Robin Williams as a con man who manages to get into a parallel universe ruled by JFK's ill-fated older brother. Peter Strauss, Barbara Parkins. (1:40) —Tues. 6:25 AM
HBO-28

Reminder

For anyone unable to Wang Chung tonight, there will be a makeup session Saturday at 10 a.m.

Thoughts Going Through My Mind As I Fall Down a Staircase

Whoah — oh crap — yep, this is really happening — ow — ow — ow — that was a bad one — ow — ow — never noticed that nice lathe work on the balusters before — ow — ow — almost halfway down! — ow — is balusters the right word for the spindly things? — oww — ow dammit — I think the balustrade is the whole thing made up of the balusters and the railing — ow — ow — oww — if I live I'm gonna look it up — ow — ow — most of the way there — ow — kind of surprised I'm still able to feel so much pain — ow — ow — I'm going to be incapacitated for quite a while, I may never fully recover — hey, nice newel post, that looks like quarter-sawn oak.

Did You Know?

The sandwich press is named for John Montagu, the 4th Earl of Sandwich, who devised it as a method for pressing his enemies to death.

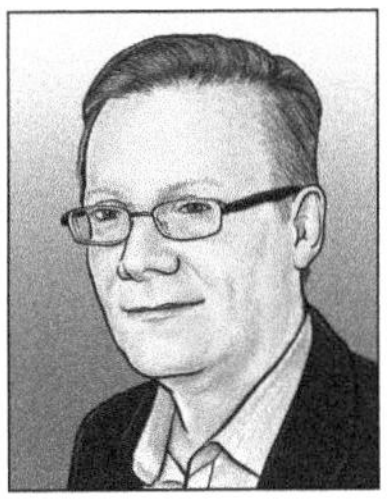

STEVE YOUNG (@pantssteve) is Oracle for *The American Bystander*.

Reasons Your Tom Bosley Fan Club Application Was Denied

- Portions of your "Why I Admire Tom Bosley" essay were plagiarized from essays praising Tom Bosley that can be found online (yes, we check these things).
- You forgot to change "Selleck" to "Bosley" when you copied and pasted your haikus which were obviously from your Tom Selleck Fan Club application.
- The recommendation letter from your Congressman came off as perfunctory and insincere.
- It's *Father Dowling Mysteries*, not *Father Downing Mysteries*, asshole.

Be a Post Office Smart-Ass!

"Well, it's a gift assortment of lithium batteries and delicate glass bottles of perfume, but I've padded everything very securely with raw meat."

Etiquette Corner

If you're wondering how much is appropriate to tip various endangered species, consult this handy list:

Sumatran rhino: $5.00
Siberian tiger: 10% of total bill
Indus River dolphin: $12.00-$15.00, depending
Leatherback turtle: nothing, and it knows why

A Few Recent Name Misspellings on Junk Mail Received by the Demon Beelzebub

Beetsburp
Bathtubz
Beltzer, Bob

What to Say If You Want to Seduce the Person Installing Your Track Lighting

...Wow, the lights can be positioned at different spots along the track? That makes me feel like literally anything can happen.

...For a long time I resisted track lighting, but now I'm at the stage of my life where I want to try different things.

...I'm feeling really confused and vulnerable because I just got out of a relationship with someone who installs recessed lighting.

Least Popular Ringtones

- Refrigerator compressor cycling on
- Hair being swept up on barbershop floor
- Rustling and coughs of classical concert audience during brief interlude

between symphony movements
• Vial of oil and vinegar salad dressing being shaken
• Someone sorting mail
• Mouse inside wall intermittently busy with something
• Deflating air mattress

Coin Collectors! Look for These Valuable U.S. Mint Errors in Your Pocket Change!

• 1996 dime depicting Roosevelt suffering from conjunctivitis
• 2014 penny with "Liberty" misspelled as "Whatevs"
• three-inch-thick 2009 nickel
• 1985 penny with front and back in opposite places (identical to regular 1985 penny, but worth much more)
• 2004 quarter depicting George Washington as made of a silvery metal alloy rather than human flesh

Uncooperative Witness Nostalgia Corner

"No, I don't remember any great vintage toys from decades ago."

"I'm sorry, I'm afraid I don't recall any favorite classic '70s sitcom moments."

"Yes, I realize I'm under oath, but while I acknowledge that there may indeed have been fashions and hairstyles that we once thought were 'cool' but which now make us laugh or cringe, I'm unable to recollect them."

"I have no memory of claiming to enjoy 'nostalgia.'"

Confidential to 'Royal Pain':

While it may be true that no real economic harm is coming to local merchants due to your occasional shoplifting, you should seek counseling in order to deal with this compulsion, Your Majesty. Remember, this is what brought down Qaddafi.

Announcement

Will the owner of a gray 2006 Toyota Corolla, New York license T6Y3VF, please get a more interesting car. **B**

KNOW YOUR BYSTANDERS

We asked. ***Joe Keohane*** *answered.*

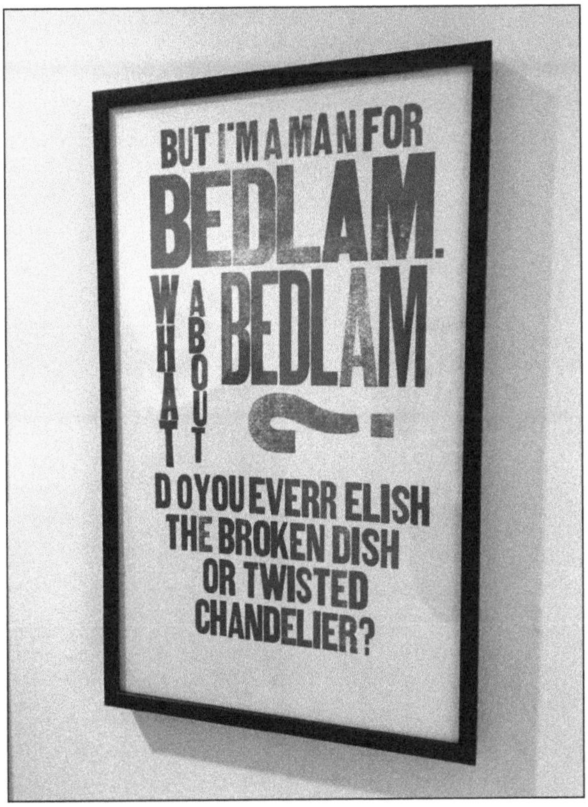
BUT I'M A MAN FOR
BEDLAM.
WHAT ABOUT
BEDLAM
?
DO YOU EVERR ELISH
THE BROKEN DISH
OR TWISTED
CHANDELIER?

When I asked for a photo of something meaningful to him, Joe sent this. "It's a letterpress print I made featuring my favorite line in my favorite book, The Ginger Man *by the late, great J.P. Donleavy. It hangs in a place of honor in my hallway." It was either that, Joe said, or a photo of his liquor cabinet.*

People ask me what I love about running humor magazines; hell, I ask myself. It's not the work (hard) or the pay (nonexistent). It's simply this: A good humor magazine is an engine for friendship. When functioning properly, these peculiar publications throw off camaraderie and pleasure like a Tesla coil sheds lightning.

Sometime around Issue #3, Joe Keohane hit Bystander's *transom like a briefcase filled with nickels and has been all over the mag ever since. Why? When you read his stuff, he sounds like a friend.— MG*

NAME: *Joe Keohane*
PROFESSION: *Journalist*
LIVES IN: *Brooklyn, New York*
RECENT PIECES: *Make A Wish* (#4); *Eight NYC Bars You Need To Drink At Before You Die Tuesday* (#4), *How To Win The War With Your Picky Eater* (#5), *Introducing Your New MTA* (#6), *The Secret Life of Walter Mitty, Firearms Enthusiast* (#6).

Where were you born, and did that have any bearing on the person you've become? I was born in Boston to an Irish Catholic family of funeral directors. That combination accounts for 97% of who I am today. Though on some days it's 110%.

What's your favorite drink? Manhattan, up. The perfect cocktail. A nation of so-called mixologists working a thousand nights in a thousand bars have never been able to top it. If vermouth isn't available: three fingers of good bourbon on an empty stomach. You can have your opioids. For me, bourbon-on-empty's the best drug there is.

By the way, what's your idea of "a good bourbon"? If I'm buying: Four Roses Small Batch; if you are, an 18-year-old Jefferson's.

Continuing the theme, what's your favorite toast? "To the confusion of our enemies." John Oppenheimer.

What are you interested in that most people haven't heard of? Civility, composure, wit and taste.

What's your favorite activity? Making my 18-month-old fall over laughing.

What's worth spending more on to get the best? Shoes. My father told me once that when it comes to shoes, cheap is expensive. They hurt, they break in badly, and you have to keep buying new ones. Don't be afraid to spend $300-plus on a good pair of shoes. Before you ask: Allen Edmonds, Grenson, and Frye for boots.

What is something that a ton of people are obsessed with but you just don't get the point of? Podcasts.

What fad or trend do you hope comes back? Print journalism.

Pure self-interest. What is the luckiest thing that has happened to you? Blundering into meeting my wife-to-be in a parking lot.

I have to hear more about that. It was a parking lot in Cambridge, MA, behind where she worked. Hilariously, I was unemployed and used to spent my days harassing friends who had jobs. One such friend worked with Jean. We circled one another suspiciously for quite some time, but it worked out well.

What subject do you wish you knew more about? Finance. But if I did, I wouldn't be a writer.

What amazing thing did you do that no one was around to see? I once got chased out of the Muslim quarter of Old Jerusalem by a gang of teenagers, and then being told to "go pray at the Wall with the rest of the Jews," which made me burst out laughing because if I were any more Irish I'd have potatoes for ears.

(continued on next page) ☛

What one thing do you really want but can't afford? Another bedroom.

What's the title of your autobiography? The Rogue Trombone.

What's something you like to do the old-fashioned way? Surgery.

What was the best compliment you've received? I was stranded on a desert island in Indonesia for three days for a magazine story. I failed to find food and otherwise demonstrated a complete inability to stay alive. All I did was rage at nature and dream of getting back to New York for a cheeseburger and a Manhattan. On the way back to catch the first of four flights to get home, I explained my failure to the driver. He told me other stories of men who had flourished in that scenario, concluding: "But you are not survivor. You are journalist." I loved that. Then, when I got home, my wife said that experiences like that typically change people in a profound way, but in my case, "You're more yourself than you were in the first place."

What fictional place would you most like to visit? Denmark.

What job do you think you'd be great at? Conceptual artist. I want to do a piece in a long, narrow, brilliantly white gallery. Visitors would enter, and proceed down this long white room toward a small doorway. Out of this doorway would come terrible fighting sounds. As you walked toward it, you'd note the occasional drop of blood on the gleaming white floor. Finally you'd get to the doorway and crouch down to look inside. There you would find my large Lithuanian friend Peter stripped to the waist, furiously fighting 2,500 pounds of meat in this tiny room. I call it "Peter Fights the Meat." And recently I was telling a friend I want to build a manger scene for Christmas in which everything is normal, except for the cradle itself, which would be hooked up to a gas line so it could blast out a column of fire. I haven't named that one yet though. Something about an everlasting flame probably.

If you had unlimited funds to build a house that you would live in for the rest of your life, what would the house be like? It would be an apartment in New York with more than one real bedroom, and more than three windows that don't look out at an airshaft caked with 800 pounds of guano.

If you could make one rule that everyone had to follow, what would it be? Don't stand in the doorway on the subway, punishable by death.

What risks are worth taking? Before 30: all of them. After 30: most of them. After 60: all of them.

What do you hope your last words will be? "I accept your apology." **B**

TRUMP STAMP

Racist Liar

KUPER

NY/NJ COMEDIC ACTOR (40s-50s) available for auditions, readings, runs of any length. Resume and pictures: **DavidCNeal.com.**

IT CAME FROM THE BOTTOM SHELF!
Bottomshelfmovies.com is a film recommendation website focusing on forgotten classics, lesser-known gems, and odd-ball discoveries. It's the video collector's resource for movie reviews, weekly new release video picks, upcoming Blu-ray/DVD announcements, sales alerts, and other cinematic news. **Bottomshelfmovies.com**

JANE AUSTEN MUSIC Live music from the English Regency era for dancing or ambience in the San Francisco area. **jameslangdell@gmail.com**

DOPEY PODCAST
On the dark comedy of drug addiction.
www.dopeypodcast.com

FREAK CHIC STUDIOS
Jewelry, Art & Accoutrements for the Eclectic Heart.
www.freakchicstudios.com that's Dubyah Dubyah Dubyah dot FreakChicStudios dot See Oh Em. Twitter: @FreakChicStudio / Instagram: Freak Chic Studios / CB Callsign: Freak 2 The Chic. Be a good human and buy my stuff! Ten-four good buddy. Keep the bugs off your glass, and the bears off your... TAIL. Over and out.

THE MISADVENTURES OF LI'L DONNIE
Making Comics Great Again - Since 2017!
donniecrys.blogspot.com or follow "Donald Littles" (w/the asterisk pic) on the facebooks!

MYXPROJEKT
Free long-form Ambient Drone music. Great for relaxation, meditation, sleep. Nod off in style! Money back guarantee.
soundcloud.com/myxprojekt

COMEDIANS DEFYING GRAVITY
Comedians Defying Gravity highlights Chicago comedy: interviews, weekly events calendar and more. CDG is part of ChicagoNow, the Chicago Tribune Media Group's blogging network.**http://www.chicagonow.com/comedians-defying-gravity**

FULL OF WIT Funny poems and more. The Killing Tree by J.D. Smith can be found at most online sellers and at the link. **www.finishinglinepress.com/product/the-killing-tree-by-j-d-smith/**

PATSY O'BRIEN
Alt-Celtic Songwriter
Award-winning
NPR - featured.
www.patsyobrienswebsite.com

¿GOT TSUNAMIS?
Or some other annoyingly inconvenient problem at your local beach, port or 5-star resort? Give a shout, we'll sort you out!
http://eCoast.co.nz
jose@ecoast.co.nz
coastal dynamics • tsunamis • erosion • wave pools • surfing reefs • resorts • marinas • marine ecology
Solutions offered worldwide!
No beach out of reach!
The absurdity of advertising coastal engineering services to a bunch of writers and English majors isn't lost on me, but hey, I like the *Bystander*, so why not?

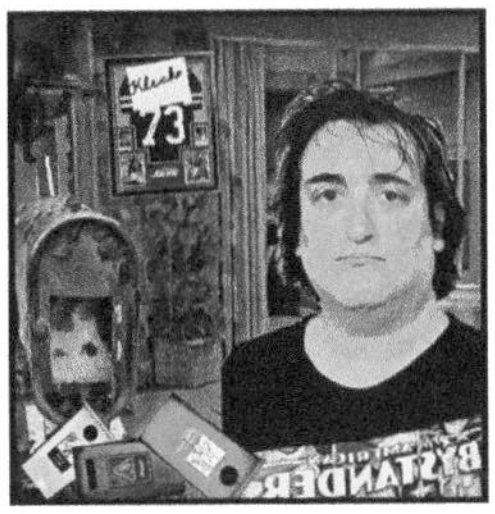

IN MEMORIAM:
Johnson Dunst, Jr., the deaf-mute imbecile who would bring our pre-separated trash and recyclables from the *Bystander* main offices to his religiously-excepted home incinerator just over the border in West Los Angeles, has died. Cause of death is believed to have been his correct knowledge that the life expectancy of a deaf-mute imbecile in AD 1732 was nine combined with his apparent, yet woefully misguided, belief that it is now AD 1732. Mr. Dunst, Jr., leaves no known next of kin, though he was known to smile for days whenever he successfully spelled the word "Klecko" in cursive. We wish him well.

TONY ISABELLA'S NEW BOOK
July 1963: A Pivotal Month in the Comic-Book Life of Tony Isabella Volume One. Obsessive nostalgic fun that inspired the career of the creator of Black Lightning, Misty Knight, Tigra and more. Available in print and digital formats from Amazon. Superman competes in the Interplanetary Olympics. The coming of the Avengers. Baby Huey's criminally negligent parents. Batman's super-powered dog. All this and so much more.

A (VERY GOOD) LITERARY AGENCY
Why, you must have stellar taste to be here. Are you also an extremely talented writer with a book idea? Let's talk. I'm Scott at **sgould@rlrassociates.net.**

---

www.kingcormack.com

DRUNK MONKEYS
America's finest "two women drinking odd liquors and talking about it" web series may be found at drunkmonkeyshow.com – only one 's', so it's Drunk Monkeys how?

CLASSIFIEDS

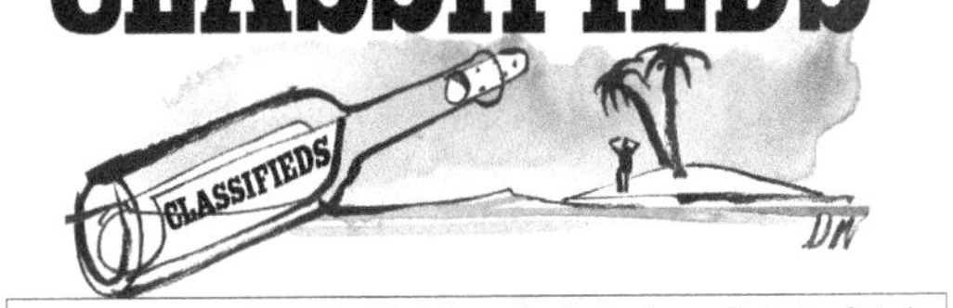

Interested in placing an ad? Email **classifieds@americanbystander.org**. The American Bystander reserves the right to reject any ad for any reason. We do not guarantee the quality of the items being sold, or the accuracy of the information provided. Ads are provided directly by sellers and are not verified.

CARTOON COMPANION
Cartooncompanion.com is a new website that discusses and rates the cartoons in *The New Yorker*. Co-hosts Max and Simon trade amusing observations and barbs with each new issue. *TNY* cartoonists have contributed to the site and praised it. Future posts will include interviews of the cartoonists and cartoons that *The New Yorker* rejected.
cartooncompanion.com

DO YOU READ THE OTHER A.B.?
Attempted Bloggery – An art blog about cartoons and other high culture. Published more or less daily since 2011.
attemptedbloggery.blogspot.com

CURRENCY CONVERSION BY MAIL
Convert unwieldy US folding money into small denominations! Send $10 bill get back $5 bill. Send *one* $20 bill receive a completely different bill. Never ask for change again! Do not delay!
Contact **@Specky4Eyes**
Serious inquiries only. No fatties.

YOU LIKE COMICS?
Sure you do! Who doesn't? (well, ignore those dweebs). For the finest in graphic storytelling, look ahead to 2018 for the premiere of BERGER BOOKS, created by the legendary Karen Berger, founding editor of VERTIGO! And the Art Director? The also legendary - except not so much - Richard Bruning! Top notch talent too. Watch for this revolutionary new imprint from indy pioneer Dark Horse.

THE COMIC TORAH
Stand-up comic Aaron Freeman and artist Sharon Rosenzweig reimagine the Torah with provocative humor and irreverent reverence. Each weekly portion gets a two-page spread. Like the original, the Comic Torah is not always suitable for children. "Hyperactive, colorful art brings the story to life." – Publisher's Weekly "If God was a comic artist, this is what She would have drawn." –Harold Ramis "Awesome!" – Alison Bechdel "Sacred & profane at the same time." – Paul Krassner
benyehudapress.com/ct or amzn.to/2npmv4V

STUDY CARTOONING and Illustration at the School of Visual Arts. We offer courses by Tom Motley, Steve Brodner, Carl Potts, and more! Fall courses are enrolling now.
www.sva.edu/continuing-education/illustration-and-cartooning

VISUAL REALIA
Photography, food and everything visual:
www.visualrealia.com.

CONFEDERACY OF DRONES POLITICAL SATIRE
Using humor to shoot down the political hypocrisy of mindless drones.
confederacyofdrones.com

LOTS OF NATIONAL LAMPOON
Lots of Nat Lamps for sale. Various monthly issues and Best Ofs. Mostly in pretty good condition. $4 each or more per issue plus postage. Email me with any particular issue you need at **bardinerman@aol.com.**
Thank you and Godspeed.

COMIC STUDIES at the University of Wisconsin-Madison http://humanities.wisc.edu/research/borghesi-mellon-workshops/past-workshops/comics2

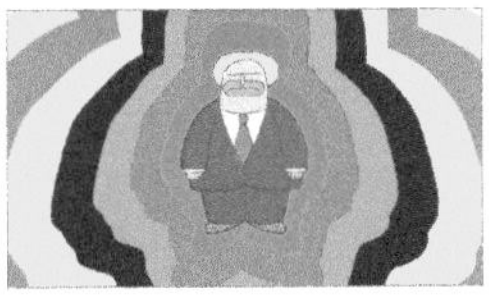

THE MAN WHO KILLED REALITY
The Prefab Messiahs explain all! Observe their hit animated musical video on the Youtubes:
youtube.com/prefabmessiahs

Alien Invasion

L	A	M	B	■	A	N	A	L	■	A	S	T	R	O
O	R	E	O	■	D	E	L	I	■	Q	U	R	A	N
S	T	A	N	L	E	W	O	K	■	U	S	A	G	E
T	E	N	N	E	S	S	E	E	■	A	A	M	E	S
■	■	■	I	N	T	■	■	■	E	R	N	■	■	■
■	■	P	E	T	E	R	U	S	T	I	N	A	V	I
A	H	I	■	■	■	E	V	A	C	U	A	T	E	S
B	O	L	A	S	■	C	U	T	■	S	H	A	N	E
B	L	A	C	K	H	O	L	E	■	■	■	L	I	E
R	A	F	A	E	L	N	A	D	A	L	E	K	■	■
■	■	■	P	L	S	■	■	■	N	A	N	■	■	■
V	A	L	U	E	■	B	A	N	D	W	A	G	O	N
A	D	U	L	T	■	B	J	O	R	N	B	O	R	G
C	I	S	C	O	■	L	A	T	E	■	L	O	G	O
A	N	T	O	N	■	S	R	A	S	■	E	D	Y	S

2018

TABLETOP TALK - a YouTube channel for gamers by gamers. We create raw tabletop gaming content by filming our games. No scripts, just gaming. **www.youtube.com/user/TabletopTalk**

TOONS BY STEV-O (by Steve McGinn). some cartoons I hope'll make ya laff! drawn fresh in ink & then posted every day - 7 days a week! look for us on Facebook and The Comx Box Syndicate.

THE AMERICAN VALUES CLUB Crossword (formerly the Onion AV Club Crossword): It's rude, it's clued, and you'll get used to it.
Subscribe at avxword.com.

Buy **THE LAFAYETTE CAMPAIGN** **mybook.to/lafayettecampaign** "Andrew Updegrove brings a rare combination of drama, satire and technical accuracy to his writing. The result is a book you can't put down that tells you things you might wish you didn't know." - Admiral James G. Stavridis, former NATO Supreme Allied Commander Europe

---

UNICORN BOOTY WANTS YOU ...to read some of the most outrageously fun news, pop culture, and opinions on the web! Unicorn Booty serves up original news, film, TV, art, sports, fashion, travel and other weird wonders from around the world. Check us out at **http://unicornbooty.com**.

THE NEW YORK REVIEW OF SCIENCE FICTION
Reading Science Fiction Like It Matters for 28 Years. The first one's free! **http://www.nyrsf.com**

HARRY BLISS

"Do me a favor and just move to the left about 18 feet."

AN ILLUSTRATED ZARATHUSTRA Hilarity ensues as excerpts and epigrams from Nietzsche's timeless classic comes to life in this madcap comic-strip-style dub version. Embrace your Fate and read it online at:
ScottMarshall.org

BOOKS, POSTCARDS, ORIGINAL art by Rick Geary, available exclusively at **www.rickgeary.com**. I also take commissions.

FREE LUNCH! NO BALONEY!
Attention all hungry cartoonists passing through Chicago:
Contact Jonathan Plotkin
Editorial Cartoonist & Illustrator
Minister of Ways and Means
NCIS Chicago Chapter
Spontoonist@gmail.com
spontoonist.com

WANTED: MURDERER I'm looking for someone to kill me please, inquiries: **@ZackBornstein** on Twitter & Instagram

---

THE VIRTUAL MEMORIES SHOW
What's the best books-art-comics-culture interview podcast you've never listened to? Discover The Virtual Memories Show at
www.chimeraobscura.com/vm/podcast-archive

GEORGE BOOTH: cartoons, illustrations. Other services: grass fires stomped out and despots deterred. **929-210-0707**

YOUR ANDREW JACKSON $20s will soon be worthless! Use one to buy our non-award-winning, non-best-selling comedy anthology, **The Lowbrow Reader Reader**, available from Drag City Books. Or check out the The Lowbrow Reader zine itself, eminently purchasable at **lowbrowreader.com**.

VEGETARIANS EATING HAGGIS PIZZA
Cosmic quarks! It's the Zen of Nimbus comic created by Michael Sloan. Nimbus, the celebrated immobile astronomer, is visited by a variety of repulsive creatures and events. Will they ever disturb his meditations? View the comic and blog, shop for Zen of Nimbus t-shirts and artwork:
www.zenofnimbus.com

EULOGIES WRITTEN ON DEMAND
Need a touching tribute...*stat*? Semi-professional eulogist offers her services. Quick turnaround guaranteed; encomium completed while the body's still warm or it's free. Little knowledge of the deceased in question necessary. Email **megan.koester@gmail.com** for rates.

WELCOME TO DISTRACTIONLAND
Too much time on your hands? Watch RANSACK RABBIT and other engaging animated entertainments. **Xeth Feinberg**, proprietor. As seen on the internet!
www.youtube.com/distractionland

UTILITY RIGHT FIELDER Available Also draws, writes. For more information contact Deerfield (Illinois) Little League. Or visit **kenkrimstein.com.**

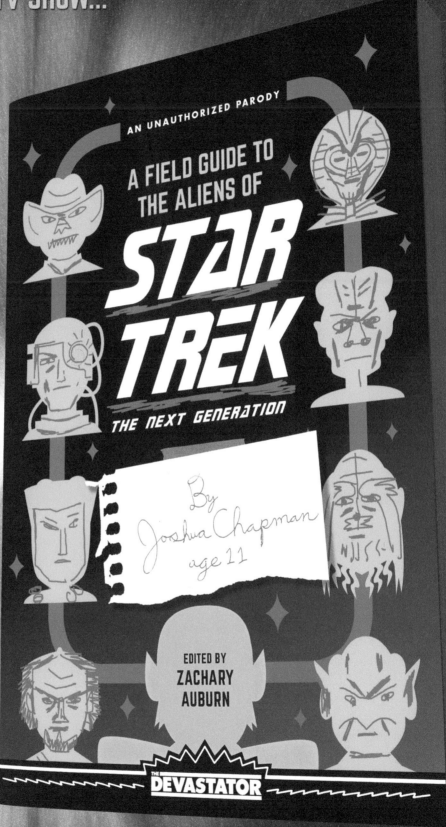

AVAILABLE NOW from Dock Street Press

"How do you make a joke out of a joke? Not easy, but Tom Toro crushes it."—*Garry Trudeau*

"*Tiny Hands* is very, very funny. And if you have any interest in keeping your sanity during the reign of the Orange Gasbag, it's also necessary."—*Roz Chast*

"Scathing work, from an expert at wielding a big-boy-sized pen."—*Emma Allen*

ORDER ONLINE: dockstreetpress.com/our-books

dockstreetpress.com

INDEX TO THIS ISSUE

Stuff you might not have noticed • By Steve Young

BY MATT MATERA & ALAN GOLDBERG

ALIEN INVASION

The truth is out there...on Page 85.

ACROSS

1. Proud Mary companion, at school?
5. Overly detail-minded
9. Member of the 2017 World Champs (hard clue for a Dodgers fan to write)
14. Cookie brand that doesn't know how to spell "stuff" or "cream"
15. Home to cutting-edge technology?
16. Holy book with 114 suras
17. *Comic book icon and frequent maker of movie cameos who now also is adorable and living on a forest moon?
19. Prescriptivist vs. descriptivist topic
20. Creator of Blanche and Stella
21. CIA's version of MacLean or Philby?
22. QB's deeply unsuccessful att.
23. Shore bird
24. *Classic portrayer of Poirot who's now blue and communes with nature?
31. ___ moment? (when you know you need to have sushi-grade tuna for dinner!)
33. Clears the area with a digital Hoover?
34. Weapons used by the Tehuelche to catch guanacos
37. Share
38. "Come back, ___" (what Heat fans might say to "no-stats all-star" Battier?)
39. Famously dense former star
41. "The answer to this clue is FIB," e.g.
42. *Master of clay court tennis who now also seeks to exterminate the Doctor?
46. Three-letter text request
47. ___ Wood Honeyman, first female congressperson from Oregon
48. Empathy, for example
51. Jump aboard to be au courant
57. ___ Swim ("Too Many Cooks" home)
58. *Swedish tennis star who apparently was always part of an e.t. hive mind?
59. The ___ Kid, or a network giant
60. 8:30 p.m., if you have young kids
61. The one for Baskin-Robbins hides the number 31
62. First name of the inspiration for "Chekhov's gun"
63. Mexican mademoiselles, for short
64. Ice cream brand with over 31 flavors

DOWN

1. Directionless?
2. Pinturas del Museo Frieda Kahlo, por ejemplo
3. Fetch movie "___ Girls"

4. Like a lovely Loch Lomond lass
5. Latin injunction sung at Christmas
6. Paper topic?
7. Popular succulent
8. Fancy synonym
9. Opening number in "Hair"
10. Accused "witch" Martin executed in Salem at age 70
11. Streetcar
12. Triggering Hulk emotion
13. "A Room of ___ Own"
18. Fast time at Ridgemont High?
23. You get the picture
24. Rice dish common in many cuisines
25. Madoff's second scam?
26. Don't try to ululate without it
27. Filled
28. Give ___ (orate)
29. First word from Caesar's salad days?
30. What the blind carpenter said when he picked up a hammer and saw?
31. 31-Down, e.g.
32. Greeting in 35-Down

35. Setting for a '63 south-of-the-border film starring Elvis and Ursula Andress
36. "Archaeological Dig Uncovers Ancient Race of ___ People" (classic Onion headline)
40. Postgraduate inst. for Barack Obama
43. Celebrity chef (and Puerto Rico recovery hero) Jose
44. The old sod?
45. Make possible
48. Cabeza de ___ (Spanish explorer who wrote about the tribes he met)
49. Score that may happen several times in one tennis game
50. "___, Caution" (Ang Lee film)
51. Unit for crude oil, for short
52. What a door is when it's not a door?
53. ___ bene (pay attention to this!)
54. "The ___ Place" (outstanding current NBC sitcom)
55. Result of 50-Down, at an extreme
56. Partners in Health and Doctors Without Borders, briefly

B

CPSIA information can be obtained
at www.ICGtesting.com
Printed in the USA
FSHW04n0052270318
45643FS

9 780692 065853